"The author should be commended for his outstanding introduction to research methods in applied linguistics. An excellent reference for researchers, this up-to-date book should also be required reading for graduate students in MA-TESOL/TEFL and applied linguistics programs."

Todd Hernández, Marquette University, USA

"A terrific textbook for new graduate students who need to learn the valuable skill of reading and evaluating research, written in an interesting and accessible way that builds readers' confidence in understanding research as it goes along. Equal attention is paid to both quantitative and qualitative methods, with some discussion of mixed methods as well. All the example studies described in the book are from research in applied linguistics which makes it much more interesting than a general research methods textbook."

Nicole Tracy-Ventura, University of South Florida, USA

"Very useful and relevant text for applied linguistics students as they become discerning consumers of research in the field. The topics and discussions covered in this book provide valuable information that lays the groundwork for successful future research."

Eric Friginal, Georgia State University, USA

Research in Applied Linguistics

Now in its third edition, this popular introduction to the foundations of research methods is designed to enable students and professionals in the field of applied linguistics to become not just *casual* consumers of research who passively read bits and pieces of a research article, but *discerning* consumers able to effectively use published research for practical purposes in educational settings. All issues important for understanding and using published research for these purposes are covered. Key principles are illustrated with research studies published in refereed journals across a wide spectrum of applied linguistics. Exercises throughout the text encourage readers to engage interactively with what they are reading at the point when the information is fresh in their minds. Intended for and field-tested in courses in MA-TESOL/TEFL and applied linguistics programs, course instructors will find that this text provides a solid framework in which to promote student interaction and discussion on important issues in research methodology. This book provides an excellent foundation for those who plan to continue in an active research agenda.

Changes in the Third Edition

- Chapter 2 revised to reflect formatting changes made by ERIC, addition of referencing and citation resources
- Chapter 8 revised to increase practicality
- Revision of some embedded exercises
- The topic of meta-analysis integrated more fully where appropriate
- Corpora research given more attention
- Many studies older than 2000 replaced with more recent studies
- Companion Website (www.routledge.com/cw/Perry) with list of journals related to applied linguistics, annotated resources to aid students and instructors for each chapter, access to screencasts and YouTube demonstrations, and a space for students and/or teachers to interact with the author.

Fred L. Perry, Jr. is Professor Emeritus of Applied Linguistics at the American University in Cairo, Egypt.

Research in Applied Linguistics

Becoming a Discerning Consumer

Third Edition

Fred L. Perry, Jr.

 Routledge
Taylor & Francis Group

NEW YORK AND LONDON

Third edition published 2017
by Routledge
711 Third Avenue, New York, NY 10017

and by Routledge
2 Park Square, Milton Park, Abingdon, Oxon, OX14 4RN

Routledge is an imprint of the Taylor & Francis Group, an informa business

First edition published by Lawrence Erlbaum Associates, Inc., 2005
Second edition published by Routledge, 2011

Library of Congress Cataloging in Publication Data
Names: Perry, Fred L. (Fred Lehman), 1943– author.
Title: Research in applied linguistics : becoming a discerning
consumer / Fred L. Perry.
Description: Third edition. | New York : Routledge, [2017] |
Includes index.
Identifiers: LCCN 2016045318| ISBN 9781138227750 (hardback) |
ISBN 9781138227767 (pbk.) | ISBN 9781315394664 (ebk.)
Subjects: LCSH: Applied linguistics—Research.
Classification: LCC P129 .P47 2017 | DDC 418/.0072—dc23
LC record available at https://lccn.loc.gov/2016045318

ISBN: 978-1-138-22775-0 (hbk)
ISBN: 978-1-138-22776-7 (pbk)
ISBN: 978-1-315-39466-4 (ebk)

Typeset in Sabon and Gill Sans
by Florence Production Ltd, Stoodleigh, Devon, UK

Visit the companion website: www.routledge.com/cw/Perry

Dedicated to my wife, Karen Kay, who has inspired me to do my best over these last 50 years. I also dedicate this book to all people who want to be discerning consumers of research.

Brief Contents

Contents

Figures

Tables

Preface

The premise of the third edition of this book is the same as for the first and second editions. Graduate students, teachers, administrators, and others working in the field of language learning and teaching need to understand research in the field—i.e., they need to be *discerning consumers* of research, regardless of whether they ever carry out a research project. The impact of research on our daily lives continues to increase more than ever. People affected by research include those developing and/or implementing language learning programs, graduate students, parents who are involved in their children's education, and politicians who need to read research before making decisions that affect us all. All of these people and others on whom research in applied linguistics has an impact need to be able to understand it to the point where they are able to evaluate recommendations based on such research.

This book is specifically written for all those who want and need to be consumers of research—graduate students, administrators, teachers. Members of the first group tend to be thrown into the deep end of the pool of research from the first day they enter their programs. This text is designed to assist them in getting up to speed as soon as possible.

The goal is to develop not just *casual* consumers who passively read bits and pieces of a research article, but *discerning* consumers who will read research reports from beginning to end with a level of understanding that can be used to address both theoretical and practical issues. Once this stage is reached, consumers will no longer look upon research journals as forbidding, boring documents that only university professors find interesting. Rather, they will regard them as important sources of evidence or counter evidence that can be used in arguing the pros and/or cons of formulating and implementing new ideas and methodologies in educational settings. They will also be able to effectively employ these valuable resources for developing their own research ideas and methodologies for their own research.

Organization of the Text

The organization of the first edition evolved over 24 years of experience in teaching people how to understand research in applied linguistics. The second edition came out five years later with changes based on valuable feedback from over that period of time. Now, another five years later, this third edition is again based on further feedback of those using the former editions to keep up with what research is doing today. I have kept the same format as the first two editions, with the focus on becoming a consumer rather than a doer of research. However, I agree with one reviewer that, once a discerning consumer, becoming a doer of research is a natural next step forward. This book works as a great foundation for advanced courses for those who want to be doers of research.

As with previous editions, this new edition is organized into two parts. Part I introduces the reader to the fundamentals required for becoming a discerning consumer. Chapter 1 distinguishes between common conceptions of the meaning of research and how it is understood among professional researchers. It also discusses the driving force behind the entire research process: the research question(s)—the question(s) that guides the choices researchers make when planning and carrying out their studies. In the third edition, I have reworded some phrases and inserted comments in strategic places to add further clarification. However, I have replaced six studies used for examples to provide more recent research.

Chapter 2 is intended to help students get a jump start on how to find research articles, through both traditional and electronic methods. Basic information accompanied by a walk-through example is provided. In the third edition, due to the changes ERIC has made in their formatting, I replaced outdated examples with six more recent examples to make them more current.

Appendix A continues to feature detailed instructions on how to write a review of research. These instructions are put in an appendix at the end of the book, rather than in Chapter 2, so that readers can complete a review of research after they have become discerning consumers, that is, on completing the entire book. Putting this material in an appendix also allows an instructor to assign reading this material at any time felt appropriate. In an additional aid, my companion website, an updated annotated list of many of the journals pertinent to applied linguistics is provided, which was formerly Appendix C in editions one and two.

In this edition, Part II continues to be structured around the order in which each component appears in a typical research report used by most research journals. Chapter 3, the first chapter of this section, maps out these components along with brief explanations, and then examines the functions of the title, the abstract, and the introduction in a typical study, along with descriptions of criteria used for evaluating these components.

I replaced 10 studies used for examples with more recent ones, deleted one exercise that I felt unnecessary, and restructured some wording and exercises.

Chapter 4 looks at the two sampling paradigms used in both qualitative and quantitative research. Under each paradigm, various commonly used methods are described with research examples provided. The major change in this chapter was replacing 10 example studies with more recent ones.

The first section of Chapter 5 (similar to the first and second editions) surveys research designs according to three research continua with recent studies provided to illustrate how they can be classified along these continua. My purpose is to help consumers develop schemata for research in order to facilitate understanding how various methods fit into the greater scheme of things. The second section surveys different research methods used to answer the two basic questions: what and why. The third section describes the important characteristic of internal validity required by all research for reasonable explanations and conclusions. Other than minor tweaking of wording, the major change in this edition is replacing 16 studies used for examples with more recent ones.

Chapter 6 looks at the different ways data are gathered according to various research methods. The chapter is divided into two sections. The first deals with the collection and evaluation of verbal data. The second focuses on the collection and evaluation of numerical data. In the second section I have added a section on meta-analysis, which has gained a lot of popularity over the five years since edition two. I also replaced 23 studies with more recent ones to bring the book up to date.

Chapter 7 follows the same structure as found in the previous two editions. My intent is for readers to be able to look into the results section of a research article with enough confidence to critically evaluate whether appropriate procedures have been used and correct interpretations have been made. This chapter is divided into two main sections. The first relates to how verbal data are analyzed and interpreted. Over recent years, there have been important strides made in how to evaluate these procedures. I provide an overview abstracted from the leading authorities in this area. The second focuses on numerical data. Because the readers of this text come from a variety of academic backgrounds and levels of mathematical sophistication, when I discuss statistical issues I aim not to inundate the reader with more information than a consumer of research needs. This topic is approached in layers according to frequency of use and relevance to the reader. The first layer is presented in this chapter. The next layer is presented in Appendix B, which contains information that is important but less common and a little more complex. (Note that nine studies were replaced with more current ones in this appendix.) In both layers, statistics are approached conceptually. My contention is that consumers of research do not need to know math formulas to understand statistical concepts but they do need to know why certain procedures are followed, how to interpret them, and whether they are appropriately used. I have made two major changes in this chapter. First, I have replaced 12 studies used for illustrating the discussion with more recent ones. Second, I reorganized the Key Terms and Concepts section at the end of the chapter and added missing information that was not in the previous editions.

As in the first two editions, I continue to aim at helping readers integrate the many aspects of research methodology by synthesizing them into graphic illustrations. They may appear to be somewhat reductionistic— that is, to leave out details some instructors might consider important— but my experience continues to lead me to understand that up-and-coming discerning consumers of research need to first develop a *big picture* schematic view of research before dealing with too many details. Once this overall framework is in place, the consumer will be able to accommodate whatever additional information is considered important as time progresses. This also prepares the consumer to become a researcher in the future.

Chapter 8, the final chapter, provides a set of criteria by which to appraise the discussion and conclusion section of the typical research report. I restructured this chapter making it, in my opinion, more useful for evaluating the final section of a study. I also replaced the two examples with more current studies.

Selection and Use of Studies for Illustrations

In this edition, I have continued to illustrate each major point in the book with at least one research study published in a refereed journal where possible. When choosing these studies, I followed five criteria, listed here in order of priority. First, the study should provide a clear example of the point being made. Second, it should be as recent as possible at the time of writing this book. In this edition, I have replaced many older studies with more recent ones. Third, the topics of the research studies should vary in order to expose the reader to some of the breadth of the issues being researched in applied linguistics. Fourth, the studies should come from a wide a variety of journals in order to familiarize readers with a good sample of the type of journals available. Finally, studies should not only look at the teaching and learning of English as a second/foreign language but also include other languages and other issues in applied linguistics.

Though most of the studies used point out how certain criteria were met, on several occasions I identify where studies might have weaknesses in relation to the evaluative criteria being discussed. My rationale is that readers' critical skills need to be sharpened to help them develop into discerning consumers of research. It is not enough to simply state that some published studies have certain weaknesses; the reader needs to see actual examples where such weaknesses could have occurred. The key word here is *discernment*, which does not mean *fault finding*. I do not want readers to become cynics who delight in slamming researchers on every little perceived weakness, but rather to develop a healthy skepticism. The objective is for readers to gain confidence in their own ability to assess research so that they will be able to evaluate the influence any one study should have on practical issues of concern. (Any researcher who has published one of the studies I used for this purpose should not take offense. No study is perfect, including my own.)

On occasion, I tried to use some subtle humor to lighten up the reading, especially when dealing with heavy issues. This is risky, I know, because humor, like beauty, varies in the eye of the beholder and is very cultural. However, I have taken some risk, though not to the extent I originally did in earlier prepublished versions, because I think research should not be perceived as a dry, boring affair. My goal is that, every once in a while, the reader might crack a smile even when reading difficult material.

Recommendation for Use as a Textbook

The motivation behind this book is to continue to provide people with a solid introduction to the foundations of research methods with the aim of helping them to become discerning consumers. I have found that this frees the instructor from having to lecture about things that students can read for themselves. It also releases class time for more interaction between students and the instructor.

The exercises distributed throughout the chapters play an important role. When used as assignments, students come to class with questions generated from their reading in preparation for these exercises. This leads to a very lively Q and A during the class period. Not only does this help individual students cognitively process the criteria about research studies, based on their own interest, but the entire class is also exposed to a variety of studies and journals. By the end of the class session, students' exposure to how these criteria have been applied to recent research studies has grown exponentially.

The strategy for using interspersed exercises throughout the chapters, rather than placing them at the end, is based on the notion of the effects of adjunct aids. Based on research I and others did some years ago (e.g., Cunningham, Snowman, Miller & Perry, 1982), we found that interspersed questions and exercises create strategic pauses for students to digest and apply what they have been reading. This creates an atmosphere that encourages readers to engage interactively with the text at the time of reading, when information is still fresh in their minds.

I have also found interspersed exercises to be convenient markers for scheduling the topics for discussion over the semester. I distributed the exercises over 16 weeks of classes (two class sessions per week) in addition to a mini-review of research (10 pages), based on Appendix A, which is the last assignment for my initial research methods class. Each chapter takes different amounts of time due to the varied density of the information in the chapter (e.g., I used seven class sessions to cover Chapter 5 on research designs). However, this distributes the number of research studies the students examine in proportion to the topics being studied.

Lastly, in my course I chose to allow students to select research articles on topics related to their own interest for each exercise rather than use a lockstep strategy of assigning readers the same article. Although using a lockstep strategy would have made things simpler for me as the instructor, in that everyone would have to respond to the same research articles, I have found that many students, especially graduate students, are not interested in topics that I think are interesting (can you believe it?). My experience is that giving students the freedom to follow their own interests increases student motivation and appreciation for the course. It also enhances their confidence in their ability to find and work with published research. Finally, it encourages autonomous thinking.

New to this new edition, a companion website is available to provide additional material for both the instructor and the student. It is organized around the themes of the book. Further readings, expansion of some of the more complex concepts, an annotated list of journals related to applied linguistics (formerly Appendix C of editions one and two), and additional help are included.

Final Comments

My hope is that the third edition of this book is even more useful for achieving the goal of helping readers who work with language issues to become discerning consumers of research. Whether it is used as a textbook or independently studied, I believe that anyone wanting to improve his or her ability to understand research will find this book instrumental for achieving this goal. However, it is also important to keep in mind that this is just an introduction with the intention of providing a framework with which to begin one's search for answers to research questions related to language matters. The book also lays the foundation upon which those who plan to do their own research can build.

References

Cunningham, D. J., Snowman, J., Miller, R. B., & Perry, F. L. (1982). Verbal and nonverbal adjunct aids to concrete and abstract prose memory. *Journal of Experimental Education, 51,* 8–13.

Acknowledgments

This third edition is the next step, following the previous two editions, for providing an effective tool to aid the development of critical consumers of academic research in applied linguistics. But, as with the previous editions, various people who have read and used the book as a classroom text have provided valuable feedback that I have built into the third edition.

First, as with the first two editions, I continue to thank my heavenly Father, without whom I would not have had the perseverance to cull through hundreds of studies on the Internet to find over 50 that I eventually used. On a more human level, I have to applaud the American University in Cairo Library, from which I was able to access online journals to obtain these studies from thousands of miles away. Second, prior to commissioning the third edition, Routledge asked three reviewers who had used the second edition to provide constructive suggestions for the third edition. I want to thank Eric Friginal, Georgia State University; Nicole Tracy-Venture, University of South Florida; and Todd Hernández, Marquette University, for taking on this task and providing me with valuable information for making this text better.

Last, I want to thank Naomi Silverman, publisher, along with her staff at Routledge, who has continued to be a source of encouragement and professional advice since this entire process began way back to the days of the first edition.

Part I

Fundamentals for Discerning Consumers

Chapter 1

Understanding the
Nature of Research

Introduction

The amount of research in applied linguistics pouring off the presses today is staggering. Over 100 journals that publish research related to applied linguistics are currently available (www.routledge.com/cw/perry). Some journals are monthly; others are quarterly. Can you imagine how many research studies have been published in just this last year?

So what is all this research about? Who is it all for? Is it important and, if so, how can we understand it better? Briefly, I will answer these questions, but the main purpose of this book is to answer the last question—how can we comprehend and evaluate it?

What Is All This Research About?

A quick answer is that this research tries to provide answers to massive numbers of research questions that are being generated around the world in the field of applied linguistics. By *applied linguistics*, I agree with the definition given by the Department of Linguistics and Applied Linguistics at the University of Melbourne, Australia, which stated on its website in 2003:

> Applied Linguistics is concerned with practical issues involving language in the life of the community. The most important of these is the learning of second or foreign languages. Others include language policy, multilingualism, language education, the preservation and revival of endangered languages, and the assessment and treatment of language difficulties.
>
> Other areas of interest include professional communication, for example, between doctors and their patients, between lawyers and their clients and in courtrooms, as well as other areas of institutional and cross-cultural communication ranging from the boardroom to the routines on an answer-phone.
>
> (www.linguistics.unimelb. edu.au/about/about.html)

In other words, research in the field of applied linguistics covers a vast domain of topics that deals with just about anything where language relates to society. This is a broad definition, which encompasses anything related to practical language problems (cf. Grabe, 2002).

Who Is All This Research For?

It is for you, the person who, for whatever reason, wants or needs to gain a better understanding about language issues that are important to you. This includes the following:

- students in applied linguistics (discourse analysis, pragmatics, socio-linguistics, etc.), educational linguistics, bilingual teacher education, teaching English as a foreign or second language (TEFL/TESL), etc;
- teachers of second/foreign languages;
- administrators of second/foreign language programs;
- parents of students in language programs;
- politicians who make decisions regarding language issues.

Is All of This Research Really That Important?

To answer a question with a question, "Is language important?" Needless to say, language is the backbone of society. It is one of the major characteristics of being human. Without it we would not know the world as we know it today. Literally everything that humanity has achieved would not have taken place without language. Consequently, to study language and all that it means in society is one of the major challenges that I believe we have before us today. For example, significant strides made in applied linguistic research have aided us in the improvement of teaching and learning of languages throughout the world. Hopefully, this will contribute to humanity's understanding of one another and improve the quality of life in an atmosphere of world peace.

If Applied Linguistics Research Is So Important, How Can We Understand It Better?

This book is specifically designed to answer this question. I have divided it into two parts. The first consists of this chapter and Chapter 2, which provide you with a foundation for working with the remaining chapters. This chapter introduces the concept of the *discerning consumer* and the meaning of research. The second chapter gives tools for finding research reports based on your own interests. Quickly mastering these simple guidelines will make accessible a wealth of information that can have a major impact on how you view and use research.

The chapters in Part II of the book are structured around the typical format used in published research. In them you are given a set of criteria with which to evaluate each component of a research study. For each criterion, you are given excerpts from published research to illustrate how it is used for evaluation. By the end of the book, you should be able to approach any published study in applied linguistics with confidence to not only understand it but evaluate its value for practical applications.

Overview

This chapter attempts to lay a foundation in building a framework for understanding a typical research study. I begin by defining the term *discerning consumer* and then argue for the importance of becoming one. This is followed by an attempt to demythologize how research is perceived by many people and then describe what it typically means to the applied linguistics community. In this description, a schematic understanding of the driving force behind research, the research question, is provided. With this perspective, you will be ready for the following chapters.

Who Is a Discerning Consumer of Research?

The term *consumer* in the business world means a customer—someone who buys and uses a product. In a similar fashion, readers of research are consumers in that they use research for specific purposes. To some degree, the readers of research might *buy into* the research product, if not actually pay money to obtain access to the research study.

There are two basic types of consumers: *casual* and *discerning*. *Casual* consumers are ones who passively read selective pieces of a research article out of curiosity. In the business world, they are the window-shoppers who look but do not buy. However, *discerning* consumers do more than window-shop. They want to use research for practical purposes; they want to read research reports from beginning to end with a level of understanding that can be used to address both theoretical and practical issues. I use the word *discerning* in two senses: *penetrating* and *discriminating*. In the first sense, discerning consumers are given the necessary tools to penetrate beyond the surface of the text to analyze the rationale behind the procedures used and the interpretations made. In the second sense, discerning consumers are able to discriminate between strong and weak research studies by applying the criteria that they will study in this book to make value judgments.

However, by discerning consumers, I do not mean *hypercritical consumers*. The key word here is *discernment*, not fault finding. I do not want readers to become cynics who delight in slamming researchers on every little perceived weakness and group all research as worthless. Rather, discerning consumers are ones who have self-confidence in their own ability to gauge research so that they can evaluate the influence that a study should have on practical issues of concern. When this objective is reached, research journals will no longer be looked upon as forbidding, boring documents that only university professors dare to read. Rather, they will be regarded as important sources of evidence or counterevidence that can be used in arguing the pros and/or cons of implementing new ideas and methodologies in the classroom.

Why Be a Consumer of Research?

Many students, teachers, and administrators are looking for practical information that will help them in their studies, teaching, or program development, respectively. They typically do not want to get overburdened with hypothetical theories. They want immediate and practical information that they can use. They want to know how to teach a foreign (or second) language such as English. They want to know what materials to use, what method works best.

However, there is no single way to teach. There is no single set of materials that can be used in every situation. We must make decisions, and these decisions must have some rationale for support. We must decide what, how, and when to teach based on the needs of the learner. We need to know how the learner thinks and feels, and what the best time is for teaching certain material via a certain methodology. To make these decisions, we must gather information, and this information is obtained through reading and doing research.

Unfortunately, I have seen many people in language teaching over the years jump on various bandwagons regarding what to teach, how to teach, and how the learner acquires a language. I have seen various charismatic experts sway audiences to accept their viewpoint as if it were the absolute truth. However, when the content of what was said was examined, little solid evidence was provided to back up the conjectures. Yet the audience pours out of the conference doors, back to their institutions, heralding the latest jargon, thinking that they have come across the most revolutionary thing they have ever heard. Programs are changed, new curricula are developed, and training sessions in new methodologies are imposed on the faculty. Yet have we really advanced in our discipline? The answer is often in the negative.

To avoid wasting time, money, and human energy, and to prevent being led down the garden path, I argue that we must attend to what is happening in research. Yes, this will slow things down. People will become frustrated that they must wait for answers. They want quick solutions to their problems. They do not want to delay until the verdict comes in through research. Maybe an answer might never be forthcoming. What then? My response is that if we are unable to see some results based on careful research to guide us, we had better not take this route anyway. Money in education is too limited to go out on wild-goose chases to find out five years down the road that the latest fad was a waste of time.

Or maybe one wants to prepare a summary of research on a given topic in order to get a better picture of what the state of affairs is. One cannot include everything and anything one finds. Decisions must be made as to which set of research studies best fit the purposes of one's endeavor.

In either of the above scenarios, we must learn to read research in applied linguistics with a discerning eye. The purpose of this book is to help do exactly this: guide you in becoming a discerning consumer.

The Motivation Behind Research

To become a discerning consumer, we need to have a clear understanding of the driving force behind the research process. However, we require a working definition of the meaning of research first. Today it has many meanings, but much of what is called *research* would not be considered so by the scientific community. The purpose of this section is to explain how most professional researchers understand research by making contrasts with more commonly used definitions of research.

Demythologizing Research

Research Does Not Mean Searching for Articles to Write Papers

Probably the most common misconception about research is confusing it with papers we were asked to write back in secondary school or during our undergraduate days at university—projects often referred to as research papers. Typically, such assignments mean that students go to the library and (re)search for a number of articles from a variety of sources. Then, they integrate the gathered information from these articles through summarizing and paraphrasing into papers addressing issues of importance with correct footnoting and referencing. However, the skills used in writing such papers, although important to research, should not be regarded as research.

The fact is that consumers of research will spend much of their time in this searching activity. Even researchers have to spend a lot of time on the Internet and/or in the library looking up research articles. Both consumer and researcher have to summarize and paraphrase research articles and then integrate them into logical arguments. Both have to document everything and take care in referencing. However, these skills are especially needed at the preliminary stage of information gathering. After this, research begins in earnest.

Working Only in Laboratories with Artificial Experiments

A second common misconception about research is to think that it only involves people in white coats working in spotless, white-walled laboratories running experimental tests on helpless rats or people. Included with this stereotype are graduate students sitting at computers analyzing statistical data hoping to graduate.

These caricatures discourage many people from either reading research or doing it. Fortunately, it is not a true representation of what research is all about. Research is done in many different environments, such as classrooms, homes, schools, and even on the street. Few people wear white coats anymore except in chemical and animal laboratories. Most researchers I know look no different from the average person on the street. As for computers, many people have them in their homes for their children to do their homework or play games. Computers have become so user-friendly now that anyone can use them for all sorts of everyday applications. As for practicality, research results have been applied to help solve some important problems in the language classroom and for developing new theoretical models.

Related to this is the misconception that you have to have a doctorate to understand published research. There is no mystery to research. It does not hide behind a veil that only those given the secret keys can unlock. Published research can be understood by anyone who is willing to take the time to understand the basic, and may I say simple, principles that are involved. This book provides these principles.

The Meaning of True Research

Research is the process whereby questions are raised and answers are sought by gathering, analyzing, and interpreting data. In some cases, answers are hypothesized, predictions are made, and data are collected to support or discredit hypothesized answers. Figures 1.1 and 1.2 combined provide a general framework that encompasses the entire research process. Figure 1.1 illustrates the first phase, how research questions are formulated, and Figure 1.2 summarizes the second phase, finding the answers.

The *heart* of both figures is the *research question*. It is the beginning of the research process and the focus of both the consumer and the researcher. Any given research question asks, explicitly or implicitly, either *what* or *why*. Below are examples of how these two generic questions typically manifest themselves:

"What" questions:
    What phenomena are of importance?
    In what context do these phenomena occur (e.g., when, where)?
    What important relationships exist between phenomena?

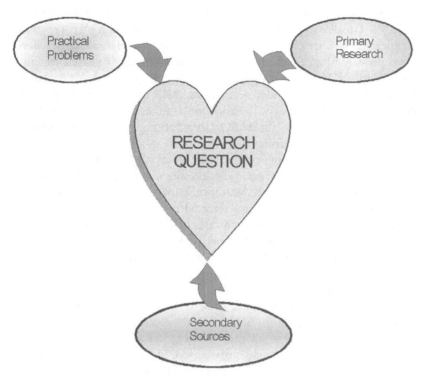

Figure 1.1 Sources for Research Questions

"Why" questions (Causation):
   Why do these phenomena occur?
   Why do people differ on certain traits?

Identifying Important Questions

The motivating force behind research is the inherent curiosity of human beings to solve problems. We see phenomena around us and we begin to ask questions: What is something made of? How did it get here? How does one phenomenon relate to another? Does one phenomenon cause another one to exist, decrease, or increase?

Our questions usually arise from several sources. Probably one of the most common sources is from observing *practical problems* (see Figure 1.1) in the language classroom. Every day, teachers and administrators are confronted with issues that require informed answers. For example, Calvert and Sheen (2015) based their study on the practical problem of teachers using language learning tasks in the classroom "because the realities of using tasks in the classroom are not always straightforward" (p. 227). This led to their research question, "How can a teacher who is inexperienced with tasks create ones that collectively engage learners, appropriately align to their level, and effectively meet shared learning goals?" (p. 227). Is this an important research question? According to Calvert and Sheen, teachers need to set tasks at appropriate levels to determine the effectiveness of a task. Similar practical issues are the focus of research promoted by the TESOL International Research Foundation (TIRF; www.tirfonline.org).

The second place where important research questions are often identified is *secondary sources*. I discuss these in more detail in Chapter 2, but for now textbooks and theoretical papers presented at conferences are examples. These sources are referred to as *secondary* because they summarize other people's research rather than provide firsthand reports by the original researchers. Authors of such literature typically raise questions that need to be addressed. For this reason, they are very fruitful places for finding current research questions being asked by the applied linguistics community.

A good example of an application of this type of resource comes from an article by Paesani (2011). She reviewed a number of research studies in order to assess whether thinking had changed regarding the impact of literature in language instruction. She found that the research in general provided evidence that there had been change "toward multi-modal language development, interpretative interaction with texts, and integration of language and literature" (p. 173). However, she then went on to raise a number of questions in three following paragraphs that need further research. Such articles provide a wealth of research questions for further research. (Take note, grad student, if you are looking for a thesis or dissertation topic!)

The third resource for identifying important questions is: *primary research* (also referred to as *empirical* research that is reported firsthand by the person(s) who actually performed the study). This is one of the most rewarding locations for discovering current questions being asked by the applied linguistics community. The better versed we are in the research literature, the more aware we become of the missing pieces in our framework of knowledge. For instance, we might notice that most of the research addressing a particular question has used a small number of people as participants. This is not unusual because it is common practice for researchers to use small groups of available students from their own programs as research participants. On careful examination, we begin to realize that important characteristics of the group of students we teach are not represented in the samples used in previous studies. This raises the question of how to generalize the findings to answer questions related to our students. We might have a suspicion that our group would behave differently. Such reasoning should lead us to be cautious toward making any practical recommendations based on such research. We would need to look for other studies using samples that are more similar to our students to see if the same results occur. More will be said on this matter in Chapter 4.

Issues other than sampling might also lead us to raise important questions from previous research. The type of material used in a treatment, the method for administering a treatment, and the way in which the data were analyzed are often places where gaps might be found. Future research is needed to help complete the bigger picture before our own questions can be answered. I address these issues in the following chapters of this book.

Besides looking for incongruities in research studies, the next best place to look for research questions is in the discussion/conclusions section of a study, usually identified by the terms *limitations* and *recommendations for further research*. Munro, Derwing, and Thomson (2015) did a two-year longitudinal study examining the segmental pronunciation difficulties between Mandarin and Slavic learners of English in Canada. In their conclusion section, they pointed out two limitations. The first had to do with a limitation in their treatment, using only single-word elicitations for their targets. The second related to their sample being limited in scope of language backgrounds. From this they suggested that further research needed to be done exploring "the longitudinal development of other aspects of L2 phonetics and should include learners from other language backgrounds" (p. 56). Someone looking for a research topic might use this as a springboard for their thesis or dissertation.

At this point, I suggest that you stop and reflect on some of the questions that you might have regarding language teaching and/or learning. Complete the following exercise and share the results with colleagues for discussion.

Exercise 1.1

1. Identify a question you have in the area of concern related to language.
2. Identify where you think this question came from:
    a. your own experience.
    b. your reading of books.
    c. the discussion section of a research article.
3. Why do you think this question is important for others beside yourself?

Where Are the Answers?

The purpose of research is to provide answers to our questions. Unfortunately, most people look for answers in the opinions of famous people before going to primary research. Such opinions are found in textbooks, published papers, and public presentations. However, before expert opinions can have any weight, they must be supported by research. Regrettably, some opinions are given without supporting research and should be recognized for what they are: educated guesses and no more. They should not be given the same status as statements that are supported by research no matter how famous the person is. However, such opinions can be used as *potential* answers and subjected to research, as indicated by the arrow going to the proposed answers oval in Figure 1.2. To draw a direct arrow from Expert Opinion to Research Question is not allowed, although some people, either intentionally or unintentionally, try to make this leap of faith.

Theories are especially developed to generate proposed answers, as Figure 1.2 exhibits. A theory is an attempt to interrelate large sets of observed phenomena and/or constructs into meaningful pictures. In applied linguistics, we do not have any all-encompassing theories that provide explanations for all the phenomena that have been observed in language learning. However, a number of mini-theories, also known as *theoretical models*, such as Chomsky's (2000) theory of generative grammar, are constantly being developed to tie subsets of observed phenomena and/or constructs together. Some more traditional theoretical models that you may encounter in your reading are Chomsky's universal grammar, Krashen's monitor model, Selinker's inter-language model (Omaggio-Hadley, 1993), and Schumann's acculturation model (Schumann, 1986). These and many more are attempts to give meaning to the many observed phenomena that we encounter in applied linguistics.

Occasionally, you will come across studies that compare and contrast various theoretical models. Carrier (1999) did exactly this. She looked at five theoretical models in her search for an answer to the question of why people vary in listening comprehension. I choose three for illustration:

- The social accommodation theory by Giles, Bourhis, and Taylor, which proposes the effects of social status on language behavior.
- Social interaction theory by Wolfson, which adds social distance to status and how they affect interpersonal negotiations.
- Interpersonal perception theory by Laing, which argues that the perceived relationship with the speaker will affect listening.

Based on her overview of these theoretical models, Carrier proposed that sociolinguistic factors, such as status, play an important role in the

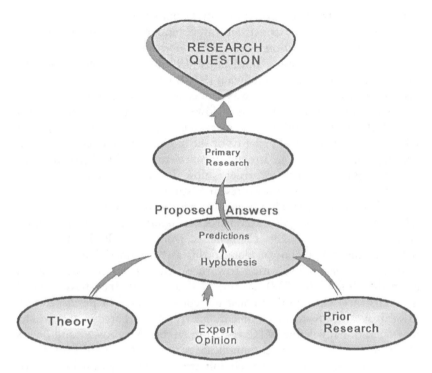

Figure 1.2 Sources for Answers to Research Questions

listening comprehension of foreign language (FL) or second language (L2) learners. However, she did not stop there. She continued by mentioning that she had begun a research study to investigate whether her suggestion had any merit.

Previously, I mentioned how theories connect various *constructs* as well as observed phenomena. A construct is a conceptual label that a given discipline (e.g., applied linguistics) has constructed to identify some quality that is thought to exist but is not clearly observable (i.e., abstract). One of the popular constructs that applied linguists have formulated is *communicative competence*.

Constructs are defined in two different ways: either *constitutively* (Gall, Gall, & Borg, 2008) using other constructs, or *operationally* in behavioral terms. For example, Canale and Swain (1980) constitutively defined the *communicative competency* construct with four other constructs: grammatical competency, sociolinguistic competency, discourse competency, and strategic competency. This does not shed too much light on what communicative competency is, except that it is now broken down into four other constructs, which are still abstract.

Before a construct like communicative competence can be of any use in research, it (or its constructural components) must be defined operationally. An *operational definition* is one that defines a construct in observable terms. Bachman and Palmer (1996), for example, refined the four constructs of Canale and Swain (1980) with further definitions. For instance, *strategic competency* was defined as consisting of metacognitive strategies (note: other constructs). However, they operationally defined one of the metacognitive strategies *goal-setting* as "identifying and selecting one or more tasks that he or she might attempt to complete and deciding whether or not to attempt to complete the task(s)" (Bachman & Cohen, 1998, p. 7). The construct is now defined in such a way that it can be observed and used for a research study.

Another construct that has been given a lot of attention in the literature related to motivation (also a construct) is *willingness to communicate* (WTC) (MacIntyre, Baker, Clément, & Donovan, 2002). MacIntyre, Baker, Clément & Donovan defined this as "an underlying continuum representing the predisposition toward or away from communicating, given the choice" (p. 538). Again, as you can see, they have defined this construct with another construct constitutively, "a *predisposition* toward or away from communicating" (p. 538). Later in the article, they operationally define WTC as a score on the "McCroskey and Baer's . . . 20-item willingness to communicate scale . . . that asked students to indicate the chances . . . of their initiating a conversation in each of 20 situations" (p. 544). As seen here, constructs are often operationally defined in terms of performance on some form of data-gathering instrument.

Going back to Figure 1.2, when theory generates a potential answer to a research question the answer is in the form of a theoretical hypothesis. These are theoretical explanations that propose how several constructs or phenomena relate to one another. To illustrate, Nielson (2014) looked at whether planning time compensated for individual differences in working memory capacity. She described several theoretical models that viewed working memory as some form of executive control for accessing information. Based on these models, she generated three research hypotheses. One, for example, was "working memory capacity will play a significant role in the accuracy of learners' performance under the – planning and + planning conditions" (p. 278). If her findings supported these hypotheses, she would have evidence to support using planning time to facilitate students with weaker memory capacities.

As Figure 1.2 illustrates, hypotheses can also come out of previous research. Often, larger theoretical models are not yet available from which to generate hypotheses. However, this does not stop researchers from trying to hypothesize why phenomena occur. When results repeat themselves over a number of studies, hypotheses can be formulated in an attempt to explain them. A study that illustrates this was done by Valeo (2013), who examined the effect of focus-on-form on learner awareness of language in a content-based language program. One of the two hypotheses they formulated was clearly from previous research. They stated "Drawing on these findings and others, it was hypothesized that instruction which included attention to form within communicative and content-based practice would be helpful for second language learning" (p. 127).

All hypotheses are some type of relationship, as illustrated in Figure 1.3. There are two basic types depending on the nature of the research question. One type is *simple relational*, which states that one construct relates to another. However, the simple relational hypothesis can be further divided into either *descriptive* or *predictive*. The *simple-descriptive–relational* hypothesis stipulates only that a relationship exists, such as "Anxiety negatively relates to language learning." In effect, this means that, as one construct changes (or varies), there is some degree of change in the other construct, but without concluding that one causes the change in the other. For instance, a student of mine formulated the hypothesis that a relationship exists between students' attitudes toward writing in English and their proficiency in English as a foreign language, based on a review of theory and previous research. The two constructs in this hypothesis were *attitude toward writing* and *language proficiency*. In other words, this hypothesis proposed that changes in student attitude toward writing occur in conjunction with changes in language proficiency. Note that this hypothesis does not say that attitude toward writing *affects* language proficiency.

An example from research is found in Préfontaine, Kormos & Johnson (2016), who studied the relationship between oral fluency variables (articulation, length of runs, pause frequency, and pause time) and overall L2 fluency ratings. This resulted in producing statistics for six relationships for three different tasks.

The *simple–predictive–relational* hypothesis states that, by knowing one or more constructs, performance on another construct can be predicted

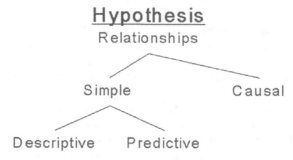

Figure 1.3 Types of Hypotheses

with some degree of accuracy. Not only did Préfontaine et al. look at a number of relationships between oral fluency variables mentioned above; they also used those relationships to predict fluency ratings. More will be said about this in Chapter 7.

The second type of relational hypothesis is *causal*, in that it states that one construct *causes* changes in a second construct. Nielson (2014), mentioned above, examined the causal relationship between working memory capacity and pretask planning time. She formulated three causal hypotheses to answer whether pretask planning offset individual differences in working memory capacity (WMC) with L2 English learners. All of her hypotheses stated that *working memory capacity will play a significant role.*

Both simple relational and causal hypotheses are either *directional* or *nondirectional*. These terms are used to specify the precise nature of the relationship between the two constructs. In the case of a relational hypothesis, a directional hypothesis will designate whether there is a positive or negative relationship. A *positive relationship* simply means that as one construct increases or decreases so does the other construct in the same direction. A *negative relationship* means that, as one construct increases, the other decreases, or vice versa. If a relational hypothesis does not state clearly whether the relation is positive or negative, then it is nondirectional, meaning that the researchers are not sure which direction the relationship will take. Yan and Horwitz (2008) studied how students' anxiety interacts with other variables in influencing language learning from the learners' perspectives. They examined the directional relationships between anxiety and achievement but made no predictions prior to the study regarding direction of relationships.

Causal hypotheses can also be directional or nondirectional. If a hypothesis proposes that one construct will cause change in a second construct in a certain direction, then it is directional. However, if it only posits that there will be a change, without stating which direction the change will take place, it is nondirectional.

On what bases, you might ask, do some researchers make directional hypotheses and others do not? The answer lies in whether there is a theory or enough previous research to warrant the assertion that the results of the study will show a specific direction. I think you will find most studies have nondirectional hypotheses, if they have them at all.

Hypotheses are usually stated in terms of abstract constructs. Yet, as mentioned previously, unless the constructs are defined *operationally* the hypotheses are difficult to test. When the constructs are transformed into operational definitions, the hypotheses become *predictions* (see Figure 1.2). In this form, the hypotheses can be tested. As mentioned earlier, Nielson (2014) used the construct *working memory capacity* (WMC) as a major variable in her study. She operationally defined this construct as the performance on an online memory task called Shapebuilder. This task involved remembering and reproducing sequences of multicolored shapes on a grid. The frequency of correct responses was used for analysis. She also operationally defined her construct *Accuracy* of student performance as percentage of error-free clauses and the error-free use of subject–verb agreement, and she defined *Fluency* as a measure of pruned speech rate. These data were collected from participants recording their stories based on two pictures. If Nielson had restated her hypothesis as a prediction after converting her constructs into their operational definitions, it would have appeared something like this: Performance on the memory task (WMC), Shapebuilder, will impact the pruned speech rate (fluency) of participants differently for those using planning vs those who do not.

Once the predictions are made, the hypothesis can be tested in primary research (see Figure 1.2). Notice here that I use the phrase *primary research* rather than *published research*, in contrast to Figure 1.1. Primary research is research reported firsthand by the researcher(s). Not all primary research is published; some research is presented orally at conferences and some never sees the light of day. I will discuss this more thoroughly in Chapter 2.

As you can see in Figure 1.2, all roads eventually lead to primary research for answering our questions. The results either *support* the hypothesis or *refute* it. Note that I did not say *prove* the hypothesis. *No theory or hypothesis has ever been proved*; although you would not get this impression after hearing some people talk about their pet theory. At best, a hypothesis may be supported, in which case we have a tentative answer to our question, not a conclusive one. If the results fail to support a hypothesis, the hypothesis is then *refuted*, meaning that it can be rejected as a possible answer. For those of you who want to get into this more deeply, I strongly recommend you reading Bhaskar's book *A Realist Theory of Science* (2008).

I need to warn you that Figure 1.2 could be misleading if we are not careful. You might get the impression that one needs all of the elements in this figure before we can answer our questions. In fact, all of the ovals in the figure, except the ones for primary research and the research questions, are not necessary. As I explain in further chapters, there are cases where researchers tackle questions without any previous theories or hypotheses. They are going in with open minds, trying to uncover new information without having their perceptions biased by expectations imposed on them by any given theory. This research is exploratory and usually is seeking answers to *What*-type questions. Do not be mistaken, however; just because there is no theory or hypothesis attached, this does not make the study inferior. In fact, you will find that there is much more exploratory research published than there is research testing hypotheses. More is said about research designs in Chapter 5.

In conclusion, the emphasis I want to make here is that there is no other place to find support for possible answers to our questions than from primary research. After a thorough search, we might find that sufficient evidence has been presented in answer to our questions. Yet, if we find that our questions have not been answered adequately by previous research, we still benefit greatly by knowing that there remains the need for more research. At least we will be prevented from going down the proverbial garden path, wasting time and resources. In preparation for your own search for studies, the next chapter shows how you can access primary research for yourself. I think you will be surprised when you discover how much is readily available for your perusal.

Before you move on to the next chapter however, I suggest you work through this next exercise to help you apply the information you have just covered.

Exercise 1.2

1. Define the following constructs each in two ways: 1) constitutively by using other constructs and 2) operationally in some behavioral terms.
    a. Motivation
    b. Anxiety
    c. Listening comprehension
    d. Attitude
2. In each of the following hypotheses, do three things:
    a. Underline the construct(s) in each hypothesis.
    b. Identify whether each hypothesis is *relational* or *causal* and explain your reasoning.
    c. Determine whether each is *directional* or *nondirectional* and explain your reasoning. If directional, is it in a *negative* or positive direction? Explain.

Hypotheses:

- Level of income influences second language acquisition.
- The more anxious L2 learners are, the slower they will learn a second language.
- The level of motivation will determine how well pronunciation is learned.
- The more positive L2 learners feel about the country of the language they are learning, the better they will do in their L2.

Key Terms and Concepts

applied linguistics
construct
  constitutively defined
  operational defined
discerning consumer
hypothesis
  causal
  directional versus nondirectional
  refuted
  relational
  supported
positive versus negative relationships
prediction
primary research
secondary sources
research versus search
theory

References

Bachman, L. F., & Cohen, A. D. (1998). Language testing—SLA interfaces: An update. In L. F. Bachman & A. D. Cohen (Eds.), *Interfaces between second language acquisition and language testing research* (pp. 1–31). Cambridge: Cambridge University Press.

Bachman, L. F., & Palmer, A. S. (1996). *Language testing in practice: Designing and developing useful language tests*. Oxford: Oxford University Press.

Bhaskar, R. (2008). *A realist theory of science*. New York, NY: Routledge.

Calvert, M., & Sheen, Y. (2015). Task-based language learning and teaching: An action-research study. *Language Teaching Research*, *19*(2), 226–244.

Canale, M., & Swain, M. (1980). Theoretical bases of communicative approaches to second language teaching and testing. *Applied Linguistics*, *8*, 67–84.

Carrier, K. (1999). The social environment of second language listening: Does status play a role in comprehension. *The Modern Language Journal*, *83*, 65–79.

Chomsky, N. (2000). *New horizons in the study of language and mind*. New York, NY: Cambridge University Press.

Gall, M. D., Gall, J. P., & Borg, W. R. (2008). *Educational research: An introduction* (8th ed.). Upper Saddle River, NJ: Pearson Education.

Grabe, W. (2002). Applied linguistics: An emerging discipline for the twenty first century. In R. B. Kaplan (Ed.), *The Oxford handbook of applied linguistics* (pp. 3–12). New York, NY: Oxford University Press.

MacIntyre, P. D., Baker, S. C., Clément, R., & Donovan, L. A. (2002). Sex and age effects on willingness to communicate, anxiety, perceived competence, and L2 motivation among junior high school French immersion students. *Language Learning*, *52*, 537–564.

Munro, M. J., Derwing, T. M., & Thomson, R. I. (2015). Setting segmental priorities for English learners: Evidence from a longitudinal study. *International Review of Applied Linguistic in Language Teaching, 53*(1), 39–60.

Nielson, K. B. (2014). Can planning time compensate for individual differences in working memory capacity? *Language Teaching Research, 18*(3), 272–293.

Omaggio-Hadley, A. C. (1993). *Teaching language in context* (2nd ed.). Boston, MA: Heinle & Heinle.

Paesani, K. (2011). Research in language-literature instruction: Meeting the call for change? *Annual Review of Applied Linguistics, 31*, 161–181.

Préfontaine, Y., Kormos, J., & Johnson, D. E. (2016). How do utterance measures predict raters' perceptions of fluency in French as a second language? *Language Testing, 33*(1), 53–73.

Schumann, J. (1986). Research on the acculturation model for second language acquisition. *Journal of Multilingual and Multicultural Development, 7*, 379–392.

Valeo, A. (2013). Language awareness in a content-based language programme. *Language Awareness, 22*(2), 126–145.

Yan, J. X., & Horwitz, E. K. (2008). Learners' perceptions of how anxiety interacts with personal and instructional factors to influence their achievement in English: A qualitative analysis of EFL learners in China. *Language Learning, 58*, 151–183.

Chapter 2

How to Locate Research

Chapter Overview

In Chapter 1, I talked about generating research questions and searching for answers by looking into previous research. This chapter shows how you can find research studies that might provide answers to your questions. I first identify some of the main sources where you can find such research, along with giving examples that walk you through the necessary steps for using them. I then give you guidelines on how to distinguish between the different types of published articles and how to weigh their value for answering questions. Finally, I provide you with suggestions for obtaining the articles you need. If this is all new to you, I have supplied a list of journals related to applied linguistics in my complementary website (www.routledge.com/cw/perry) for your perusal to help you get started.

Where to Look and What to Look For

Remember the main goal is to find *primary research*. As stated in Chapter 1, primary research is the only way we can test proposed answers to our research questions. The amount of research currently published is overwhelming. New journals arrive on the scene practically every year dedicated to new areas of interest in the research community. Accessing this research can be challenging.

Do not despair. Today is the day of personal computers and the Internet, which make the task of finding relevant research much easier. If you have not yet developed an appreciation for these two technological advances, I strongly recommend that you take advantage of any training you might be able to get. It is well worth the investment in time and money.

These days you can often sit at your computer at home and access the information you need. Not only are you able to find what and where studies are published, but you can download them onto your computer for reading and printing. What used to take many hours of work can be done in a matter of minutes. No longer do you have to go to the library to page through gigantic indexes trying to read type so small that you need a magnifying glass. The only disadvantage is that you miss the physical exercise of going to and from the library, not to mention the running around within the library looking for material.

There are three places where you can locate primary research: *preliminary sources*, *secondary sources*, and *tables of references/bibliographies*.

Preliminary Sources

Fortunately, a number of people have gone to the trouble of preparing resources to help find research. Publications that lead to primary research are known as *preliminary sources*. Some of the more traditional ones that can be found in bound copies in most university libraries (although this format is quickly becoming obsolete) are *Educational Index, Current Index to Journals in Education* (CIJE), *Language Teaching, Linguistics and Language Behavior Abstracts* (LLBA), *Modern Language Association* (MLA) *International Bibliography, Social Science Index, Psychological Abstracts*, and *Resources in Education* (RIE). Both the CIJE and the RIE are produced by the Educational Resources Information Center (ERIC). All of these sources are organized by a set of *keywords*, which reveal the focus of the study.

Keywords are very useful for locating research articles. If you have an idea about what you are interested in, use the substantive words contained in your research question to guide you in looking up related studies. For example, let's say that you have formulated the question: "What is the relationship between anxiety and language learning?" The keywords in your question are *anxiety* and *language learning*. Now you search the above sources using these two key terms to locate relevant studies.

However, thanks to the computer age, many of the bound preliminary sources have now been converted to electronic databases and put into websites on the Internet. *ERIC*, the *LLBA, Modern Language Association International Bibliography*, and many others, such as *Academic Search Complete, PsychInfo*, and *Sociological Abstracts*, are available on the Internet through your library. Another database, *JSTOR*, not only contains some valuable data; it goes back as far as the 1800s. Last but not least, do not forget to use *Google Scholar*, which also has an advanced research option. My students have found this database very useful for finding research articles.

How Databases Work

To familiarize you with the use of an electronic database in your search for studies, I chose ERIC as an example. Although there are many other useful databases, this one and Google Scholar are the most accessible ones on the Internet from almost any location. Moreover, both the *CIJE* and *RIE* have been made available online through ERIC.

If you are near a computer and have access to the Internet, try following the steps as you read along.

1. Go to the website, https://eric.ed.gov; you will be taken to the home web page for ERIC. This screen welcomes you to the ERIC database, which is the gateway to more research than you will ever be able to read in your lifetime! The database currently contains research from 1966 onward and is updated often.
2. Put the cursor in the box that says "Search educational sources," type in the word *anxiety*, and click **Search**. This should result in over 17,000 references.
3. Obviously, there are many articles in this list that do not relate to your research question. To narrow the list down to articles pertinent to your question, look at the lists on the left margin. Here you can limit your search in a number of ways: Publication Date, Descriptor, Source, etc. In the **Publication Type(s)** window, scroll down to **Journal Articles** and note the number of articles on the right that are available in journals with *anxiety* still in the keyword space. When I searched, there were 11,830 references published since 1966 that contained the word anxiety.
4. Now add *language learning* separated by an *AND* in the search box. The word AND is an **Operator**. (To get more information on research operators, click on **Searching Tips**.) When I did this, the computer responded with 842 studies that deal in some way with these two terms from 1966 until 2016.
4.1. However, if you are only interested in the research done within a certain time gap, you can click on the relevant time frame under **Publication Date**. When I limited this search to "Since 1998," ERIC returned 625 references.
5. If you choose the **Advanced Search** option you will have more choices to guide your search. You can use more terms, varying your choices of **Keywords, Author** names, **Titles** to articles, and much more. You can also combine categories with the operators *AND, NOT,* or *OR*. Check out their video, which you can access from there.

The output will provide you with a list of references. This makes it easy to quickly survey various related articles and select the ones you might want look at in greater detail. First the title of the paper is given followed by the authors, the location of the article, and the year. The beginning sentences of the abstract are given along with the descriptors (keywords). The little box on the right shows whether the article has been peer-reviewed and how you can access the article. If it shows "Direct link," click it and the next page will give you a URL that will take you to where you can get the full text of the article. If it offers "Download full text," then you can get it direct. Note that you can save or export the search output by clicking on the appropriate button in the upper right corner.

If you want more information on any article, click on the title. You get the full abstract with a fuller list of descriptors (note: these descriptors can give you more keywords to use in finding more research studies). The other information is self-explanatory, except for the ERIC number, which begins with ED or EJ. The former means that it is a document not necessarily found in a journal, whereas EJ indicates that the paper is published in a journal.

Citation Management Programs

Cite This for Me: www.citethisforme.com
Evernote.org
Mendeley: www.mendeley.com
Paperpile: https://paperpile.com/welcome
Zotero: www.zotero.org

To make things even better, you can save this information on some form of portable external memory (e.g., flash drive), if you are doing this from the library's computer, to peruse when you have more time on your own computer. You can also e-mail the retrieved information to yourself, which I prefer to do. If you are working from your own computer, you can download the information onto your hard drive. Being able to censor through all of the articles that your search produces will save you many hours of rummaging through a library, only to realize that many of the studies are not what you wanted. To top it all off, you can save your searches into a citation management program such as Mendeley or Google Scholar which will put your results into whichever format (e.g., APA) you need for your finished work. (See www.routledge.com/cw/perry for more information.)

Once you have listed out all of the studies that you think would be of interest, you can go to the library to read the entire article, if it has the journal on its shelves, or use the **Full-Text Availability Options** to find out where you might get a copy of the full article. Increasingly, many of the studies are now available electronically and can be downloaded to your computer, if your library has subscribed to such services.

The other online databases that I have mentioned previously, such as *Academic Search Complete, IBSS, Ingenta Connect Complete, JSTOR, LLBA, MLA, ProQuest,* and *PsychInfo,* work similarly to ERIC. However, these are not as accessible as ERIC and Google Scholar. So far,

I have only been able to access these databases through university websites, which require identification codes and passwords. If you are a student at an educational institution, you might have access to your own institution's website or gain access to an outside website to use these databases.

Through my university library via the Internet, 12,000 km away, I used the same keywords and time frame with the *MLA* database as used above and received 55 references. Again, I repeated the same with the *LLBA* database and got 226 citations. In the case of the latter, I obtained more references to studies done internationally. The same search with *PsychInfo* turned up 90 articles. It is always wise to search several different databases to make sure that there is not some important study out there in cyberspace that would be essential for the purpose of your search.

A Walk-Through Example

Let us ask the following question based on our own observations when visiting homes where parents speak only in their L1 while their children are trying to learn an L2 outside the home: *How do parents' L1 influence their children's learning of an L2?* As outlined above, the first thing to do is search for primary research that addresses the problem. To do this:

1. Identify the search terms. There are two phrases in our question that may guide us: *"parents' L1 influence"* AND *"children's learning of an L2."* I used these as the search terms in an ERIC search. (Note: when entering keywords that consist of more than one word, enclose them with quotation marks so they are treated as one phrase.) The results were zero hits, i.e., no articles came up for viewing. Now, what do we do?

2. Play with various combinations of words until some combination produces desirable results. A useful tool to aid us at this point is a *thesaurus*, which most databases such as ERIC provide.

2.1. I clicked on ERIC's **Thesaurus tab** and typed *parent* in the **Search For** box. When I clicked on the **Search** button, it opened another screen with 34 related *descriptors* about parents. I could scroll down this list to find terms more in line with my interest. Another way to do this, which I used, was to choose the **Browse** button back at the **Thesaurus Search**. This displayed a series of alphabetical **letter buttons** that take you to keywords beginning with the letter you choose. I clicked on **P** and scrolled down until I came across descriptors beginning with the word *parent*. I clicked on **Parents as Teachers**, then examined the descriptors listed under **Related Terms**. I found one of interest: **Parent Influence**. I entered these two phrases into the search box separated by the operator *OR* because I wanted the search to use one of these phrases, not necessarily both. Had I used *AND*, both phrases would have had to appear in the same article before a study would have been selected.

2.2. Next, I needed to find some alternative descriptors for *children's learning of an L2*. I tried *children's language learning* but captured no hits. I began with a broader term by typing *language* in the **Thesaurus** box and chose **Language Proficiency**. From the results, I selected two additional terms: *Language Aptitude* and *Second Language Learning*, which I used instead of L2.

2.3. Now I have all the terms I need. The final search phrase that I used is: "parent influence" OR "parents as teachers" AND "language proficiency" OR "language aptitude" AND "second language learning."

In Box 2.1 below I provide a summary of three searches using this search phrase with three different limiting conditions.

This example helps you realize that phrasing questions may need some imagination if you are to produce fruitful literature searches. I dare say that if a question has any importance, there will be primary research to be found. By playing around with the thesaurus, you will be able to

---

BOX 2.1 ERIC Search Summary

Search One

Delimiters: none
Input: "parent influence" OR "parents as teachers" AND "language proficiency" OR "language aptitude" AND "second language learning"
Results: 206 documents found

Search Two

One delimiter: Journals
Input: Same descriptors as above
Results: 55 documents found

Search Three

Delimiters: Journals and years 2007 to 2016
Input: Same as above
Results: 32 documents

unleash a wealth of material out there in cyberspace. The following exercise gives you another opportunity to put the above procedures into practice.

Exercise 2.1

1. Write down a question you think important for teaching another language.
2. Underline the key phrases.
3. Do an initial search using ERIC or some other database.
   a. How many articles did it turn up? Too many, or too few?
   b. If too many, add delimiters to reduce them down to a manageable size. If too few, go to the next step.
4. Look into the ERIC Thesaurus, or the thesaurus of the database available to you, and identify related terms to the ones you have chosen. Plug those into the Search box and repeat steps one to three.
5. When satisfied with your search, print out your results with a report on how you obtained the final list.

Secondary Sources

Besides primary research, your search using preliminary sources will turn up another category of literature, referred to as *secondary sources*. As mentioned in Chapter 1, secondary sources are ones that refer to or summarize primary research through the eyes of someone other than the person(s) who did the study. For this reason, they are valuable places to find references to primary research. These are commonly found in the form of research reviews, position papers, and books.

Reviews of Research

One of the most useful secondary sources is a well-written review of research (aka literature review). This is a very important piece of work that summarizes a number of primary studies related to a particular research issue. A well-written review tries to make sense out of research that has been done in a given area. It compares and contrasts various studies and identifies areas that still need more research. I advise people to look for reviews of research as the first thing they do when trying to find out what research has already been done on a topic and what researchers have concluded so far.

An example of a recent research review is Dooly and Masats's (2015) paper, entitled "A critical appraisal of foreign language research in content and language integrated learning, young language learners, and technology-enhanced language learning published in Spain (2003–2012)."

They provided an overview of research over 10 years on three areas that have impacted education policy in Spain: context and language integrated learning, young language learners, and technology-enhanced language learning. You can find more articles like this through an ERIC search or on Google Scholar with the keywords *review* AND *"language learning."*

Some journals only publish research reviews. The *Annual Review of Applied Linguistics* is dedicated for this purpose in applied linguistics. It comes out once a year, and each volume contains reviews around one general theme in the discipline. Another journal that contains only reviews is the *Review of Educational Research*, which occasionally contains reviews of research related to issues in applied linguistics. Research reviews are also published in journals that contain primary research.

Let me interject a warning here regarding working with secondary sources. There is no substitute for firsthand reading of primary research. This means that we cannot totally rely on summaries of research studies in secondary sources such as a review of research as a substitute for actually reading a primary study. The reason is that reviewers select information only relevant to their focus and leave out the rest. The selection process might have a particular bias that influences the spin that reviewers put on the information they are summarizing. Using this material in our own work would perpetuate this bias and misrepresent the original study. I strongly recommend that you do not yield to any temptation to shortcut the process, but that you make the extra effort to track down the articles that you want to examine and read them for yourself.

Position Papers

Another type of secondary source commonly found is the position paper (aka opinion papers). Often, they resemble a literature review but with a much more focused purpose. In this type of paper, writers argue their particular viewpoints, or positions, on various issues by providing short summaries of research as support. For example, one article I found in a literature search restricting my search to *Opinion Papers* on ERIC was McLean's (2016) paper entitled "The Importance of Supporting Inferences with Evidence: Learning Lessons from Huffman (2014) in the Hope of Providing Stronger Evidence for Extensive Reading." This was published in a research journal but was not primary research. Rather, McLean argued the position that the effects of extensive reading providing comprehensible input for foreign language learners can be bolstered by improvements in research designs. He cited a number of studies to warrant his position. However, for reasons outlined below, we cannot conclude that he has proven his position.

Because position papers are not primary research, we cannot use them as direct evidence to support answers to our research questions. The reason is that authors usually draw the proposed answers (i.e., formulated hypotheses) out of the research studies they cite (see Figure 2.1). However, the research they cite cannot then be turned around to support their positions (represented by the dotted curve line). In other words, the same research cannot be used for both things: proposing answers and justifying answers. If I generate a hypothesis (i.e., a possible answer) from existing data and then turn around (the dotted curve line) and use the same data to support my hypothesis, I have fallen into the trap of circular reasoning (Giere, 2004). There is nothing wrong with the first part (i.e., generating a hypothesis based on existing research), but I cannot use the same data to support the hypothesis from which it was derived. To test a hypothesis, I must do subsequent research to find support, as illustrated on the right side of the vertical dotted line in Figure 2.1.

Let me reiterate here that we cannot use a position paper to support a possible answer on the basis that the people giving the papers are famous or authorities in their field. Somewhere we seem to have picked up the notion that because people are famous what they say must be true. Unfortunately, many people have been led down many a wrong path by relying on someone's fame or charisma. Therefore, unless these famous *someones* back up what they say with solid research, they are just giving their own opinions, which cannot be used as evidence.

As with reviews of research, we cannot substitute position papers for personally reviewing primary research with our own eyes. In presenting his argument, McLean (2016) summarized several primary research studies to generate his suggested answer. The temptation for us is to use his summaries rather than take the time to find the primary studies and summarize them ourselves for our own work. However, we cannot use such summaries as substitutes for summarizing primary research our-selves because it is not uncommon to only focus on information for the

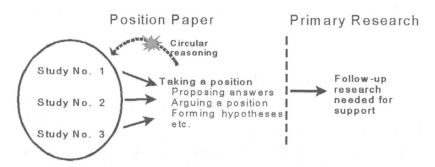

Figure 2.1 The Relation Between a Position Paper and Primary Research

specific purposes of the position paper—important information critical for our purposes may have been left out.

Books

The third secondary source that can provide information about previous research consists of published books. Typically, books are used to provide people with foundations for the issues being considered in a given area. In the process of doing this, they cite and summarize large quantities of primary research. Yet, again the discussion of such research has been run through the cognitive filter of the author(s) and cannot be relied upon as unbiased. Such material can help us become aware of existing research, but it cannot substitute for firsthand reading of such studies. However, there is one exception. Some books are compilations of primary research studies. As long as the research reported is firsthand from the researcher, it can be treated as primary research.

Other Places

Do not forget the reference librarian at your library. This person is a valuable source of information who can help you with ideas and locate other sources. Also, don't forget your professors and peers, who can spur your thinking and advance your list of keywords.

Tables of References/Bibliographies

Other profitable places to find research studies, often overlooked, include tables of references/bibliographies of research articles that we already have found. Often I find *benchmark* (or seminal) studies this way. A benchmark study is one that either sparked interest in a particular issue or marked a pivotal directional change in the way research moved on a given subject. One tactic I use to identify a benchmark study is frequency of citation. When you notice that just about every article you read cites a particular study, you can be fairly sure that it is an important one in the history of the area you are investigating.

Is All Primary Research of Equal Weight?

I have stated that primary research is the only place where we can find evidence to answer our questions. However, not every piece of primary research that you find in your database search is of equal weight for supporting a proposed answer to a question. Figure 2.2 lists the various venues in which primary research can be found. The higher the venue is in Figure 2.2, the more weight it has. Two criteria are directly relevant to the weight: 1) whether the submissions for publication are refereed and 2) whether the referee is blind toward who wrote the study. A referee is usually someone who is either at the same academic level (thus the term *peer evaluation*) as the person submitting the study for publication, or higher. They are considered by the journal publishers to have enough experience in research to give meaningful evaluations. A *blind* referee is one who does not know the researcher's identity when reviewing the article.

There are three general venues: published research, conference presentations, and databases. Under published research, there are three types of journals plus doctoral dissertations. Journals are divided into blind/nonblind, refereed or nonrefereed. Most journals have editorial boards that review every manuscript that is submitted for consideration before being accepted for publication. Yet the rigor with which a manuscript is evaluated varies with the journal.

To add to the problem of weighting different sources, not all journals are equal in prestige, despite the referees being blind. Some journals are considered more important than others. There are several sources evaluating a journal's importance today: the GISI Journal Impact Factor and Srimago Journal & Country Rank. Both take into consideration the number of journal citations in relation to the number of articles published over a designated period of time; however, the latter uses a procedure that provides better information regarding the prestige of a particular journal.

Exercise 2.2

1. Go to the Srimgo website (www.scimagojr.com/journalrank.php).
2. Use the pull-downs to access the following menus:
   a. Subject area: *Social Sciences*
   b. Subject categories: *Linguistics and Language*
   c. Region & Country: *All*
   d. Year: *2015*
3. Locate the journal that you want to find the ranking for.

Consequently, more weight should be given to studies that have been critiqued by qualified referees who are blind than those which have not received this scrutiny. If you can also find the ranked position of a journal's prestige in the field, this adds to the weight of the research article. This type of information will be made more available as the discipline advances.

Notice in Figure 2.2 that I have placed doctoral dissertations higher than nonrefereed journals. The reason I have done this is that doctoral dissertations typically go through rigorous screening by doctoral committees and are not accepted until everything is in good order—at least, that is what is supposed to happen. These dissertations are available, although not as readily as articles in research journals. They are also typically voluminous, which makes them much more difficult to work with. They can be ordered on microfiche, which saves on postage and storage but requires a microfiche reader. They are also becoming more accessible through websites (Google *doctoral dissertations*). Eventually, some of these will be summarized and submitted for publication in research journals. However, you might not want to wait that long.

Primary research can also come in the form of papers read at conferences (see Figure 2.2). If you have ever attended any conference related to applied linguistics (e.g., AAAL, ACTFL, IATEFL, TESOL, etc.), you will find many sessions where primary research is presented. At paper sessions, researchers present 15- to 20-minute summaries about their

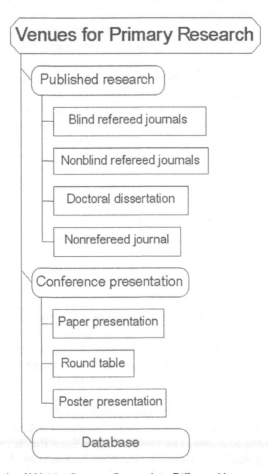

Figure 2.2 Levels of Weight Given to Research in Different Venues

research; at round tables, various researchers present short summaries of their research on a common theme and are available for questions; and at poster sessions researchers (often graduate students) exhibit their studies on poster boards and are available to explain their research to anyone interested. Notice in Figure 2.2 that I have put them in order based on the degree to which they are critiqued. Although there is some degree of scrutiny applied before papers are accepted at conferences, research presented at this venue does not have the same weight as a study that has been published in a journal. The reason is that they have not gone through the same degree of rigorous evaluation prior to presentation. Yet some work presented at conferences is usually evaluated by discussants and certainly by those who hear the presentations. The problem for the consumer is that, unless present at the time of the presentation, these evaluations are not personally heard or read.

Least weight is given to any primary research that appears in a database that has neither been published in a journal nor presented at a conference. Some databases provide references for books, theses, dissertations, speeches, viewpoints, reports, and conference papers, as well as primary research. They do not require any of these works to be published or presented at conferences. Therefore, some primary research referenced in them has been submitted by the researcher so that others might see what was done. For example, individuals can submit summaries of their research to ERIC, which references them for all to see and even provides full-text copies free of charge. A case in point is Al-Sayed, Abdel-Haq, El-Deeb, and Ali's (2016) study on the use of a WebQuest model to develop English language planning strategy in the classroom. From what I can see in the reference, it has not yet been published or presented at any conference. However, it is available through ERIC's website, www.eric.ed.gov, free on a PDF file.

This is not to suggest that articles such as this are not useful research. There is a lot of important research that has not been published nor presented at conferences. However, because it has not gone through some form of peer review, it cannot carry the same weight as research that has. As you develop into a discerning consumer, you can review these articles for yourself and determine their value for answering your questions.

A third criterion you want to keep in mind when gauging the usefulness of a research study for answering your question is how recent the study is. Studies that are 10 years old or older do not usually carry the same weight as more recent studies unless they are seminal studies. When searching, you will want to begin with the most recent and work your way back. The most recent research will bring you up to date on what is happening.

The order of recentness usually goes like this: conference presentations, research journals, and secondary sources. The first is the most recent.

If you are trying to get the latest research on a topic, the place to go is a research conference (e.g., AAAL, IATEFL, & TESOL) where people are reporting their own research, often still in progress. You can usually obtain complete research studies directly from the author(s) at these conferences. If authors do not have full reports or have run out of them, they are usually more than happy to send you a copy. Less recent are journal articles, which may appear anywhere from six months or more from the time the research has been accepted for publication. Most journals take six months to a year before an article is published. Remember that the study itself may have been completed much earlier; therefore, the actual data could be three to four years old before you see the study in print.

The least recent research is material that is cited in secondary sources. Under this classification, literature reviews and position papers are less dated than books. The review cited earlier by Dooly and Masats (2015), for example, reviewed studies between 2003 and 2012. In contrast, books have older references simply because it takes much longer to publish a book than to get a literature review or a position paper presented.

Differentiating Primary from Secondary

One problem my students complain about is the difficulty in identifying primary research from position papers and even literature reviews when searching preliminary sources. My suggestion is that the first thing to examine is the title of the article. In the following reference, for example, from an ERIC search, Molyneux, Scull, and Aliani (2016) informed us that their article is primary research by using the term longitudinal study in their title:

> Bilingual Education in a Community Language: Lessons from a Longitudinal Study. (EJ1100970)

However, we cannot infer whether the following title (Ariani & Ghafournia, 2016) is a primary research article from the title:

> The Relationship between Socio-Economic Status, General Language Learning Outcome, and Beliefs about Language Learning. (EJ1090 138)

Are the authors collecting data or presenting an overview about relationships between socioeconomic status, general language learning outcome, and beliefs about language learning? Fortunately, ERIC provides us with the first sentences of the abstract to gather more information (provided below). We could click on the title of the article, which would provide an unabbreviated abstract if we needed to. Here, we look for key phrases that will give us a clue regarding the nature of the article. The following abstract for Ariani and Ghafournia's study, taken from ERIC, is:

> The objective of this study is to explore the probable relationship between Iranian students' socioeconomic status, general language learning outcome, and their beliefs about language learning. To this end, 350 postgraduate students, doing English for specific courses at Islamic Azad University of Neyshabur participated in this study. They were . . .

The phrase in the abbreviated abstract that shows that the article is a primary study and not a position paper or a review is, "The objective of this study . . ." Not every abstract uses these exact words, but something is said to the same effect.

Often, position papers give clues in the titles as we see in the next ERIC reference.

> Saying what we mean: Making a case for "language acquisition" to become "language development." (EJ1075823)

Here. Larsen-Freeman (2015) lets the reader know it is a position paper by the phrase "making a case for." The abbreviated abstract confirms this:

> As applied linguists know very well, how we use language both constructs and reflects our understanding. It is therefore important that we use terms that do justice to our concerns. In this presentation, I suggest that a more apt designation than "multilingual" or "second language acquisition" (SLA) is "multilingual . . ."

How to Obtain Research Articles

Although finding references to research articles has now become much easier, there continues to be the major challenge to access actual journal articles. Databases, such as ERIC, provide information as to how to locate such material. Increasingly, this is the way most people are now accessing research.

If you cannot find a full-text version online, the next best place is your nearest university library. There, the article you want is either accessible in their collections or obtainable from another library through an interlibrary loan. Finding a good library that has helpful staff is like finding a gold mine.

If you do not have access to articles through a library, ERIC, LLBA, or other databases give you an order number where you can order any article that they have in their database for a small charge. I recommend you order an electronic copy rather than a paper copy because it is cheaper, easier to post, and saves trees.

What Journals Are Related to Applied Linguistics?

There are many research journals that can be used for different areas of interest in the field of applied linguistics. The reason is that applied linguistics is multidimensional; that is, many different disciplines are related to this broad field. You will find research related to applied linguistics in journals dealing with anthropology, computer assisted learning, linguistics, psychology, sociology, and many more areas.

To give you a good head start, several of my graduate students have worked with me to put together a list of journals with brief descriptions of their stated purpose to aid you in your search. These will give you a good idea of the variety of journals and their purposes. I recommend that you check to see how many of these are easily accessible to you. They are found on my companion website (www.routledge.com/cw/perry).

To apply what you have been reading, do the following exercise. The objective is for you to train your eye to look for terminology that will speed up your ability to distinguish between the various types of literature you will encounter in your searches.

Exercise 2.3

1. Choose a topic related to applied linguistics that interests you.
2. Go to one or more preliminary sources and select several references to articles related to your topic.
3. Examine the titles of these and try to determine whether they are primary studies, position papers or literature reviews. What terminology helped you to decide?
4. Now look at the abstracts given by the preliminary source and try to confirm whether your decisions were correct. What statements provided you with further information regarding the nature of the study?
5. Lastly, decide from the title and the abstract whether each article you have listed is relevant to the topic you chose and defend your choice.

Key Terms and Concepts

delimiter
keyword
literature review
operator
position paper

preliminary sources
primary research
secondary sources

References

Al-Sayed, R. K. M., Abdel-Haq, E. M., El-Deeb, M. A., & Ali, M. A. (2016). Enhancing English language planning strategy using a WebQuest model. Retrieved from ERIC database (ED565328).

Ariani, M. G., & Ghafournia, N. (2016). The relationship between socio-economic status, general language learning outcome, and beliefs about language learning. *International Education Studies, 9,* 89–98.

Dooly, M. & Masats, D. (2015). A critical appraisal of foreign language research in content and language integrated learning, young language learners, and technology-enhanced language learning published in Spain (2003–2012). *Language Teaching, 48,* 343–372.

Giere, R. N. (2004). *Understanding scientific reasoning.* Graton, CA: Wadsworth.

Larsen-Freeman, D. (2015). Saying what we mean: Making a case for "language acquisition" to become "language development". *Language Teaching, 48*(4), 491–505.

McLean, S. (2016). The importance of supporting inferences with evidence: Learning lessons from Huffman (2014) in the hope of providing stronger evidence for extensive reading. *Reading in a Foreign Language, 28,* 143–147.

Molyneux, P., Scull, J., & Aliani, R. (2016). Bilingual education in a community language: Lessons from a longitudinal study. *Language and Education, 30*(4), 337–360.

Part II

The Major Components of Published Research

Chapter 3

Understanding the Framework of a Primary Research Article

Chapter Overview

Research articles typically follow a standard format for presentation in research journals. I have used this format to organize the following chapters.

The purpose of this chapter is to provide you with an overview of this framework as an introduction to the rest of the book. I begin by describing what a typical research study looks like with a brief explanation of each component. The first three parts—title, abstract, and introduction—are discussed more fully in this chapter, whereas separate chapters are dedicated to the remaining components. I provide you with examples of current research from different journals and have interspersed some exercises to help you develop an overall schema of the basic structure of a research article.

The Framework of a Research Article

Most research articles adhere to the following format:

1. Title
2. Author(s) and institution(s)
3. Abstract
4. Introduction
5. Method (Methodology)
6. Results
7. Discussion/Conclusions
8. References

The Title

Although many readers might not think the title is very important, it is in fact crucial. Titles either attract potential readers or dissuade them from reading the article. A well-written title should give enough information to inform the consumer what the study is about. It might suggest what the research question is or even what hypothesis is being tested, but there should be no doubt what issue is being investigated.

The title should indicate what type of article it is. There should be no unnecessary guessing as to whether the study is primary research, a review of research, or a position paper. For example, there is little doubt what Li's (2015) study is about: "Connecting reading and writing: A case study." It is a primary study that examines the reciprocal relationship between reading and writing. In contrast, Tonne and Pihl's (2015) paper entitled "Morphological Correspondences in the Reading–Writing Relation among L2 Learners" is unclear as to whether it is primary research or a review of research. It could be either. The reader has to go to the abstract or the body of the introduction to find out which it is.

At the same time, the title should not require unnecessary reading. Some titles are short and succinct, clearly telling the readers what they want to know, such as Li's (2015) study, mentioned earlier. Others can be quite long and complex, such as the study entitled "The Relations Between Word Reading, Oral Language, and Reading Comprehension in Children Who Speak English as a First (L1) and Second Language (L2): A Multigroup Structural Analysis" (Babayigit, 2015). Although this title clearly indicates what the study is addressing and that it is a primary study, I wonder if it could have been truncated to facilitate reading for the consumer. However, I am getting off topic into the art of title writing.

In summary, the three criteria to look for in a title are: focus of the article, type, and succinctness. The first two are the most important, because they quickly inform you whether the paper is what you are searching for. The third is more of a stylistic issue, which you should keep in mind if you ever have to title a paper of your own.

The Abstract

The abstract in a research article is written by the author(s) of the study. This is not always the case with the abstract written in preliminary sources, such as ERIC or LLBA. For this reason, the abstract in the article is usually much more reliable to identify the content of the study.

A well-written abstract should summarize five essential things to help the reader know what the study is about: 1) the purpose of the study, 2) the source(s) from where the data are drawn (usually referred to as the sample), 3) the method(s) used for collecting data, 4) the general results, and 5) general interpretation and/or applications of the results. Some abstracts may contain more than these things, but unfortunately some abstracts do not contain some (if not all) of these essential elements.

With this information, the consumer will know from the abstract whether the article is of interest. To illustrate, I extracted the above five pieces of information from the abstract of a study by Li, Zhu, and Ellis (2016), set out below, which looked at whether corrective feedback, immediate or delayed, facilitated learning the English past passive construction. Table 3.1 shows the parts of the abstract verbatim that address these five points.

The article reports on a study investigating the comparative effects of immediate and delayed corrective feedback in learning the English past passive construction, a linguistic structure of which the learners had little prior knowledge. A total of 120 learners of English as a foreign language (EFL) from 4 intact classes at a Chinese middle school were randomly assigned to conditions: immediate feedback, delayed feedback, task-only, and control. The 3 experimental groups attended a 2-hour treatment session where they performed 2 dictogloss (narrative) tasks in groups, each followed by a reporting phase in

Table 3.1 Abstract Analysis Grid

Important points	Content
Purpose of the study	"investigating the comparative effects of immediate and delayed corrective feedback in learning the English past passive construction"
Sample	120 learners of English as a foreign language (EFL) from 4 intact classes at a Chinese middle school
Method used for collecting data	The 3 experimental groups attended a 2-hour treatment session where they performed 2 dictogloss (narrative) tasks in groups, each followed by a reporting phase in which they took turns telling the narrative to the class. The 2 feedback groups received either immediate or delayed corrective feedback in the form of a prompt, followed by recasts of utterances containing errors in their use of the target structure
Results	No effect for the corrective feedback was found on elicited imitation test scores, but both the immediate and delayed feedback resulted in gains in grammaticality judgment test scores, with immediate feedback showing some advantage over delayed feedback
Interpretations	We interpret these results as showing that the feedback only aided the development of declarative/explicit knowledge and that the advantage found for immediate feedback was due to the learners using the feedback progressively in the production of new past passive sentences, whereas this did not occur in the delayed feedback condition
Applications of results	Not available

which they took turns telling the narrative to the class. The 2 feedback groups received either immediate or delayed corrective feedback in the form of a prompt, followed by recasts of utterances containing errors in their use of the target structure. No effect for the corrective feedback was found on elicited imitation test scores, but both the immediate and delayed feedback resulted in gains in grammaticality judgment test scores, with immediate feedback showing some advantage over delayed feedback. We interpret these results as showing that the feedback only aided the development of declarative/explicit knowledge and that the advantage found for immediate feedback was due to the learners using the feedback progressively in the production of new past passive sentences, whereas this did not occur in the delayed feedback condition.

(p. 276)

As you can see, this abstract provided more than enough information to decide the relevance of the study for the reader's purpose.

There is nothing like firsthand experience to get a better grasp of the prior discussion. The following exercise provides you with a framework for analyzing and evaluating research abstracts.

Exercise 3.1

Find a recent research study of interest and examine the **abstract** carefully. Fill in the abstract analysis grid in Table 3.1 above and answer the following questions:

1. What other information is in the abstract? Summarize it in your own words.
2. Was the abstract succinctly written?
3. Was it easy to understand?

The Introduction of a Study

The introduction is the *brain* of the study. In it we should find the topic being investigated, why it is important enough to be studied, the research question(s), any theory being considered, any hypothesis being proposed, and any predictions made. In addition, constructs and special terminology that are used throughout the study should be defined.

Typically, the introduction should provide historical context to the issue being investigated and bring in any theory that may be relevant to the reader. Often this is referred to as the *literature review* of the study (although not necessarily referred to as such), in that it summarizes and references a number of articles to introduce the reader to the study (e.g.,

Kessler & Plakans, 2008). However, this is not a review of research, such as referred to in Chapter 2, which is a complete document that provides a broad overview of research and thinking on a given area. Rather, a literature review within the introduction of a study is a highly orchestrated, logical argument consisting of a number of propositional statements to provide the reasoning behind the study. With each statement a study is summarized and/or referenced for support of the statement. At the end of the argument there should be a conclusion in the form of at least one research question and possibly a hypothesis or several hypotheses. Hypotheses, in turn, should be operationally defined and translated into predictions.

In logic (Giere, 2004), a statement is either true or false and is used in a logical argument as one of the premises of the argument (see my complementary website for a more detailed explanation). Each statement needs to be supported by findings from at least one study to warrant the statement as a premise of the argument. If no support is provided, then the statement is no more than a hypothesis itself and needs to be tested before it can be used as a premise in any argument. For example, if I want to make the statement "Women are better language learners than men" as one of the premises of my argument, I had better cite at least one study to back this statement up. If there is no primary research to back this statement up, it cannot be used as one of the premises of my argument. It becomes itself a hypothesis that needs to be tested in a study of its own.

The support for each statement will be in the form of at least one reference to a primary study that you can look up to see if the statement has support. If there is no reference to a study after a statement, the statement should be treated with suspicion. Statements without support weaken the overall argument.

However, not every reference that follows a statement is a research study. Sometimes references only cite the opinion of someone else. For example, Sheen (2008) included the following statement in the introduction to her study on recasts, anxiety, and language learning: "It is argued that recasts create an optimal condition for the cognitive comparison needed for learning to take place (Doughty, 2001; Long, 1996)" (p. 836). The two references that she cited are not studies supporting the statement but are articles that made an argument for an opinion. She is very clear in her introduction to distinguish between citations that are supporting studies and citations that reference opinion.

A well-written paper lets the reader know in the text whether the reference is a study or an opinion. If you are not sure, look at the title in the full reference section to see whether you can identify which one it is. If that does not work, and you are really curious, you need to look at the abstract of the study provided in one of the preliminary sources (e.g., ERIC) or the study.

To illustrate the argument process, I analyzed the introduction section of Luo and Liao's (2015) study, entitled "Using Corpora for Error Correction in EFL Learners' Writing." The analysis is presented in Box 3.1

As can be seen in this example, the authors built their argument so that the reader can understand why this particular study was needed. After every premise, they supplied references to studies that provided support except for premise 2/sub-premise 2: "a considerable number of teachers

---

BOX 3.1 Analysis of the Argument for a Study

The problem:
"A lack of grammatical or lexical accuracy in writing is a major problem for English as a foreign language (EFL) learners."

The argument:
Context: Data Driven Learning (Johns, 1991), which uses corpora to help students inductively discover correct lexico-grammatical patterns, has been shown to reduce errors in writing. "Over the past decade, corps consultation in the classroom has been regarded by some L2 writing researchers as one of the most promising areas that can inform L2 writing pedagogy and broaden language teaching and learning (Bloch, 2007; Conrad, 2008; Granath, 2009; Yoon, 2011)."

1st premise:
"Numerous studies (Coxhead & Byrd, 2007; Flowerdew, 2010; Tribble, 2009) have shown that corpus examples are effective in helping learners with lexico-grammatical patterns to enhance L2 learner writing performance."

2nd premise:
"However the empirical studies about actual corpus use in learners' writing in China are rarely seen due to the following reasons"
  Sub-premises:
  1. "corpus tools are not easy enough for learners to use (Kosem, 2008) and texts sampled in corpora are so difficult that learners can hardly comprehend, especially for lower-level learners."
  2. "a considerable number of teachers don't have a pedagogical background in using corpora."
  3. "many EFL learners in China are accustomed to being told directly what to do by a teacher and not willing to assume the responsibility for their learning (Boulton, 2009b)."

Conclusion 1:
"To tackle this problem, the corpus for learners to use should be carefully selected and sufficient training is also necessary to help learners benefit as much as possible from using corpora in writing."

Literature Review (the argument continues):

3rd premise:
"writing should be learned through the writing process itself and concentrates on the development and expression of ideas for the purpose of developing the writers' ability of discovering, analyzing and solving problems so as to improve their writing ability (Deng, et al., 2003)."

Sub-premises:
1. "some researchers mainly focus on students' lexical errors." Todd (2001).
2. "some studies concerning various types of errors which include lexical errors, grammatical errors, and capitalization errors." Chambers and O'Sullivan (2004)
3. "not all types of errors were appropriate for correction by consulting corpora." Tono, Y. et al., (2014)
4. "teachers' guidance and instruction especially for lower-level students" is needed. Chang & Sun (2009)
5. "the selection of corpus should be cautious. Firstly it should be easy to handle just like Google, and then it should meet learners' needs." Chang (2014); Pérez-Paredes, Sánchez-Tornel & Alcarez Calero (2012)

Conclusion 2:
"It can be clearly seen from the above studies that although these factors such as error types, learners' language proficiency, teachers' guidance or training, types of corpora may influence the outcome of corpus use, it is also rewarding to apply corpora in error correction in writing. However, are corpora better than the traditional resources as reference tools in helping learners correct errors?"

Hypotheses: None

Research Questions:
1. "Which one is more useful in helping learners reduce errors in free production, consulting corpora or consulting the online dictionary to correct errors?"
2. "Is corpora-assisted error correction more useful in making the right corrections compared with dictionary-assisted error correction?"
3. "What are EFL learners' attitudes toward the corpora-assisted error correction?"

don't have a pedagogical background in using corpora." They did not cite a study that supported this premise. Maybe they felt it was so obvious that it did not need a study to back it up. This is the only weak link in the argument and does not look too damaging. Note that there was no hypothesis generated from the argument. However, there was a list of research questions. These clearly were supported by the argument.

A detailed analysis of the argument in the introduction is not something consumers will do every time they read an article. However, to help develop a mind-set for reading introductions in this fashion, I suggest you do the following exercise. It is not an easy exercise, but you will find that it focuses your mind more than usual when you read an introduction to a study. After doing this several times, you will find that you will be doing this automatically.

Exercise 3.2

Find a recent research study of interest and examine the introduction carefully. Perform the following tasks:

1. Identify the purpose of the study.
2. Outline the argument with the main points (see Box 3.1).
   a. List the premises of the argument.
   b. Indicate what support is given for each premise by citing one reference to a primary research study. If there is no supporting reference, indicate this.
   c. State your opinion on how well you think the points logically relate to one another.
   d. Are there any gaps in the logic? If so, what are they?
3. Identify the conclusion of the argument that should be in the form of questions and/or hypotheses/predictions.
4. State your opinion on how well you think the conclusion logically relates to the preceding argument.

Method

The *method* (or *methodology*) section consists of the skeleton of the study. If it is well written, others should be able to replicate the study exactly. The ability to replicate the study is the principal criterion used for judging the quality of this component of a research report.

The method section tells us who were studied, what was studied, and how the information was collected and analyzed. The following outline lists the typical subsections that are under this heading. Studies vary in what subsections authors include under the method section, but the information contained in the following subsections should be presented in some manner. The following chapters discuss many of these subsections in detail, but I provide a brief definition for each in the following:

- Sample
- Research design
  - treatment(s) (optional)
  - techniques (optional)
  - materials (optional)
- Data-collection procedures
  - instruments (optional)
  - observational methods
- Procedures followed

Sample

This subsection of the method section describes the participants/subjects or the objects of the study from which the data were gathered. A well-written sample section should provide as much detail as needed about the participants/objects. It should also explain the rationale used for selecting the participants so that the reader may be able to assess whether the resulting data are valid for the purpose of the study.

For example, Luo and Liao (2015) used participants and described them as 30 students (20 males, 10 females). They continued by providing information about the fact that they were native Mandarin Chinese speakers who had been ESL students for seven years. They were carefully selected so that they did not differ in language proficiency or motivation. With this information, the reader can decide whether the results of the study are applicable to the question under consideration.

However, there are studies that look at *objects* rather than participants, such as when a discourse analysis study is being done on a corpus of text. Rett and Hyams (2014) used "the corpora of 45 American English-speaking children in the CHILDES database (McWhinney & Snow 1985)" (p. 173) in one of three studies they reported which looked at syntactically encoded evidentiality in English. (Hey, this is new word for me too.) They extracted 70 declarative statements containing elements important to their study from corpora that included children between the ages of two and seven. Note that the researchers were not interested in the *who* but the *what* (i.e., the corpus of the text itself, rather than the children who produced the utterances).

Chapter 4 expands more on a number of important issues regarding the sample subsection of which the consumer will want to be aware. Although this segment of the study, on face value, appears to be routine, these issues will either add to, or detract from, the credibility of the study's results.

Research Design

The research design subsection, often referred to as *design*, explains the overall structural design used in the study. There are a number of designs available, and each one has its appropriate use. Each has its strengths and weaknesses depending on how well the data answer the research question(s).

In a well-written design section, the *variables*[1] of the study are clearly identified and defined. In fact, the term *construct* is usually replaced by the term *variable*. If something does not vary, then it is not a variable. For example, *language ability* is a construct that varies (i.e., people vary in language ability). Therefore, it is referred to as a variable when used in a study, regardless of whether the word *construct* is used. Variables can take four different forms or scales. They can vary by discrete categories, rank order, continuous scores on some measure but no meaningful zero, or continuous scores with a real meaningful zero. Gender is an example of the first (e.g., male vs female); rating one's writing ability from 1 to 5 illustrates the second; scores on a language proficiency test is the third; and reaction time to some stimulus the fourth (see Appendix B for more detail).

Variables can have different classifications. A variable may be *descriptive, correlational, independent, dependent, moderating*, or *extraneous*. How a variable is classified depends on the role the variable plays in a study and the type of research design being used, which is determined by the research question(s). In other words, the same variable can be descriptive in one study, correlational in another, independent in a third, dependent in a fourth, moderating in a fifth, and extraneous in a sixth. To make things more challenging, research studies vary in how many of these different types of variables are present.

Although I explain more about variable classification within the context of my discussion of the different research designs in Chapter 5, let me give you a brief overview of these different types of variables. *Descriptive variables* are variables that are *observed* and *described* without looking at the effect of one variable on another. These variables are mostly used to answer the *What's out there?* question. The data recorded on these variables are usually in the form of detailed verbal descriptions and/or frequency of occurrence. A study by Canale (2016) provides a clear example of a study that solely examined descriptive variables. It is clear from the title, "(Re)Searching Culture in Foreign Language Textbooks, or the Politics of Hide and Seek," that the principal variables of interest were culture and foreign language textbooks. Data were in the form of verbal descriptions and frequencies extracted from nine textbooks as the data source. More will be said about this study under the heading of meta-analysis.

Correlational variables (CV) are collected for the purpose of finding relationships between two or more variables. The variables are typically measured by counting their frequencies of occurrence or by scores on instruments that measure the variables. To illustrate, Vandergrift (2005) examined relationships between metacognitive awareness, motivation, and listening comprehension. He used a questionnaire to identify the degree to which participants used different metacognitive strategies, another questionnaire to discover the motivation behind participants studying French, and total scores on a multiple-choice test to assess listening comprehension. To answer his research questions, he correlated all of these measures in different combinations.

An *independent variable* (IV) is regarded as a *variable of influence*—that is, it *affects* the variation (or change) in another variable. The variable being influenced (or changed) is labeled the *dependent variable* (DV), in that its variation *depends* on changes in the independent variable. These two variable labels are found in research designs that look at causation.[2] The way you can identify the two variables is to note which one is thought to affect (i.e., impact, change, cause, influence, etc.) the other. The one doing the affecting is the independent variable, and the one being affected is the dependent variable. Often you can spot them in the title of the study, for example in the title of Machida and Dalsky's (2014) study, "The Effect of Concept Mapping on L2 Writing Performance: Examining Possible Effects of Trait-Level Writing Anxiety." The IV is concept mapping. The DV was trait-level writing anxiety. The DV was operationally defined as the score on a modified "Daly–Miller Writing Apprehension Scale (WAS)."

A study can have more than one independent variable and/or dependent variable as well. For instance, Moskovsky, Alrabai, Paolini, and Ratcheva's (2013) study entitled "The Effects of Teachers' Motivational Strategies on Learners' Motivation: A Controlled Investigation of Second Language Acquisition" used 10 motivational strategies for IVs, and several DVs (learners' motivation behaviors).

Some research designs have what is referred to as a *treatment* or maybe even several treatments. This is usually done when the researcher(s) *manipulates* an independent variable and looks at its effect on a dependent variable. The treatment may involve some *technique*, as demonstrated in Sheen's (2008) study, in which she provided feedback in the form of recast to both high- and low-anxiety students and compared these students to those who did not receive feedback. The treatment was the feedback.

The treatment might also consist of some type of *material*. The material can be in the form of written, audio, or visual information presented to the participants. This is illustrated by Yanguas (2009), who examined the effects of different types of glosses (textual and pictorial) on reading comprehension and acquiring vocabulary. The type of gloss was the treatment.

The *moderating variable* (MV), as the name suggests, works as a go-between from one variable to another; that is, it moderates the relationship between two CVs or influences the degree to which an IV affects a DV. Figure 3.1 shows the mediating role the MV plays in a study involving an IV and a DV. An MV can be in any of its possible forms: categorical, ordinal, or continuous. For instance, a study by Rahmani and Sadeghi (2011) "examined the effects of note-taking strategy training on Iranian EFL learners' comprehension and retention of written material, with gender as a moderating variable (ERIC: EJ955182)." The IV was *note-taking training*, and the DVs were *comprehension and retention of written materials*. However, they used an MV as well: *gender*. They wanted to know whether the effect of the note-taking training on comprehension and retention was different depending on whether the participants were male or female (i.e., whether gender moderated the effect).

Extraneous variables (EV) are any variables that the researcher does *not* want to influence the relation between two CVs or the effects on a DV other than by the IV. As Figure 3.1 illustrates, these variables (aka confounding variables) are lurking around a study trying to creep in to distort the results. In some studies, researchers may not want their data influenced by differences in such variables as gender, age, level of language proficiency, intellectual development, and so on. The design of the study, if planned appropriately, should keep the influence of these variables at bay. Chapter 5 provides a detailed description of many types of EVs that

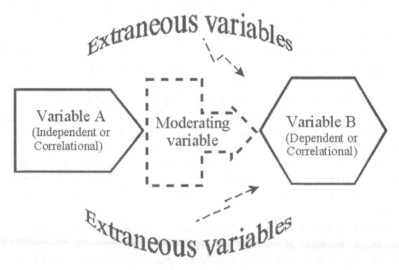

Figure 3.1 Relationships Between Variable Types

can mess up a study. A well-written study mentions what EVs threaten the results and states what was done to prevent their effects.

Identifying variables of a study is not a straightforward task. For this reason, I have included the following exercise to give you an opportunity to identify variables and classify their types in studies that you have found. I suggest that you use Figure 3.1 as a guideline for making your decisions.

Exercise 3.3

Task: Use a recent journal related to applied linguistics. Find a research study of interest and examine the introduction and the method sections carefully. Perform the following tasks:

1. Summarize the purpose of the study in your own words.
2. Classify the variables according to the previous definitions.
3. Identify the forms (scales) of the variables.
4. Provide a rationale for your classification.

Data-Collection Procedures

This subsection explains in detail how the information is collected for the purpose of a research study. Most studies involve either instruments and/or observational procedures.

Instruments specifically relate to the devices used to collect the data. These are usually in the form of surveys or tests. They can be presented in written, audio, or visual format. Responses can be gathered via paper-and-pencil tests, computer-administered tests, video camera, or audiotape recorder.

Other studies may not involve any data-gathering instruments but may involve personal observations of participants or objects. These studies typically use video or audio recording to keep a record of the data in case there is need for validation, but the actual data collection is done by an observer or a group of observers.

In some studies, confusion between the instruments and the materials used in the treatment can occur if the reader is not careful. One might think of the material as the stimulus that elicits the behavior that is measured or observed by the instrument. For example, Luo and Liao (2015), cited earlier, studied whether the use of corpora would decrease errors in writing. They used a web-based corpus analysis tool as part of the treatment in their study. They classified it under *instruments* along with an online dictionary. These were not used to collect the actual data that were analyzed but rather were part of the treatment in the study. The data collection was done by trained teachers who tabulated the errors in the subsequent writing output. Chapter 6 provides a more detailed discussion on this.

Procedures Followed

This subsection is a detailed explanation of how the complete study was executed. In some studies, the data-collection procedure subsection and this section are the same. The procedure subsection describes when and how the treatment (if any) were administered, when and how the instruments (if any) were given, and/or when and how observation methods were used. The main criterion for judging the quality of this subsection is whether we have enough information to replicate the study if need be. In Luo and Liao's (2015) procedures section, they gave a very detailed explanation about the three steps that they used for both the treatment and control groups. The reason is that, if anyone wanted to replicate this study, they would be able to compare their results with those of this study.

To give you a feel for what has just been discussed, I recommend you doing the following exercise.

Exercise 3.4

Task: Use the same research study that you used for Exercise 3.4. Examine the method section carefully. Complete the following tasks:

1. Briefly summarize the procedure that the researcher(s) went through to collect their data.
2. Estimate whether you could replicate this study if you had the facilities. If you could not, explain what pieces of information you would need to repeat this study.

Results

In this section, the results of any analysis of the data are given. Depending again on the nature of the research design, different methods are used to try to make sense of the data. One common method is to use statistics. Often, many readers jump over this section, thinking it is only for the mathematically inclined. However, one of my goals in Chapter 7 is to help the consumer of research not to be intimidated by strange Greek symbols, tables full of numbers, and graphs full of lines.

Not all studies have results sections filled with statistics. In some studies, which I later refer to as *qualitative studies*, the results section contains verbal data consisting of detailed descriptions of what was observed. Researchers spend extended amounts of time gathering large quantities of verbal data, with the main purpose of identifying patterns and trends that will guide in answering the research questions of the study. Occasionally, some descriptive statistics are used to help illustrate these patterns. More is said about the issues involved in this type of analysis in Chapter 7.

The results section of a study is important and should not be avoided. The strengths and weaknesses of a study can often be found in the choice of a data analysis procedure that affects the results. Conclusions based on faulty results cannot be used to answer our research questions. Chapter 7 expands on the results section more. It compares how verbal and numerical data are treated and the criteria that need to be used when evaluating whether they have been properly used.

Discussion/Conclusion

The final section of a research study discusses the results and concludes the study. If the discussion is exceptionally lengthy, the conclusions may be separated from it. Here is where the results are interpreted in light of the research question(s) being asked and/or any hypothesis being tested.

A well-written discussion/conclusions section also relates the findings of the study to previous research that has been done and to any theorizing that has been going on regarding the research topic. In addition, authors should evaluate their own study by pointing out its strengths and weaknesses. This section characteristically concludes with what further research needs to be done and suggestions on how it might be done. Chapter 8 spends more time describing what constitutes a well-written discussion section.

Key Terms and Concepts

abstract
data-collection procedures
instruments
material
method
observational methods
participants/objects
premise
research design
sample
treatment
variables
   correlational
   dependent
   descriptive
   extraneous
   independent
   moderating

Notes

1. A *variable* is simply something that varies, usually corresponding to one of the constructs in a study.
2. Studies that look at predictive relationships also distinguish between IVs and DVs, but cannot conclude causation.

References

Babayigit, S. (2015) The relations between word reading, oral language, and reading comprehension in children who speak English as a first (l1) and second language (l2): A multigroup structural analysis. *Reading and Writing: An Interdisciplinary Journal, 28*, 527–544.

Canale, G. (2016). (Re)Searching culture in foreign language textbooks, or the politics of hide and seek. *Language, Culture and Curriculum, 29*, 225–243.

Giere, R. N. (2004). *Understanding scientific reasoning.* Graton, CA: Wadsworth.

Kessler, G., & Plakans, L. (2008). Does teacher's confidence with CALL equal innovative and integrated use? *Computer Assisted Language Learning, 21*, 269–282.

Li, S., Zhu, Y., & Ellis, R. (2016). The effects of the timing of corrective feedback on the acquisition of a new linguistic structure. *Modern Language Journal, 100*, 276–295.

Li, Z. (2015) Connecting reading and writing: A case study. *English Language Teaching, 8*(6), 150–158.

Luo, Q., & Liao, Y. (2015). Using corpora for error correction in EFL learners' writing. *Journal of Language Teaching and Research, 6*, 1333–1342.

Machida, N., & Dalsky, D. J. (2014). The effect of concept mapping on L2 writing performance: Examining possible effects of trait-level writing anxiety. *English Language Teaching, 7*(9), 28–35.

Moskovsky, C., Alrabai, F., Paolini, S., & Ratcheva, S. (2013). The effects of teachers' motivational strategies on learners' motivation: A controlled investigation of second language acquisition. *Language Learning, 63*, 34–62.

Rahmani, M., & Sadeghi, K. (2011). Effects of note-taking training on reading comprehension and recall. *Reading Matrix: An International Online Journal, 11*, 116–128.

Rett, J., & Hyams, N. (2014). The acquisition of syntactically encoded evidentiality, *Language Acquisition, 21*, 173–198.

Sheen, Y. (2008). Recasts, language anxiety, modified output, and L2 learning. *Language Learning, 58*, 835–874.

Tonne, I., & Pihl, J. (2015). Morphological correspondences in the reading-writing relation among l2 learners. *Reading Matrix: An International Online Journal, 15*, 206–219.

Vandergrift, L. (2005). Relationships among motivation orientations, meta-cognitive awareness and proficiency in L2 listening. *Applied Linguistics, 26*, 70–89.

Yanguas, I. (2009). Multimedia glosses and their effect on L2 text comprehension and vocabulary learning. *Language Learning & Technology, 13*, 48–67.

Understanding Where Data Come From

The Sample

Chapter Overview

The first subsection in the methodology section of a study typically informs the reader where the data come from (i.e., the sample). You might ask, "What is so important about a sample of participants that we have to spend a whole chapter on the topic?" As I hope you see while reading this chapter, what initially appears to be an insignificant portion contained in the methodology section of a study proves to be one of the foundation stones upon which the study is evaluated regarding its usefulness.

The purpose of this chapter is to provide you, the consumer of research, with an overall understanding about the importance of and the thinking that goes on when choosing a sample. I first provide some initial definitions of terminology, which are essential for understanding the rest of the discussion. These definitions are followed by two segments that discuss the two major sampling paradigms found in research in applied linguistics. The choice of paradigm, as you might suspect by now, is guided by the research question being asked by the researchers. The chapter ends with a discussion of the ethics of using human participants in a research study.

Sampling Terminology

The *sample* is the source from which data are drawn to answer the research question(s) and/or to test any hypothesis that might be made. The sample consists of one or more *cases*. In most studies the cases are made up of human beings, referred to as *subjects* or, more currently, *participants*. For example, Luo and Liao (2015) used 30 students (20 males, 10 females) in their study investigating the effects of using corpora to correct errors in EFL students' writing.

In other studies, the cases might be inanimate *objects* from which researchers extract their data. Examples are *corpora* of verbal discourse such as an accumulation of newspaper articles, or when researchers cull their data from transcriptions of taped dialogs. Rett and Hyams (2014), for instance, used the corpora of 45 American English-speaking children in the CHILDES database in their study of the acquisition of syntactically encoded *evidentiality*. They extracted 70 perception verb similatives (a type of sentence) out of the database for their data. Interestingly, they put this under the heading of "Subjects." Although the corpora constituted the verbal output of 45 children, the children were not the participants of the study; the corpora were the source of the verbal data. They narrowed the corpora down to 70 statements, which were their final sample (i.e., the objects of the study).

Sometimes the reader can be confused as to what makes up a sample, as seen in the Rett and Hyams (2014) study. The answer is determined by which data source is used to answer the research question(s). If it is directly from the participants, then the qualities of the participants need to be reported. If it is from objects like corpora, then the qualities of the corpora should be summarized. For reasons outlined next, there are different uses, which demand different combinations of participants/objects to answer different questions.

Sampling Paradigms

There are a number of ways that a sample is chosen to do research. Table 4.1 provides a list of some of the most commonly used techniques along with the main purposes for using them and brief definitions. The two general paradigms I refer to are *representative (probability)* and *purposeful (nonprobability)*. The first consists of techniques that try to capture a sample that best represents a defined *population* based on probability theory. The second attempts to identify samples that are rich in specific information. Representative sampling (more commonly referred to as probability sampling) has one aim: finding a sample that reflects salient characteristics of a specific population so that the results of the study can be generalized to that population. Purposeful sampling (also referred to as nonprobability or *purposive* sampling) is more concerned with the unique characteristics of the sample itself aside from any larger population—which is not to say that the results cannot be applied to other situations (more on this later). Before going further, I want to state that purposeful sampling is the paradigm that is most commonly used in applied linguistic research. However, I am presenting the material in the following order because I believe that the section on representative sampling lays down foundational principles for understanding sampling theory.

Table 4.1 Sampling Terminology

Paradigm	Purpose	Sampling Strategy	Definition
Representative (probability) sampling			A sample representing the target population
	Generalizability		Inferring the results of the study from the sample to the population
		✓Simple random	Everyone has an equal chance to be chosen
		Systematic random	Cases are selected across the population in an orderly fashion
		Stratified random	Cases selected within different strata in the population
		Proportional	Selected to reflect the proportions of the strata in the population
		Nonproportional	Selected to reflect the strata but not the proportions
		Cluster	Intact groups are randomly selected. All cases within the selected groups are used
		Multistage	A combination of cluster sampling combined with another random selection technique
Purposeful (nonprobability) sampling	In-depth information gathering		Focus on the quality of the information
		Convenience sampling	Cases selected because they are readily available
		Extreme/deviant case	Cases that are atypical
		Intensity (expert, critical case)	Ones that contain high amounts of the characteristics being studied
		Snowball/chain sampling	Rare cases are found via other rare cases
		Criterion sampling	Cases used which meet specific criteria
		Typical case (modal)	Ones that represent the average
		Maximum variation sampling	A cross section of cases that represent a wide spectrum
		Stratified purposeful sampling	A few cases from each strata
		Homogeneous sampling	Cases that are very similar
		Volunteers	Individuals who offer to participate

The Representative Sampling Paradigm

As previously mentioned, in the representative sampling paradigm the goal of the researcher is to generalize the findings and interpretations of the study to a larger population. The sample is a portion of a larger population. The word *population* usually means everyone in a country or a city. In research, this word has a more technical use; although similar, *population* means *all* the members of the group of participants/objects to which researchers want to generalize their research findings. This is referred to as the *target population*. In other words, the criterion for defining a target population is determined by the group of people to which researchers would like to generalize the interpretations of the study. For example, the population might be all learners of English as a foreign language (EFL) or it might be a more limited group of all learners of EFL who attend an English-medium university. For another study the target population may be entirely different.

Typically, having access to the entire target population to which researchers want to generalize their findings is impossible. For example, having access to all learners of EFL who attend English-medium universities throughout the world is, in practice, impossible. However, researchers may have access to English-medium universities in their own country. Whatever is available for use becomes the *experimentally accessible population* (Gall, Gall , & Borg, 2008). It is to this population the findings of a study can be directly generalized, not to the entire target population. The only time that researchers could make inferences from the findings of their study to the target population is when they can show that the experimentally accessible population possesses similar characteristics to the larger target population. For the rest of the book, I use the phrase target population with the understanding that I am referring to the *experimentally accessible* population.

Selecting a representative sample is important for making use of the findings of a study outside of the confines of the study itself. This is because the degree to which the results of a study can be generalized to a target population is the degree to which the sample adequately represents the larger group—the degree to which a sample represents a population is determined by the degree to which the relevant attributes in the target population are found in the sample.

Figure 4.1 illustrates the relationship between the sample and the population. I have used different graphic symbols to represent different attributes of a population. These attributes could be gender, age, level of education, level of language proficiency, and so on. Notice that the attributes in the sample (A, B, C, D, F) almost match exactly the attributes in the population; however, attribute E is missing in the sample. In this case, the sample is not 100 percent representative of the population, but it is very close. Most likely we could conclude that the population was representative enough to make *tentative* generalizations. However, there would always remain caution due to the missing attribute E.

The degree to which findings of a study can be generalized to a larger population or *transferred* to similar situations is referred to as *external validity* (or *transferability*: Miles & Huberman, 1994). To achieve this type of validity, researchers must demonstrate that the samples they use represent the groups to which they want to apply their findings. Otherwise, without this important quality, the findings are of little use outside of the study. The more representative the sample is to the population, the greater the external validity. In other terms, the more similar the characteristics of the sample are to other situations, the better the transfer of conclusions.

Identifying the target population is not always easy. For example, Hong-Nam and Leavell (2007) examined the language learning strategies of bilingual and monolingual students. The authors described the participants as 428 monolingual Korean university students (223 males and 205 females, aged 18–28) and 420 bilingual Korean–Chinese university students (182 males and 238 females, aged 20–28). They also provided information about the bilingual participants, which included the number of students using either Korean or Chinese at home or with friends, and overall proficiency (beginning, intermediate, or advanced) in both languages. Then they compared the two groups on gender, English proficiency, years of study, years studying English, test-taking experience, and travel abroad.

You can see rather quickly that the sample becomes more complex as the authors add more details about the participants. Without a careful read of the article, it can quickly become confusing about who the target population is. In this study, the target population is identified in their

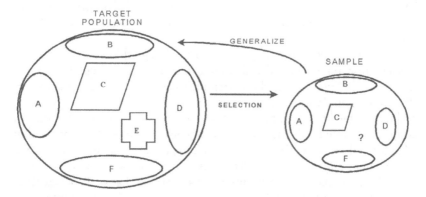

Figure 4.1 Illustration of a Sample Partially Representing a Target Population

research questions as monolingual Korean and bilingual Korean–Chinese university students. All of this additional information is important to the study, but does it add to or distract from clarifying the target population? Is it all bilinguals who use more complex strategies to learn when compared to monolinguals or is it only bilinguals with more extensive English backgrounds? These questions are important to answer if the researchers want to generalize their findings to larger populations than these subgroups represent.

The problem of researchers not identifying their target populations is not uncommon in published research. However, without this information, the consumer cannot evaluate whether correct generalizations are being made.[1]

An additional note is that choosing a representative sample is used not only for quantitative research. Some qualitative studies also seek this quality in their samples. To illustrate, Ożanska-Ponikwia (2016) used 97 Polish L2 adult learners of English in their study of the effects of immersion in the L2 culture on the Polish culture-specific emotion of *tęsknota* in the qualitative part of their study. They took care in describing their participants in great detail so that readers could transfer their findings to similar groups. However, they also warned in their conclusion section that the sample was still too small to generalize to the target population.

Sampling Strategies for Making Generalizations

There are a number of strategies used to try to achieve a representative sample (see Table 4.1). Because the manner in which a sample is chosen is so important, published studies in applied linguistics should inform the reader how the samples were selected. The following is a summary of the more common sampling strategies and the rationales used to warrant them. Note that all methods under this heading use the word *random*. This term technically means that the procedure used gives every member of the pool from which the sample is being taken an equal chance of being selected.

The ideal strategy for statistical purposes, though this is rarely achieved in social research in general and applied linguistics in particular, is *simple random* sampling. This method attempts to ensure that every member of the target population has an equal opportunity for being chosen. In addition to facilitating obtaining representative samples, this method can control unwanted influences from extraneous variables. As mentioned in Chapter 3, these are variables that could impact the variables being studied and produce spurious results. The reason that simple random sampling controls the impact of these nuisance variables is that it disperses their effect throughout the sample. For example, if a researcher is not interested in whether males behave differently than females, yet gender could affect the dependent variable in some undesirable way, the researcher would want to ensure that the sample consisted of approximately half males and half females. One way to do this is to obtain a sample randomly. If the sample is randomly chosen (and large enough), there is a high probability that both genders will be equally represented, which would wash out any gender effect when the data from the two groups were combined.

However, as just alluded to, simple random selection on its own does not guarantee a representative sample; sample size is also a consideration. Obviously, a sample of one person would not represent a population of language students, even if randomly selected. The target population might consist of males and females, but a sample of one is not representative because only one of the sexes is represented. Or, if the sample of one is male but the dependent variable does not behave with males as it does with females, then the findings would be misleading. To avoid these two problems, you need to use a larger sample. The maxim in research that aims to make generalizations is *the larger the sample the better*. In Chapter 7, when I discuss some statistical issues, I show the relationship between size of sample and the risk of getting a nonrepresentative sample. But suffice it to say here that the larger the random sample the greater the probability of getting a representative sample.

The negative impact of an overall small sample size is exacerbated if there is any *attrition* (i.e., loss of participants). An example of how this might be a problem is Lee-Johnson's (2015) study, which looked at the effects of out-of-class social interactions between ESL learners and their native-speaking counterparts on their overall learning experiences. She used five ESL students for the main participants to be observed by various methods over a five-month period. Any time the data are being collected longitudinally, there is a possibility of losing one or more participants. If this had happened in this study, how would it have changed the data and subsequent conclusions? Fortunately, this did not happen in Lee-Johnson's study.

In Table 4.1, I list another procedure, *systematic random sampling*, which I will not elaborate on here because I have rarely seen it used in applied linguistic research. If you are interested in knowing more, explore the term on Google or some other search engine.

However, a procedure that you might see in the research literature is one form of *stratified random sampling*. This method is especially useful when the population consists of subgroups such as males/females, various language proficiency levels, or different ethnic backgrounds that the researcher wants to control. In this scenario, one of two forms of *stratified random sampling* can be used: *proportional* or *nonproportional* (Gall et al., 2008).

Proportional stratified random sampling attempts to choose cases that represent the proportion of each of the subgroups in the population. For example, suppose researchers want to survey the attitudes of elementary school students in Egypt toward learning English as a second language. However, the population of students consists of substantially different proportions of children in public schools (i.e., grammar schools) versus semiprivate schools. To ensure that the sample needed for the survey reflects these proportional differences, the researchers will randomly survey from each subpopulation the number of students that reflect these proportions. In concrete terms, if 70 percent of the students attended public schools and 30 percent semiprivate schools, a sample of 1,000 students should contain approximately 700 randomly selected from public schools and 300 randomly selected from semiprivate schools. The results can then be generalized to the whole population of elementary school children in Egypt. Had the researchers used a simple random sampling procedure, they would most likely not obtain these proportions.

On the other hand, if the main intent was to compare the subgroups with one another, the researchers need to have equal numbers of participants for each group. To do this they should use a *nonproportional stratified random sampling* strategy. That is, the researchers will randomly sample the same number of participants from each of the levels. In the example above, it would mean 10 participants from each level.

Koyama, Sun, and Ockey's (2016) study exemplifies the use of the nonproportional stratified sampling strategy. They examined the relationship between previewing test items and video-based multiple-choice listening assessments. They stated that they used a stratified sampling method to ensure that participants from eight classes did not differ in listening proficiency when assigned to three testing conditions. They did not say whether their strategy was proportional or nonproportional, but their goal was to have equal numbers in each listening condition ($n = 8$), so their strategy was nonproportional. The distinction is not important in this study, though, since the class sizes were fairly equal to begin with.

A sampling strategy used to help manage very large populations is *cluster sampling* (see Table 4.1). Rather than trying to randomly sample from every member of a population, researchers randomly sample groups from within the population, such as schools or programs. Once these clusters are chosen, all the members of the clusters are used as participants. A permutation of this method is the *multistage* method, which initially selects clusters randomly followed by use of another random selection procedure within the clusters chosen. For example, Donista-Schmidt, Inbar, and Shohamy (2004) combined cluster sampling with proportional stratified random sampling in their study of the effects of teaching spoken Arabic on attitudes and motivations of Israeli students. They stated that

The schools were selected by using stratified random sampling with the strata being socioeconomic status (i.e., the schools represented both lower and higher socioeconomic levels) and degree of religious observance (i.e., Israeli State schools are comprised of secular State schools—about 70%—and religious State schools—about 30%).

(p. 221)

They argued from this that their sample adequately represented the elementary schools of Tel-Aviv. In their discussion section, they were confident that the results of their study could be generalized to all elementary schools in Israel.

The following exercise gives you the opportunity to find a study that used the representative sampling paradigm.

Exercise 4.1

Select a study of interest that used one of the representative sampling techniques previously discussed.

1. Summarize the purpose and the research question(s) of the study.
2. Define:
    a. The target population to which findings were intended to be applied. You most likely have to infer this from the questions, hypothesis, or discussion section.
    b. The experimentally accessible population.
    c. How the sample was chosen (e.g., simple random method, stratified random method, etc.).
    d. The size of the sample.
    e. Characteristics of the sample.
3. Evaluate the sample as to whether the sample was representative of the target population. Defend your answer.

The Purposeful Sampling Paradigm: Sample Strategies for Maximizing Information

The purposeful sampling paradigm focuses on the specific characteristics of whom or what is selected for the sample. The question that decides this is "Does the sample contain the needed information being sought?" These can range from one participant/object, as in a case study, to larger numbers. However, with this approach, the emphasis is more on the *quality* of the information taken from the sample. I discuss this approach more fully in the next chapter.

As previously mentioned, I am convinced that the purposeful sampling paradigm is more commonly used than representative sampling in the area of applied linguistics. Although one particular genre of research methodology, *qualitative research* (see Chapter 5 for more on research designs), uses this type of sampling paradigm almost exclusively, researchers using *quantitative* designs in applied linguistics also use it over 90 percent of the time. For this reason, I want to spend more time on the various strategies used under this heading than is commonly found in textbooks on research methodology.

Rather than trying to find a sample to represent some population as with representative sampling, purposeful sampling stresses strategies for selecting samples for in-depth data gathering. Gall, Borg, and Gall (1996, pp. 231–236) summarized 15 *purposeful sampling strategies* (cf. Patton, 2015) for deliberately choosing a sample to supply the most information possible regarding the research question. While reviewing these, I found a fair amount of overlap between the 15 strategies. In Table 4.1, I have regrouped these to reduce the redundancy, and included two that are not normally included under purposeful sampling: *convenience* and *volunteer sampling*. In addition, you will see that these strategies are not mutually exclusive. They are often used in combination to select the best sample.

The first purposeful sampling strategy I discuss is *convenience sampling* —though sometimes associated with representative sampling. In practice, having access to all members of even an experimentally accessible population to obtain a representative sample is often impossible due to time or financial constraints. Instead, researchers access participants from those immediately available, but they do not do this randomly. They select their conveniently available sample so that it fulfills the purpose of the study. Because the sample is not randomly chosen it lacks generalizability, but it does not lack purpose. For example, if my target population is all learners of EFL who attend an English-medium university, but I am only able to have access to a sample from learners of EFL who attend the English-medium university where I teach, I will use this group because it is convenient. For this reason, I have placed this sampling strategy under the purposeful sampling paradigm because the sample is usually biased and is not representative (nonprobabilistic) of a larger population. In addition, it is purposeful in that the researcher determines that the sample is the right one for gathering the data needed for the study—this is not to be confused with haphazard.

Whether one can apply one's findings from a convenience sample to a larger target population depends on how well one can show that the sample corresponds to the larger population on important characteristics. This is done by providing clear descriptions of how the sample shares these features. Often the researcher gathers this information through surveys and tests prior to the implementation of the study.

From the many studies that my students and I have seen, our conclusion is that many studies use *convenience sampling* when using other criteria for selecting a sample. I found that over 3,390 studies used convenient samples from 2012 to 2016 when doing a search EBSCOhost. One such study that clearly used a convenience sample was done by Ahmed, Aftab, and Yaqoob (2015), who investigated undergraduate students' motivations toward learning the English language. They stated "From the accessible population, a convenient sample of 199 students has been . . . taken as a sample of this research because they were easily available." This has important implications if any statistics are used, which will be discussed in Chapter 7.

Let me encourage you regarding your attitude toward studies using convenience samples. You should not think that such studies have little value, but, rather, you need to take the findings from such studies with the understanding that they need to be replicated with different samples. I think that it is safe to say that very few studies use samples that pass all of the criteria for a good sample. For this reason, the consumer needs to look for similar studies using different samples to see if the results are repeated. If so, you can have more confidence in the answers to your questions.

The second strategy listed in Table 4.1, *extreme/deviant case*, selects cases that stand out either above or below the average. The purpose is to look for characteristics in cases that are unusual and then contrast/compare these traits with average cases. For example, Samimy (2008) studied the personal characteristics and attributes of an advanced language learner of a language other than English. She stated that she used a purposeful convenient sampling strategy. She chose a person who was clearly very proficient in Arabic. She clearly stated her reason: "Mark was an advanced language learner. I was not interested in theory building nor in generalizing the findings to other cases. But what can we learn from a single case" (p. 405). I love it when researchers are clear about what strategy they use and why they use them.

The next strategy in Table 4.1 is *intensity* sampling, within which I have included *expert* and *critical case* sampling. The main goal is to use cases that concentrate the trait(s) being studied. For instance, expert teachers may be chosen to study what characteristics make them to be considered as experts. As an example, van Compernolle and Henery (2015) did a case study in which they examined one teacher's learning and use of Vygotsky's "concept-based pragmatics" approach for teaching second language (L2) pragmatics. They deliberately chose a person who had specific qualities critical for their study. They stated,

Although Mrs. Hanks was an experienced language teacher (she had taught French for several years) and was familiar with current language teaching practices as well as L2 learning research (she was completing her PhD in second language acquisition with an emphasis of L2 French pragmatics), she was new to Vygotskian sociocultural theory (SCT) in general and to CBPI in particular. Her integration of CBPI was collaborative in nature: she and a more expert teacher-researcher, who had originally developed the approach, designed the course together, and Mrs. Hanks received support (e.g., through interviews, stimulated recalls, and role plays) throughout the semester from him.

(p. 352)

Clearly, this teacher, in van Compernolle and Henery's opinion, was an appropriate person to study to provide the information needed—this participant was *information-rich*.

Another strategy listed (see Table 4.1) is *snowball* or *chain* sampling. For those in climates that have not seen snow or made snowballs, let me try to explain. You first pack a little snow into a ball in your hand and then add more snow, making the ball bigger. Once it gets big enough, you roll it on the ground until you end up with a big snow ball. It is very similar to how the dung beetle builds up a ball of dung—maybe we should call it the *dung beetle sampling method* for those in warmer climates. This strategy is helpful for finding individuals who are normally difficult to find to use for a sample. Lam and Rosario-Ramos (2009) studied how young migrants from different cultural backgrounds in the United States use digital media to structure relationships socially and interact with news and media products both in the United States and their native countries. They initially located 18 participants who had previously indicated in a survey that they corresponded with friends from their country of origin. After interviewing them they asked if they knew of others who were immigrants and stayed in contact with people back in their home countries. The result was that they added 17 more people to their study.

The next strategy listed in Table 4.1 is *criterion* sampling. This strategy uses one or more criteria to determine whether or not to select an individual as part of the sample. Vasilopoulos (2015) studied language learner investment and identity negotiation in a non-English setting (Korea). She selected 10 young adult Koreans who lived in Korea for her sample. Her selection was based on one critical criterion, bilingualism. She defined this as "the ability to converse naturally and fluently with native to near-native ability in both English and Korean" (p. 66). Although she stated in the abstract that she used purposive homogenous sampling techniques, the 10 participants varied on a number of factors that she summarized in her Table 1, except for the criterion mentioned above. I think that *purposive criterion sampling* might have been more indicative of how she sampled her participants, though it is not something that hinders her study.

If researchers wanted to select a sample that represented the average person or situation, they would use the typical case (modal)2 strategy (see Table 4.1). Palmer, El-Ashry, Leclere, and Chang (2007) purposefully selected a nine-year-old Palestinian boy for their study because he represented "a growing population of Arabic-speaking children who are entering U.S. public schools . . . This population includes many students like Abdullah, who must acquire enough facility with the English language to meet the academic requirement of their new country" (p. 8). Clearly, the researchers considered Abdullah an example of a typical person of the group they were concerned about and one who had the information they needed for their study.

Other studies use a *maximum variation* sampling strategy (see Table 4.1) to see what type of information might be collected over a wide variety of individuals. Guilloteaux and Dörnyei (2008) examined how teachers' strategies for motivating their students influence student motivation. They clearly stated their sampling strategy: "The main criterion for our specific sampling was to generate as much diversity as possible in terms of school location and the teachers' age, qualifications, experience, and level of English proficiency" (p. 60). They also employed the use of snowball sampling to obtain an adequate number of participants. The result was a sample consisting of 20 schools, 27 teachers, and 1,381 students in 40 classes. One might think that with such large numbers the researchers would be using a representative sampling paradigm. However, they were very explicit in stating that they were using a purposeful sampling paradigm with the goal to obtain information-rich data. For example, "we focused on examining the quality of the teachers' overall motivational teaching practice by generating a composite index of the rich observational data" (p. 60).

Another strategy that is similar to the maximum variation sampling strategy is the *stratified purposeful* sampling strategy. However, rather than trying to maximize the variation of the sample, its aim is to ensure that there is at least one participant from each stratum of a population. This sounds very much like stratified random sampling under the representative sampling paradigm heading (see Table 4.1), but it differs in that it does not select participants randomly from the different strata and does not necessarily have to use large samples. Csizer and Kormos (2008) used this method in gathering their sample for investigating how direct and indirect cross-cultural contact with targeted language groups affects Hungarian students' attitudes and motivation. Although they stated that their data were "based on a national representative survey of 1,777" (p. 166) students, they selected 237 from this group who had "the highest level of inter-cultural contact" (p. 166). They also stated that the larger number represented a *stratified sample*, but, because they did not specify that this was randomly selected, I have to classify this sample as a *stratified purposeful* sample. Although their subsample of 237 does not allow for generalizing to all second language learners, according to the researchers, it does provide them with a large enough sample to use a particular analysis technique for their purposes.

On the opposite side of maximum variation sampling is the *homogeneous sampling* strategy. The aim of this strategy is to select participants who share the same attributes. Bell (2005) studied types of interactions that take place during humorous interchange between native speakers (NSs) and non-native speakers (NNSs) and their role in second language acquisition. She drew her data from her dissertation where she used three NNSs participants who were homogeneous on four criteria that she had previously defined: regularly interacted with NSs, willing to audio-record such interactions over long periods of time, had a high level of English proficiency, and had no difficulties with L2 humor.

Last, in Table 4.1 I have listed the use of *volunteers*. Many research methods textbooks list volunteers as a separate sampling strategy, including the first edition of this book (see Table 4.1). However, I believe that this can no longer be used as a separate sampling strategy for the simple reason that all participants or their parents/guardians have to agree to participate, i.e. volunteer, in any study. This is due to laws that are now in place for the protection of human rights, as outlined in the following section of this chapter on ethics. Regardless of which previously discussed sampling paradigm is used, participants must in essence volunteer. Traditionally, volunteer samples were considered biased for reasons outlined in texts like Gall et al.'s (2008). However, what makes a sample biased depends on the sampling paradigm. Representative sampling should result in unbiased samples and purposeful sampling will almost always produce biased samples.

In summary, whichever sampling paradigm researchers use, they should give attention to precision in describing why a sample was chosen and what steps were taken to ensure that the best sample was selected. The more precise the description the more credence can be given to the interpretation and application of the results. For further reading on sampling theory, I suggest you read Gall et al. (2008).

What about sample size and purposeful sampling? The rule *the more the better* also holds true for this paradigm—although for different reasons than for representative sampling. As stated previously, the purpose of using this paradigm in research is to do in-depth investigations, which need information-rich samples. So, it is logical to conclude that larger samples should lead to more information-rich data.

The last point I want to make is that, although researchers using the purposeful sampling paradigm are not generally concerned with *generalizing* their findings to larger populations, they are usually hoping that the interpretations of their data can be *transferred* to other situations.

With a sample of one, for example, van Compernolle and Henery (2015) did not try to generalize their findings to all teachers; however, their findings were informative and certainly promising for further research. More is said about the issue of transference in Chapters 5 and 7.

I suggest that you do the following exercise so that you can get firsthand experience looking at a study which has used the purposeful sampling paradigm.

Exercise 4.2

Locate a study of interest that used the purposeful sampling paradigm and complete the following:

1. Summarize the research questions under investigation.
2. What purpose did the researcher(s) state for selecting the sample?
3. How was the sample selected?
4. Summarize the characteristics of the sample.
5. Explain how you think the sample was appropriate for the purpose of the study.

As I conclude this chapter, I trust that you have gained a healthy appreciation regarding the need for researchers to provide a clear description of the samples they use in their studies. The sample subsection should describe detailed characteristics of their sample and indicate the conditions under which it was selected. The two main criteria are, first, whether you are able to identify the sampling paradigm(s) that researchers use and the reason(s) for its use. The second is whether you have enough information to decide whether the findings of the study can be generalized/ transferred (see Figure 4.1) to the target population or similar situations. The choice researchers make will guide how you evaluate the conclusions and applications suggested by the findings of the study. In addition to these basic criteria is the need for researchers to point out what precautions were taken to ensure the safety and the confidentiality of any human participants. The final thought is, although the sample subsection in a research article may consume little space, the implications have profound effects on the rest of the study.

Ethics in Sampling Human Participants

Ethical issues are involved with everything that is discussed in the following chapters. When using human participants in a study, there are a number of ethical issues that must be addressed. The main concern is that the rights and privacy of human participants are protected. This is such an important issue that the US government set up a commission in

1974, which produced the Belmont Report in 1979. In 1991, a number of US government agencies adopted a number of regulations to protect human participants (AERA, 2000). In fact, they established the Office for Protection from Research Risks inside the Department of Health and Human Services to monitor any misuse of participants.[3] Every research institution and university Institutional Review Board (IRB) must examine and approve any research using human beings. (Take note, those of you planning a thesis or dissertation.)

In essence, these guidelines can be summarized in the following statement. "The 'rights' of a research subject include reading and discussing the informed consent with study staff, answering any questions, voluntary participation, and a right to information about the study's procedures, risks, and benefits" (AERA, 2000, paragraph 5).

There are some situations where these rules do not have to apply. They are listed below (AERA, 2000, paragraph 5):

1. Research conducted in established or commonly accepted educational settings.
2. Research involving the use of educational tests, surveys, interviews, or observation of public behavior.
3. If the human participants are elected or appointed public officials or candidates for public office.
4. Research involving the collection or study of existing data, documents, or records.
5. Research and demonstration projects that are conducted by or subject to the approval of Department or Agency heads, and which are designed to study, evaluate, or otherwise examine public benefit or service programs.

As seen in these five exceptions to the rule, there is a lot of latitude, which keeps researchers from being overly tied up in red tape. However, it is important that participants are protected from research that violates their rights to privacy.

Key Terms and Concepts

attrition
case
cluster sampling
convenience sampling
criterion sampling
experimentally accessible population
external validity

extreme/deviant case sampling
homogeneous sampling
information-rich
intensity (expert, critical case) sampling
generalizability
maximum variation sampling
multistage sampling
objects
participants
proportional/nonproportional stratified random sampling
purposeful (nonprobability) sampling paradigm
representative (probability) sample paradigm
sample
simple random sampling
snowball/chain sampling
stratified purposeful sampling
stratified random sampling
systematic random sampling
target population
transferability
typical case (modal) sampling
volunteers

Notes

1. I believe that all journals should add to their criteria for publication a clear statement by researchers that identify the target population if the researcher plans to generalize his or her findings.
2. Modal refers to the Mode, i.e., the average.
3. If you are interested in getting more details regarding this, I suggest that you go on the Internet to the site of the Department of Education, www.ed.gov/offices/OCFO/humansub.html. From there you will be able to locate a number of documents that will spell out clearly what these regulations are.

References

AERA (2000). *Code of Ethics*. Available online at http://c.ymcdn.com/sites/www.weraonline.org/resource/resmgr/a_general/aera.pdf.

Ahmed, M., Aftab, M., & Yaqoob, H. (2015). Students' motivation toward English language learning at undergraduate level. *Advances in Language and Literary Studies*, 6, 230–238.

Bell, N. D. (2005). Exploring L2 language play as an aid to SLL: A case study of humour in NS—NNs interaction. *Applied Linguistics*, 26, 192–218.

Csizer, K., & Kormos, J. (2008). Modelling the role of inter-cultural contact in the motivation of learning English as a foreign language. *Applied Linguistics*, 30, 166–185.

Donista-Schmidt, S., Inbar, O., & Shohamy, E. (2004). The effects of teaching spoken Arabic on students' attitudes and motivation in Israel. *The Modern Language Journal, 88*, 217–228.

Gall, M. D., Borg, W. R., & Gall, J. P. (1996). *Educational research: An introduction* (6th ed.). White Plains, NY: Longman.

Gall, M. D., Gall, J. P., & Borg, W. R. (2008). *Educational research: An introduction* (8th ed.). Upper Saddle River, NJ: Pearson Education.

Guilloteaux, M. J., & Dörnyei, Z. (2008). Motivating language learners: A classroom-oriented investigation of the effects of motivational strategies on student motivation. *TESOL Quarterly, 42*, 5–7.

Hong-Nam, K., & Leavell, A. G. (2007). A comparative study of language learning strategy use in an EFL context: Monolingual Korean and bilingual Korean-Chinese university students. *Asia Pacific Education Review, 8*(1), 71–88.

Koyama, D., Sun, A., & Ockey, G. J. (2016). The effects of item preview on video-based multiple-choice listening assessments. *Language Learning & Technology, 20*, 148–165.

Lam, W. S. E., & Rosario-Ramos, E. (2009). Multilingual literacies in transnational digitally mediated contexts: An exploratory study of immigrant teens in the United States. *Language and Education, 23*, 171–190.

Lee-Johnson, Y. L. (2015). A qualitative study of the out-of-class learning opportunities constructed by five ESL freshmen and their native speaking peers in a college town. *Journal of Ethnographic & Qualitative Research, 10*, 120–134.

Luo, Q., & Liao, Y. (2015). Using corpora for error correction in EFL learners' writing. *Journal of Language Teaching and Research, 6*(6), 1333–1342.

Miles, M. B., & Huberman, A. M. (1994). *Qualitative data analysis: An expanded sourcebook* (2nd ed.). Thousand Oaks, CA: SAGE.

Ożanska-Ponikwia, K. (2016). The influence of immersion in the L2 culture on perception of the L1 culture-specific emotion of tęsknota. *International Journal of Bilingualism, 20*, 116–132.

Palmer, B. C., El-Ashry, F., Leclere, J. T., & Chang, S. (2007). Learning from Abdallah: A case study of an Arabic-speaking child in a U.S. school. *The Reading Teacher, 61*(1), 8–17.

Patton, M. Q. (2015). *Qualitative research & evaluation methods integrating theory and practice* (4th ed.). Thousand Oaks, CA: SAGE.

Rett. J., & Hyams, N. (2014). The acquisition of syntactically encoded evidentiality. *Language Acquisition, 21*, 173–198.

Samimy, K. (2008). Achieving the advanced oral proficiency in Arabic: A case study. *Foreign Language Annals, 41*, 401–414.

van Compernolle, R. A., & Henery, A. (2015). Learning to do concept-based pragmatics instruction: teacher development and L2 pedagogical content knowledge. *Language Teaching Research, 19*, 351–372.

Vasilopoulos, G. (2015). Language learner investment and identity negotiation in the Korean EFL context. *Journal of Language, Identity & Education, 14*, 61–79.

Chapter 5

Understanding Research Designs

Chapter Overview

The research design, as mentioned in Chapter 1, is the overall plan for carrying out a research study. This design is like the blueprint for building a house. Its purpose is to guide researchers in constructing the strongest and most efficient structure to provide the most useful data to answer the research question(s). Just like a poorly designed blueprint, which results in a house full of problems and possible structural collapse, a poorly designed research study produces results containing many flaws, and consequently has little practical use.

The goals of this chapter are to help you understand the technicalities of the design subsection of a study and be able to determine whether the appropriate design was used. There are a number of different research designs that are currently being used to answer a wide variety of questions. This is where things can be a little confusing, and remembering them all can be somewhat overwhelming. In addition, there might be several *equally appropriate* research designs to answer the same question. For this reason, one needs to develop a discerning eye. As you will see, one should judge a design's suitability by whether it answers the research question.

To aid in accomplishing the previously stated goals, I have divided this chapter into three sections. Section 1 provides a conceptual framework for classifying various types of research designs to help reduce the confusion. Section 2 describes in more detail the various research designs used for finding answers to the two basic research questions: *what* and *why*. Section 3 discusses the factors that can interfere with the results of a study under the heading of *internal validity*. Examples of published research are given to illustrate the main points of the discussion.

Section 1: Classifying Research Designs

Life would be so simple if we had only one kind of everything, but it would also be very boring. In keeping up with the rest of life, research does not provide just one simple type, or even a choice between only two types. Rather, research can be classified, at least, by three intersecting continua: *basic–applied*, *qualitative–quantitative*, *and exploratory–confirmatory* (see Figure 5.1). Although these continua are independent of each other, any given study can be classified somewhere on an intersection of the three. This means that a study would appear at some point out in the three-dimensional space, represented by Figure 5.1. Each continuum is first defined with an explanation showing how a study can be located on it. An example is then given of how one study can be classified on all three continua simultaneously and what this might look like in three-dimensional space.

The Basic–Applied Continuum

This continuum represents research that ranges from the highly theoretical (basic) to the very practical (applied). At the basic end of the continuum, researchers focus on the theoretical, dealing mainly with highly abstract constructs. These studies are not, at first sight, very appealing to the classroom teachers who are looking for immediate ways to improve their

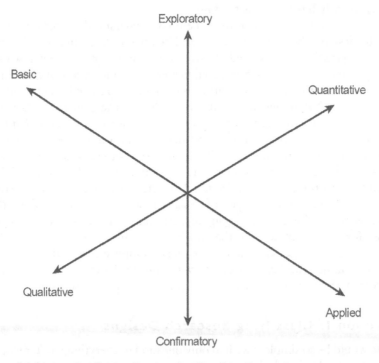

Figure 5.1 Intersecting Design Continua for Classifying Research

students' learning. Nevertheless, these studies are very important for looking at the underlying linguistic, psychological, or sociological mechanisms that might be eventually applied in the classroom. In fact, one might argue that this type of research reveals the theoretical foundations upon which all other research rests. For example, unless we have demonstrated in basic research that the brain processes information in a certain way, it would be difficult to promote a teaching method that elicits this type of brain processing.

Some studies can be identified immediately from their titles as basic research. For example, Gabriel and Kireva's (2014) study, entitled "Prosodic Transfer in Learner and Contact Varieties," appears to be near the end of the basic continuum. Based on the title, it does not look too practical for the language classroom teacher. That was not their intent. They clearly stated their goal was "to test McMahon's (2004) transfer hypothesis with respect to speech rhythm and intonation, more precisely with regard to the tonal shape of yes–no questions" (p. 258). This does not mean, of course, that this research is of little value. They saw this as part of the bigger picture that "will hopefully shed more light on the intriguing interplay of markedness and pragmatics in the acquisition of L2 prosody" (p. 276). Hence, in line with our first impressions, I placed it near the basic end of the continuum, as shown here.[1]

Basic ⟵————————⟶ Applied

At the other end of the same continuum is applied research. As you would expect from the previous discussion, research that is directly applicable to the teaching/learning situation would be placed here. Studies that deal with teaching methods, or ones that try to address immediate problems in the classroom, would fit at this end of the continuum.

The research genre called *action research* (AR), which has received a lot of recent attention, is one of the purest forms of applied research (cf. Burns, 2010). There is even a journal dedicated solely to this type of research, entitled *Action Research*. Burns (2010) defined it as research in which

> a teacher becomes an "investigator" or "explorer" of his or her personal teaching context. . . . One of the main aims of AR is to identify a "problematic" situation or issue that the participants . . . consider worth looking into more deeply and systematically.
>
> (p. 2)

She continued by saying, "The central idea of the *action* part of AR is to intervene in a deliberate way in the problematic situation to bring about changes and, even better, improvements in practice" (p. 2). She emphasized that such recommended improvements are based on systematic data collection.

A study that illustrates action research was done by Palmer, El-Ashry, Leclere, and Chang (2007). They based their study on the concerns of one of the researchers, Sara Chang, who taught ESL in an elementary school in Florida. She specifically noticed that one of her students was having reading difficulties (i.e., a problematic situation) and decided to study how she could help him improve. She formed a research team with some more experienced educators and systematically gathered data, which they used to develop a plan to bring about improvement in the student's reading ability. This study clearly can be placed at the applied end of the continuum.

Basic ⟷ Applied

However, other studies might be placed somewhere between these two extremes. If a study is built on a heavy theoretical base, yet has clear practical implications, it would fall somewhere in the middle. For example, Moskovsky, Alrabai, Paolini, and Ratcheva (2013) examined the effects of teachers' motivational strategies on the motivation of students. They provided a good overview of various motivational theories in their introduction, which makes it lean toward the basic end of the continuum. However, their study was done using teachers and students in live classrooms, making it lean toward the applied end. Based on this, I would place the study near the middle of the continuum.

The prior discussion illustrates that the consumer of research should read research with this continuum in mind. One type is not more important than another. For this reason, journals contain research covering the entire spectrum on this continuum (cf. *Action Research* with *Journal of Phonetics*).

The Qualitative–Quantitative Continuum

The qualitative–quantitative continuum has received a lot of attention over the past 30 years, usually accompanied by much controversy. When you read articles dealing with this debate, you might think that this is not a continuum but two distinct armed camps. However, as you become more familiar with the research available, you will find that many studies are neither purely qualitative nor quantitative. This is in line with Larsen-Freeman and Long (1991), who described these two terms as two ends of a continuum that have different data-collecting procedures along with different degrees of subjectivity in interpreting data. My students' findings concur with this opinion, in that they have classified many studies somewhere between the two ends of this continuum.

The problem is that epistemological issues regarding the nature of reality have been wedded with these two methodologies, resulting in the polarization of a number of researchers into *camps*. I agree with Miles and Huberman (1994), however, who stated, "We believe that the quantitative-qualitative argument is essentially unproductive . . . we see no reason to tie the distinction to epistemological preferences" (p. 41). Therefore, I am not going to address the related philosophical issues of positivism and postpositivism in this book because I do not believe that they are important for the consumer of research at this time. However, if you are interested in reading more about this, I recommend Chapter 1 in Tashakkori and Teddlie's book (1998).

I try to use the terms *qualitative* and *quantitative* in ways that separate them from this philosophical spat—getting into epistemology is not necessary. However, you should be aware of the designs and methodologies that are typically associated with quantitative and qualitative approaches. Familiarization with these methods will enable consumers of research to be eclectic and versatile, ready to digest whatever research method comes their way. Only then will the consumer be better able to find potential answers to research questions.

The two ends of this continuum mostly have their origins in different disciplines. Quantitative research has come mainly from the field of psychology, where there has been heavy emphasis on the use of statistics to make generalizations from samples to populations, thus the label *quantitative methods*. However, most methods under qualitative research have originated with anthropologists and sociologists who rely heavily on verbal description rather than numbers. Consequently, quantitative research is characterized by the use of numbers to represent its data, and qualitative research is characterized by verbal descriptions as its data.

I would add, in light of the discussion in Chapter 4, that sampling paradigms also help distinguish between the two. Quantitative research frequently uses representative sampling strategies for generalizing findings to larger populations, whereas qualitative research works to uncover information from small purposeful samples.

Although some mistakenly think that qualitative research does not use any numbers or statistics, this is not necessarily so. A number of qualitative studies involve numbers in the form of frequencies of occurrence of certain phenomena and are analyzed by such statistical methods as chi-square. In fact, a number of books have been written (e.g., Agresti, 2012) describing statistical procedures for qualitative research.

Another misunderstanding regarding the differences between qualitative and quantitative approaches is that the former is atheoretical, whereas the latter is not. Although most qualitative research studies do not begin with theoretical hypotheses, developing theory (or, to be more precise, a theoretical hypothesis) is often their goal. For instance, an approach referred to as *grounded theory*, which arose out of anthropology, has become part of the qualitative research repertoire in applied linguistics. The express goal of this method is to develop a theoretical hypothesis from descriptive data as the data accumulate from the ground up. A good example is Kubanyiova's (2015) qualitative study, part of which analyzed a corpus of ethnographic data drawn from one EFL teacher in Slovakia. She stated,

> My aim, instead, was to construct a grounded theory of the invisible dimension of Tamara's discursive practices in the classroom by examining how her cognitions were embodied in her descriptions of everyday experiences and events. ... I analysed the ethnographic data iteratively, generating larger and more abstract concepts out of a set of initially identified recurrent themes, interrogating the relationships between them, and moving back and forth between data and existing theories in the fields of applied linguistics, teacher education, and psychology to generate theoretical explanations for the emerging empirical insights.
>
> (p. 569)

So, what is *qualitative research*? Miles and Huberman (1994, pp. 5–8) defined what they thought to be common features across different manifestations of qualitative research are. I have extracted and summarized them in the following list. Data are gathered:

- in natural settings;
- through concentrated contact over time;
- holistically—"systematic, encompassing, integrated";
- from deep inside the situation trying to hold preconceived notions in check;
- by the researcher, who is the "main 'measurement device'";
- to analyze for patterns, comparisons, and contrasts;
- with interpretations constrained by theoretical interests and/or "internal consistency"; and
- consisting mainly of verbal data.

In other words, any study that is done in a real-life setting, involving intensive holistic data collection through observation at a very close personal level without the influence of prior theory and contains mostly of verbal analysis, could be classified as a qualitative study.[2]

However, there are differing opinions as to what constitutes qualitative research. Gall, Borg, and Gall (1996) list under their section on qualitative research such things as case studies, along with a list of 16 research traditions that are typically referred to as *qualitative research*. Among these are methods such as ethnography, protocol analysis, and discourse analysis—all commonly used methods in applied linguistics. Wolcott illustrated over 20 strategies in his famous tree diagram (Miles & Huberman, 1994, p. 6). Tesch organized 27 strategies into a flowchart under four general categories (Miles & Huberman, 1994, p. 7). Nunan (1992) included ethnography, case studies, introspective methods, and interaction analysis in his book.

Consequently, it is difficult to provide a simple overview of all of these qualitative research strategies for the up-and-coming consumer. Other texts are better designed to do this (e.g., Creswell, 2013; Denzin & Lincoln, 2011).

Case Studies

These types of studies are frequently found in applied linguistics research. Gall et al. (1996) define a *case study* as

> the in-depth study of instances of a phenomenon in its natural context and from the perspective of the participants involved in the phenomenon. A case study is done to shed light on a phenomenon, which is the processes, events, persons, or things of interest to the researcher. Examples of phenomena are programs, curricula, roles, and events. Once the phenomenon of interest is clarified, the researcher can select a case for intensive study. A case is a particular instance of the phenomena.
>
> (p. 545)

Notice that the focus of a case study is on a specific phenomenon. Remember van Compernolle and Henery (2015), mentioned in Chapter 4 and that they did a case study where they examined one teacher's learning and use of Vygotsky's "concept-based pragmatics" approach for teaching second language (L2) pragmatics? The phenomenon they focused on was the teacher's "development in terms of her internalization and transformation of relevant pedagogical content knowledge" (p. 351). Their main data source was six 15- to 20-minute video recordings of the teacher's classroom on days that she engaged her students and three 60-minute video recordings of mentoring meetings between the teacher and her collaborator. The data that they worked with were mainly verbal transcriptions of the video recordings. Being a case study that involved only one teacher, the researchers recognized that their findings were not generalizable to larger populations. However, they believed that their findings were valid to transfer important implications for teaching and for stimulating future research

Ethnography

The term originally comes out of anthropology and means the study of human societies and culture. In applied linguistics, it focuses on cultural issues related to languages. An ethnographic study is characterized by the researcher(s) getting as close as possible to the culture under study over an extended period of time. Data are gathered from a number of sources (e.g., notes from observations, interviews, transcriptions of video and audio recordings, etc.), resulting in large quantities of verbal information. For example, Johnson (2010) did an ethnographic study over a three-year period investigating the impact of applied linguistic research on bilingual education policy and program development. He described how he used observation and extended field notes in a variety of meetings with teachers and administrators. He also used formal and informal interviews and recordings of natural conversations in meetings, and analyzed many documents for *triangulation*.[3]

Recently there has been a revival of Hymes's work in the 1960s in the form of *linguistic ethnography*. According to Jacobs and Slembrook (2010), it "has rapidly secured itself a place among the most commonly used paradigms for analyzing language in use" (p. 235). Creese (2008) stated that it is the joining of anthropology, applied linguistics, and sociology in research regarding communication. Also known as the ethnography of communication, Toyosaki's (2004) study, entitled "Ethnography of cross-cultural communication: Japanese international students' accounts of US-American culture and communication," employed this method for examining Japanese international students' perceptions of American culture and communication. Such methods fall under the qualitative end of the continuum.

Discourse and Conversational Analysis

These two methods are related in that they analyze connected discourse. However, they differ in the scope of the discourse they analyze. In fact, some argue that conversational analysis (CA) is a restricted form of discourse analysis (DA) (cf. Paltridge, 2006). DA is more an umbrella label that subsumes a number of ways to study connected discourse, whether written, spoken, or sign language (see Paltridge, 2006, for an excellent summary), whereas CA is a specific fine-grain analysis of limited spoken discourse. Both aim at identifying patterns in discourse that provide new insights into relationships within the discourse.

An example of discourse analysis is the study by Johnson (2010), previously mentioned, which used "intertextual discourse analysis to analyze the connections between the various layers of policy discourse" (p. 75)—in addition to ethnography. He specifically stated that "The goal here is to trace the intertextual links between federal and local language policy discourse by focusing on a particular theme: the role of Applied Linguistics research and/or researchers in language policy creation, interpretation, and appropriation" (p. 76). More is said in Chapter 6 about the gathering of these types of verbal data.

A more restricted type of DA is CA,[4] which uses transcriptions of oral discourse from conversations between participants. Lazaraton (2003) explained that

> CA insists on the analysis of real, recorded data, segmented into turns of talk that are carefully transcribed. Generally speaking, the conversation analyst does not formulate research questions prior to analyzing the data. The goal is to build a convincing and comprehensive analysis of a single case, and then to search for other similar cases to build a collection of cases that represent some interactional phenomenon.
>
> (p. 3)

Lazaraton continued by stating that the CA procedure approaches the study from a totally inductive perspective by not relying on any prior knowledge about the context of the participants. She added that they seldom use any coding system and do not condense the data into groupings.

Gan, Davidson, and Hamp-Lyons (2008) used CA to examine how Cantonese-speaking ESL students negotiated topic organization—a type of oral interaction—in an assessment context. They purposefully sampled one video recording out of a large data bank that best exemplified the assessment process. The recording was an eight-minute discussion of four secondary school participants who were given the task of choosing a gift for the main character of a film. The researchers only used two excerpts from this recording for their analysis. They proceeded to do a detailed analysis of topic initiation, development, and transition in the oral discourse of the four students. As you can see, the researchers used a microscopic approach on a very limited set of oral output. Needless to say, this study would be placed at the qualitative end of the continuum.

Qualitative ←——————————→ Quantitative

Protocol Analysis

Another qualitative approach mentioned by Gall et al. (1996) has its origin in the field of cognitive psychology. Gall et al. define it as "asking individuals to state all their thoughts as they carry out a challenging task, so that the researcher can obtain a holistic overview of their cognitive activity as recorded in their verbal reports" (p. 596). This is commonly

known as the *think-aloud* approach. Similar to other qualitative procedures, audiotapes are made as participants think aloud. The tapes are
transcribed and analyzed. Bowles (2010) provides a very good overview
of the think-aloud method and the controversy regarding validity, and
shows how it has been used effectively in applied linguistic research.

An example of a study that used protocol analysis was done by Valeo
(2013), who investigated whether focus-on-form (FF) instruction has any
impact on language awareness in a content-based language program. She
compared one group, who received both FF and meaning-focused
instruction, with another, who got only meaning-focused instruction over
a 10-week period. Valeo's data consisted of retrospective protocols that
she gathered after the lessons. The protocols were coded and analyzed to
see whether the FF group attended to form language more than the non-
FF group. She listed a number of constraints regarding the participants
she used in the study, which she clearly stated limited the transferability
of the findings of her study to larger populations. However, she also listed
a number of issues that need further research as a result of her study. I
would place this study clearly toward the qualitative end of the continuum.

At the other end of this continuum is the *quantitative approach*. As you
would expect from the label, the data for this approach are some type of
numbers. These numbers can be frequencies, percentages, proportions,
rankings, and/or scores on some type of test or survey. Further-more, the
method for analyzing the data is some form of statistical procedure.[5]
Finally, quantitative studies ideally use large representative samples. However, realistically many studies use smaller purposeful samples—often
convenient samples. Studies located toward this end might test hypotheses
or only gather information to answer questions.

A study that I would place toward the quantitative end of the continuum
is one done by Koyama, Sun, and Ockey (2016), mentioned in Chapter 4.
They examined relationships between previewing test items and video-
based multiple-choice listening assessments. Their stratified random
sample was 206 Japanese university English-language students. They
used a statistical procedure called analysis of variance (ANOVA) (see
Chapter 7), which marks this study as clearly quantitative. However, they
warned in their conclusion section that their sample was too homogeneous
to generalize to a population, and too small for one of the statistical
procedures they did on their test items.

Qualitative　◄————————►　Quantitative

Often you will find studies that fall somewhere in the middle of the
continuum. They land in between the two extremes, depending on how
much of each methodology they use. These are referred to as *mixed-method*
approaches (Creswell & Plano Clark, 2011; Teddlie & Tashakkori, 2009),

which combine both qualitative and quantitative methodologies in one study. The following study illustrates this point.

Ożanska-Ponikwia's (2016) study, which I mentioned in Chapter 4 to illustrate the use of qualitative data, also used quantitative data. She stated clearly in her study that she used a mixed-method design. "Data from 97 Polish–English late bilinguals and Polish L2 users of English were analysed qualitatively and quantitatively" (p. 116). When I looked more closely, I noticed that the quantitative side of her study was descriptive. That is, the numbers she used (e.g. percentages, means, etc.) described her data. There was no use of any inferential statistics (see Chapter 7). As a result, I place this study more toward the qualitative side of the continuum.

Qualitative ⟷ Quantitative

The mixed-method paradigm seems to be the latest bandwagon in some areas of applied linguistic research these days, which I personally applaud. However, my students have found several studies, though claiming to be mixed-method, that are either quantitative studies with a little verbal data from an interview with a couple of participants or qualitative studies with numbers in the form of frequencies. These are not fully mixed-method studies. To qualify for a true mixed-method study, there needs to be clear sections that follow the procedures for both quantitative and qualitative studies. Compare Lee, Wong, Cheng, and Lee (2009) with Lin (2008) and note the difference.

The Exploratory–Confirmatory Continuum

The third independent continuum is labeled *exploratory–confirmatory* (Figure 5.1). The main characteristic of this continuum is whether a study is trying to find information to answer research questions without any hypothesis or to find evidence to support (i.e., confirm) a hypothesis.

On the confirmatory side of the continuum, Valeo's study (2013), mentioned previously, had one research question: "What effect does FFI have on learner awareness of language in a content-based language programme?" She proposes two answers in the form of hypotheses (predictions):

(1) Learners will be able to report awareness of both content and language in instruction that includes a focus on grammatical form and content meaning, and (2) learners reporting higher degrees of language awareness will show stronger outcomes on language measures than learners who report a lower degree of awareness.

(p. 131)

Her study can easily be plotted near the confirmatory end of the continuum, as shown here.

The other studies cited in this chapter (i.e., Koyama et al., 2016; Ożanska-Ponikwia, 2016) did not test any hypotheses. They were exploratory. They attempted to find out what was happening without trying to support any particular hypothesis. They should all be located toward the exploratory end of the continuum. However, just as an additional note, there are studies that can be placed more in the middle of this continuum if they have more questions than they have hypotheses to answer them.

As Figure 5.1 illustrates, the three continua intersect. This means that any given study can be plotted along all three continua at the same time. I have tried to show how this might be done in Figure 5.2 with Kubanyiova's (2015) study. Point A shows where the study represents the point of intersection between the basic–applied and the exploratory–confirmatory continua. It is an exploratory study that is quite basic. Point B at the intersection of the basic–applied and qualitative–quantitative continua points out that the study is qualitative and quite basic. Point C at the intersection of the exploratory–confirmatory and qualitative–quantitative continua means that the study is qualitative/exploratory. You will have to use your imagination a little to see where a study intersects when all three continua are taken into consideration. Point D attempts to show this, although it is difficult to display a three-dimensional graph on a two-dimensional piece of paper. The study is qualitative, exploratory, and quite basic.

After all of this discussion, I hope you understand that using *only* one of these continua is somewhat simplistic for describing research. The picture is even more complicated than this. I can think of three other continua—authenticity (natural–contrived), focus (unrestricted–restricted), and behavior (external–mental)—but, for the moment, I have used the three continua discussed here to illustrate that there is more to a research study than what we might first be led to believe (e.g, qualitative–quantitative).

You might ask why this information is important for consumers to know. The importance lies in the fact that a researcher's system for choosing procedures and an interpretative framework for their study is based on how their study is designed. For consumers, knowing where a study intersects on these continua provides an overall framework for understanding the remainder of a study.

To help you become more familiar with the classification system I have just outlined, do the following exercise.

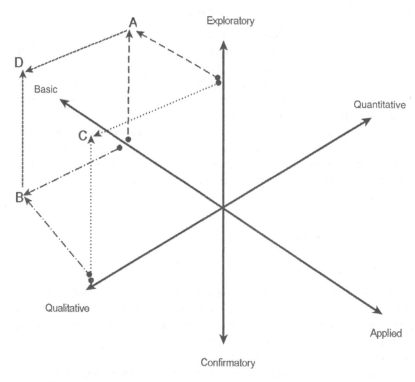

Figure 5.2 Example of Classifying Kubanyiova's Study (2015) on the Three Design Continua

Exercise 5.1

Find a recent study that interests you.

1. Plot the study on the three different continua below based on your perusal of the study.
2. Provide a rationale for each placement based on what you find in the study.

Basic _____ Applied

Exploratory _____ Confirmatory

Qualitative _____ Quantitative

As you read research with this system in mind, you will develop an understanding of why researchers do what they do. You will also realize when a researcher does something out of the ordinary.

Section 2: Questions and Designs

Some research methodology books can give the impression that various research designs are independent from one another by the way they present them (i.e., a chapter per method; e.g., Gall et al., 1996; Martella, Nelson, Morgan, & Marchand-Matella 2013). However, in my opinion, a more useful way to understand research designs is by organizing them around the type of research question under investigation.

As outlined in Chapter 1, the two generic questions found in research literature center around *what* and *why*. The second section of this chapter is structured around these generic questions and their sub-questions. For each question type, I present the most common research designs found in applied linguistics research.

The WHAT Questions

What Phenomena Are Important?

To answer this question, researchers use designs that are usually classified as either qualitative/exploratory or quantitative/exploratory. These designs can be placed anywhere on the applied–basic continuum. In such studies, there is no hypothesis to test. Rather, the researcher is trying to gather information not known previously. The purpose might be to develop a hypothesis during the investigation, as in grounded theory ethnography, or to fill in missing information, but it is not to confirm an existing hypothesis.

To illustrate, Lee-Johnson (2015) did a (qualitative/exploratory/applied) study that looked at the effects of out-of-class social interactions between ESL learners and their native-speaking counterparts on their overall learning experiences. She used five ESL students as the main participants to be observed by various methods over a five-month period. She had three research questions with no hypotheses. Her data consisted of field notes, interviews, participant observations, participant diaries, and artifacts. She then analyzed the verbal data by looking for patterns and themes. Based on this she drew her conclusions.

However, quantitative designs are also used to answer *What* questions. Koyama, Sun, and Ockey's (2016) study, as you might remember, examined relationships between previewing test items and video-based multiple-choice listening assessments. They addressed three research questions and had no hypotheses. A quick glance at their results section confirms the quantitative nature of this study. Their study appeared to be addressing a practical problem. So, all combined, this study is a quantitative/exploratory/applied one.

Before moving on to another research question, with its corresponding research methodologies, do the following exercise to provide you with firsthand experience in examining an article that applies the prior discussion.

Exercise 5.2

Find a recent study that tries to answer the following question: what phenomena are of importance (i.e., *neither* correlational nor cause/effect)?

1. Classify it on the three continua.
2. State the research question(s).
3. Identify the variables in the study.
4. Summarize the methodology of the study by explaining in your own words how the researcher(s) designed the study to answer the research question(s).

What Simple Relationships Exist Between Phenomena?

Except for research that only wants to identify and describe phenomena, all other research is in one way or other looking at relationships between phenomena (see Figure 1.3 and related discussion). Some researchers want to know if there are any *simple relationships* between constructs. However, by *simple* I do not mean the relationships are unimportant or lack complexity. Here the term means a relationship between two variables. Many simple relationships have profound implications for the language classroom.

A synonym commonly used for a simple relationship is *correlation*. This is not to be confused with the term *correlation coefficient* (see Chapter 7), which is a specific statistic used to indicate a correlation (i.e., a type of simple relationship).

Research on this question can be classified anywhere on all three of the classification continua. It can be confirmatory or exploratory, qualitative or quantitative, basic or applied. Different from the previous *What* question, researchers might have a hypothesis to test for answering the question. Following the research question "What relationships exist?" for instance, they may hypothesize that a relationship between certain variables does exist. The researchers could do this based on theory or the findings of previous research.

The most common design used to examine simple relationships gathers data on two or more variables and then correlates data sets using various statistical procedures. Akbari and Hosseini (2008) examined possible relationships between eight multiple intelligences with six language-learning strategy types for EFL learners. To answer their research question, they analyzed the relationship between each pair of variables, illustrating the use of the *shotgun* method. That is, all of the data for all of the variables are processed in one go. The resulting 8 × 6 matrix of correlation coefficients revealed that there were some relationships between the components of the two constructs. The advantage of this method is that a lot of relationships can be explored at the same time.

Another type of simple relationship study mentioned back in Chapter 1 (see Figure 1.3) is *predictive*. Based on simple pair-wise relationships between variables, a researcher can explore what variables can be used to predict behavior on another variable. For example, Venkatagiri and Levis (2007) examined whether there was any relationship between phonological awareness and speech comprehensibility. They hypothesized that

> learners who show greater phonological awareness do so because they are better at noticing patterns in phonological input. An extension of this hypothesis is that those L2 speakers who are better at noticing phonological patterns will also be judged as more comprehensible to NS listeners.
>
> (p. 265)

Regarding the above correlational studies, however, I want to reiterate a very important principle here. Finding a relationship between two variables is not enough to conclude that one variable causes the other to change. Akbari and Hosseini (2008) could not (and did not) conclude from their data that the multiple intelligences variables actually *caused* the differences in performance on language learning strategy usage. The reason for this is that correlations are symmetrical, meaning that variable A correlates with variable B in the same direction and magnitude as variable B correlates with variable A. But now I am getting into issues that I discuss more fully in Chapter 7.

For a similar reason, prediction studies do not show cause-and-effect relationships. Venkatagiri and Levis (2007) based their predictions on simple relationships that are symmetrical. Although intuitively one might think that phonological awareness might impact speech comprehensibility, such conclusions cannot be based on these data. Venkatagiri and Levis were careful to not make this type of error in their study.

I recommend that you take this opportunity to do the following exercise to give you another example of a study looking for simple relationships. To help locate one more quickly, I suggest you look for the keyword *relationship* in the title.

Exercise 5.3

Find a recent study that investigates the following question: Are there any important simple relationships between phenomena?

1. What relationships were being examined?
2. State any hypothesis and/or prediction made (if any).
3. Identify the variables in the study.
4. Summarize the methodology of the study by explaining in your own words how the researcher(s) designed the study to answer the research question(s).

The WHY Questions

Once we begin to understand what phenomena are out there, or what relationships exist between variables, we begin to ask *why*. Why do people vary in the phenomena that we observe to be important to a particular issue? Why do certain variables relate with one another? The essence of this type of question is *causation*. Causation indicates a more specific type of relationship between variables than only a *simple* relationship. Causal relations delineate how variables (i.e., constructs) affect other variables. Why do some people learn languages better than others? What makes people good readers? Does using computers affect the way people write? If only we could discover why, we might be able to help improve desirable abilities and discourage undesirable ones in language learning.

To refresh your memory from Chapter 3, the variable(s) that is suspected of causing variation in another variable(s) is the *independent variable(s)*. The variable(s) that is being influenced by the independent variable(s) is the *dependent variable(s)*. Sometimes the intent of the researcher is made clear in the title of a study and the variables are easily identified. Machida and Dalsky's (2014) study expressly states in its title "The Effect of Concept Mapping on L2 Writing Performance: Examining Possible Effects of Trait-Level Writing Anxiety" its IV and DV. Concept mapping is the IV, and L2 writing performance is the DV. However, the last phrase, "examining possible effects of trait-level anxiety," confused me at first. Is this another IV? Upon scrolling down their study to the research question ("Is concept mapping more effective for improving writing proficiency for students with high writing anxiety or low writing anxiety?" (p. 30)), it became clear that writing anxiety is a moderating variable (MV). Other researchers might use terms in their titles such as *impact, influence, improve, change, role of*, and so on when they are investigating whether variables cause changes in other variables. But they are all referring to causation.

Such studies have at least one independent variable and at least one dependent variable. Machida and Dalsky's (2014) study had one of each. Other studies might have more than one IV and/or DV. I cite some examples later.

Research into causal relationships is not restricted to any one end of the three continua discussed in Section 1 of this Chapter. Causal studies can be placed anywhere on the basic–applied, exploratory–confirmatory, and qualitative–quantitative continua. The key characteristic of this type of study is that it is looking for one or more causal relationships.

Causal Qualitative Studies

Some mistakenly believe that causal relationships can only be studied using quantitative approaches. However, Miles and Huberman (1994) have clearly described how causal relationships are studied using qualitative research designs. A study that illustrates this is one by Yang and Kim (2011). Their qualitative study examined two L2 learners' belief changes due to change in study abroad contexts. The independent variable was study abroad contexts and the dependent variable was belief changes. They collected the data from two ESL students consisting of "pre- and post-study abroad interviews and monthly-collected journals with other triangulating methods such as L2 learning autobiographies and stimulated recall tasks" (p. 325). By analyzing the verbal output of each of these participants and identifying commonalities, Yang and Kim were able to identify possible causative factors that make a difference. I classified this study as qualitative/exploratory/applied on our three intersecting continua.

Causal-Comparative Designs

On the more quantitative side, one common research design that is used to examine causal relationships is the *causal-comparative* design. However, as is made apparent below, the findings from this design might suggest cause/effect, but they cannot answer for sure whether the variation in the dependent variable is caused by the independent variable. The reason is that the IV comes already packaged with a lot of other variables (i.e., extraneous variables) that might be the real influencing variables. When researchers cannot manipulate the IV, they cannot control for such nuisance variables by this design.

Let me first illustrate the causal-comparative method with an actual study. MacIntyre, Baker, Clément, and Donovan (2002) investigated the causal relationship between two independent variables (sex and age) and four dependent variables (one at a time): willingness to communicate, anxiety, perceived competence, and L2 motivation. Part of the title of the study, "Sex and Age Effects on . . .," strongly indicates a cause-and-effect study. However, the researchers did not manipulate the independent variables. Sex and age cannot be manipulated. They are taken as is; males and females are found in nature at given ages. The sex and age of a participant are givens. In other words, if an independent variable is found already in existence and is not manipulated by the researcher, as is the case with sex and age, the research design is labeled *causal-comparative*.

Why does this make any difference, you might ask? The reason is that by not being able to control or manipulate the independent variable, other variables associated with this variable might be the real cause behind any variation in the dependent variable rather than the independent variable itself. Take *age*, for example. MacIntyre et al. (2002) found, among other things, that willingness to communicate in French as a L2 increased from seventh to eighth grades (i.e., their operational definition of age) but leveled off between grades eight and nine. However, can they conclude that difference in age, even though only between seventh and eighth grade, *caused* the increase? Not with much confidence. The reason is that some other variable could have contributed to the change between grades seven and eight at the particular school where the participants attended other than age. Did something happen during this two-year span other than the participants getting older? Most likely, a lot happened. For this reason, MacIntyre et al. cannot—and did not—make strong causal conclusions based on their study, which used a causal-comparative design.

For practical or ethical reasons, many independent variables cannot be manipulated. For example, if researchers want to know whether economic status influences language learners' use of reading strategies, they cannot manipulate the economic status of the participants. In other words, they cannot choose random groups of people who have no economic status and then randomly assign each group where they increase or decrease participants' economic level. Participants already come from different economic levels when they participate in the study. So, researchers take random samples from each economic group and then examine whether the participants differ on what reading strategies they choose (i.e., the dependent variable). As with sex and age, the difficulty here is that economic groups differ in a number of other ways that might influence how they choose reading strategies.

The validity of any causal conclusions based on results from a causal-comparative study increases with the amount of care the researcher takes when designing the study. For this reason, you need to attend carefully to how the researcher tries to control for any competing alternative explanations for the potential results. MacIntyre et al. (2002) were careful to inform the reader that the three grade levels were housed in the same building and that the participants came from the same community and had similar previous exposure to French as an L2. This information rules out that any age difference was due to the grade levels being housed in separate buildings, or representing students from different communities. However, it would have been helpful if they would have also reported whether any special events had occurred for the seventh graders that were different for the eighth graders to rule out any other possible factors that may have produced differences.

Now let us see if you can find a causal-comparative study for your own by doing the following exercise. The keywords to look for in the title, abstract, or research questions in the introduction of the studies you peruse are: *effect, impact, influence,* and so on, along with variables that cannot be manipulated, such as sex, age, language level, nationality, and so on.

Exercise 5.4

Identify a recent study from a research journal that answers a WHY question using a causal-comparative design.

1. State the research question.
2. Identify the independent variable(s) and the dependent variable(s).
3. State any hypotheses and/or predictions made (if any).
4. Study the introduction and methodology section. In your own words, explain why you think this is a causal-comparative study.
5. Identify any strategies used for controlling for any alternative explanations of the results.
6. How strong were the conclusions in your opinion? Were they justified?

Experimental and Quasi-experimental Designs

As you might expect, if there are variables that cannot be manipulated, there are other variables that can be. Designs that manipulate independent variables are grouped under the heading of experimental or quasi-experimental designs. Both experimental and quasi-experimental research designs involve manipulating the independent variable(s) and observing the change in the dependent variable(s). The goal of this genre of design in comparison to others is that researchers try to control changes in the variance of the independent variable(s) without allowing the intervention of other unwanted variables. In one of the simpler designs, there is one group of participants that gets the treatment and another group that does not (i.e., the control group). For example, Hung (2015) examined the effects of *flipping the classroom* (i.e., rearranging the order of events) on English language learners' academic performance, learning attitudes, and participation levels. She stated that she used a posttest-only quasi-experimental design. Her IV was the flipped classroom approach, which had three different formats of treatment, which included one control group. Note that the three formats of treatment make up three levels of one IV. The DVs were the students' academic performance, measured by the end-of-lesson assessments; learning attitudes, measured by a questionnaire and interviews; and participation levels, measured by lesson study log. She randomly assigned one of each of the three levels of treatment to each of three intact classrooms. One level was the full flipped classroom treatment, the second was a partial flipped classroom, and the third received a conventional classroom experience. The difference between experimental and quasi-experimental research has to do with how the sample is selected. If the samples for the treatment and the control groups are randomly selected, then the design is experimental. If not, it is quasi-experimental. This is an important difference because any sample that is not randomly sampled could be biased and thereby could unintentionally allow extraneous variables to affect the results of the study. *Bias*, here, has a specific meaning. If there is a systematic difference in the makeup of either the treatment group or the control group that might affect the results of the study, other than the treatment variable, the samples are biased.

Hung's (2015) study, mentioned above, would be classified as quasi-experimental because the samples were not randomly chosen. She used three intact classes. The question arises as to whether there were any important differences between the treatment and control groups other than receiving or not receiving the treatment. She tried to control for this by testing the participants on a number of traits that might have interfered. The three classes did not differ on any of these, giving Hung confidence that any differences were due to the treatment levels.

Purely experimental studies are uncommon in applied linguistic research, mainly because of the difficulty to randomly select participants from experimentally accessible populations (see Chapter 4). There are two characteristics that identify them: whether the independent variable was manipulated by the researcher(s) and whether some form of randomization was used in selecting the participants. One example is a study by Martin, Claydon, Morton, Binns, and Pratt (2003), which investigated the effects of orthographic and phonological strategies on children's ability to decode words developmentally. The researchers randomly sampled 191 children from grades 1 to 10 from four high schools and five elementary schools in differing socioeconomic areas in southern Tasmania. By doing so, they increased the external validity (see Chapter 4) of generalizing the findings of the study to the target population. Second, the researchers manipulated two independent variables: the modality in which words were presented (visual vs oral) and the instruction type (phonological vs orthographic). This study is clearly classified as experimental.

Random selection of participants is sometimes thought to be substituted by another randomization procedure called *random assignment*. Instead of randomly selecting participants from a pool of possible participants, the treatment is randomly assigned to participants who may have been part of a convenient sample. Note, however, that this use of randomization does not necessarily increase the *external validity* of the study. The researcher might assign treatments randomly to participants within intact groups, such as classrooms. Such groups are not usually representative of a larger target population to which generalizations can be made. Conclusions, therefore, may not be directly generalizable to the target population.

Experimental/quasi-experimental studies come in a variety of designs. I counted over 12 designs presented in Chapters 12 and 13 of Gall et al. (1996). The reason that there are so many different designs is that there are many extraneous variables, other than the independent variable(s), that might cause the dependent variable to vary. Each design tries to control a specific set of these unwanted variables. I will not go into detail here, but suffice it to say that each design is defined by various combinations and ordering of the treatment and control groups along with random or nonrandom sampling. If you would like more detail, I recommend websites such as www.socialresearchmethods.net/kb/desexper.php.

Section 3: Internal Validity

When discussing cause and effect in research, no matter where the study fits on the three continua discussed in Section 1, the internal validity of the study is of critical importance. The extent to which extraneous variables affect the change in the dependent variable is the extent to which the internal validity is influenced. Whereas *external validity* relates to the degree to which findings can be generalized/transferred to populations or situations (see Chapter 4), *internal validity* is concerned with the degree to which the results of the study are due to the independent variable(s) under consideration and not due to anything else. Researchers favoring more qualitative approaches use the term *credibility* to mean the same thing as internal validity (Miles & Huberman, 1994).

Internal and external validity are not mutually exclusive. The degree to which a study lacks internal validity limits the degree to which the findings can be generalized to a target population (i.e., external validity). In other words, for a study that looks at causation, internal validity is a necessary requirement for external validity. Obviously, if the changes in the dependent variable are not due to the independent variable, then you certainly cannot generalize any findings to some target population. Nevertheless, having internal validity is not sufficient for establishing external validity. That is, a study might be designed so that the independent variable is the only thing that could cause change in the dependent variable, but, because the sample is not representative of the target population or comparable to any other situation, the results of the study cannot be generalized/transferred to that population or situations. The following may be of some help.

As previously mentioned, there are a number of extraneous factors that can affect the results of a study that will lower the internal and external validity of a study. Gall et al. (1996) gave a very good overview (Chapter 12) of the work done by Campbell and Stanley (1963), Cook and Campbell (1979), Bracht and Glass (1968), and others that try to identify most of the extraneous factors that can play havoc when exploring causal relationships. They listed 12 factors related to internal validity and 12 factors under external validity. Miles and Huberman (1994) presented a very similar list of factors from a qualitative research perspective in their Chapter 10 (sections B and C).

I have reworked these lists to try to remove redundancies and make things more manageable. I have also subordinated some of the factors to show how they relate to one another. As a result, I list 14 threats to internal validity, along with nine subordinate ones. I illustrate these extraneous factors with the *Research Minefield* presented in Figure 5.3. A well-designed study will weave around these hazards to capture a more accurate picture of how the independent variable(s) influences the dependent variable. The following is a brief explanation for each of the 14 *mines*, with examples of studies that have either avoided them or hit them.

History

This refers to the influence of events that take place at different points in time on the dependent variable other than the independent variable. Any study that takes considerable time to be completed can be affected by this if care is not taken. For instance, suppose researchers are running a study on improving the L2 of young children using some new teaching methodology over a period of several months. During that time, a new bilingual (L1/L2) program is put on national TV. If the researchers found any difference between the treatment and control group, could they be certain that the results were only due to the new methodology? Could the new methodology have interacted with the new TV program in such a way as to produce the results? Had the program not appeared when it did, the new methodology might not have produced the same results. Consequently, the researchers could not be sure what caused the changes in language behavior, if any were observed.

Longitudinal studies (i.e., studies that are done over a period of time) are vulnerable to the history mine. An example is the study done by Moeller, Theiler, and Wu (2012), who reported a quasi-experimental study of the relationship between goal-setting and student second language achievement in the Spanish-language classroom over a five-year period. They refer to their study as quasi-experimental in their abstract, which

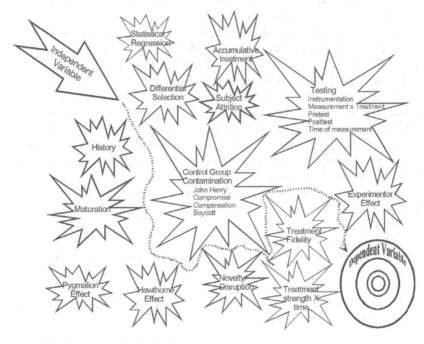

Figure 5.3 The Research Minefield

means that they are looking for a causal relationship, though they did not mention this in their research questions. The independent variable was LinguaFolio goal-setting process consisting of three stages: "setting goals, establishing an action plan for goal attainment and reflecting on relative attainment of goals" (p. 158). The dependent variables were teacher-independent scores based on an online proficiency assessment, which provides a comprehensive score for reading, writing, and speaking. The sample consisted of 21 teachers from 23 high schools and varying number of students depending on the level of class (one to four) and year of the study. For example, there were 106 total students in 2005 compared to 527 in 2007. In 2006 they had one third-year student, and in 2008 they had 158. The study began in 2005 and was completed in 2009. Although the researchers were careful to describe many factors about the study, they did not report whether there were any significant events or changes in policy that took place during this five-year period. One historical factor that might have had some influence on the study is that during this period there was a large migration of immigrants to Nebraska, where the study was done, many of whom were from Spanish-speaking countries. Could this have had any impact on students' Spanish ability? To give more confidence to the results of longitudinal studies, it is always wise for a researcher to inform the reader if anything of possible importance had occurred historically. Even if nothing happened, this should be reported so that the reader is made aware that this precaution was given attention.

Maturation

This is similar to history but it deals with the natural changes that take place over time in the participants other than what is under study. Such areas as physical coordination and strength, emotional states, and cognitive structures change as people grow older. Studies that take place over longer periods of time are potentially subject to this interference. For example, according to Piaget, young children who are at the preoperational (Ormrod, 1995) stage, between the ages of two and six, "confuse psychological phenomena with physical reality" (p. 175). In the next stage, concrete operational (6 to 11/12 years), children are able to think logically, but only with visible concrete objects. If Piaget's thinking is valid, we would have to take great care in the use of visual objects when using them to examine language ability of children across these stages (cf. Perry & Shwedel, 1979, an oldie but a goodie, though I'm biased).

The longitudinal study by Moeller et al. (2012) might have had this problem. Cognitive maturation over a five-year period most likely took place. The researchers suggested that increase in motivation over time might have played a role in their results. The point is that, if there is something about the treatment that interacts with certain developmental stages, then different results could be found.

Differential Selection

Hitting this mine can occur whenever researchers do not randomly select their samples when forming different groups for comparison purposes. Any preexisting differences between groups caused by choosing dissimilar participants could result in differences between groups not due to the variable being investigated. The classic situation where this might occur is when two intact classrooms are used, one for the treatment group and the other for the control group. Chances are that there are preexisting differences between the classes. Accordingly, these prior differences, and not the treatments, could account for any difference in the dependent variable between groups.

Hung (2015) did not use random sampling to select her participants for her study, but she was careful to test the participants in the three intact classes to ensure that they did not differ in language proficiency. The participants were around the same age, had been learning English around 10 years and had no previous experience with the treatment. However, the results of Hung's study might still have been influenced by *differential selection.* Possible problems might have arisen if differences between groups were due to the effects caused by other differences. Any time you see a quasi-experimental study, this is always a potential problem. The researchers, as Hung did, almost always warn the reader that causal conclusions are only suggested.

Statistical Regression

This is a fancy name for a phenomenon found in research where participants chosen from either of two opposite ends of an ability continuum, usually based on performance on some test, have a high probability of scoring closer to the middle of the continuum on the second testing without any outside help. This movement of scores toward the middle is referred to as *regression toward the mean* or *statistical regression.* This can manifest itself when a researcher selects participants who initially score very low on a language ability test and test them again after administering some form of treatment to raise their ability level. Any increase in performance after the treatment could not be conclusively attributed to the treatment because it might be due to the statistical phenomenon of regressing upward toward the mean (i.e., the middle of the ability group). Why does this happen, you might ask? The reason is that test scores are not exact measurements of a person's ability. Many people who initially do badly on a test may have done badly for a variety of reasons—maybe they were not feeling well or something disturbing happened on the way to the test. If they had taken the test on another day, they might have done better. This is just one possible explanation of this phenomenon.

However, in the case of qualitative research, the extreme cases might be exactly what researchers are focusing on (Miles & Huberman, 1994). If they are trying to obtain a sample that contains information-rich data to answer the research question, then this strategy is the correct one. Statistical regression is not a factor.

Subject Attrition

When there is a loss of participants during a research study (also known as *experimental mortality*), this can occur. The results can be affected and misleading because attrition does not commonly occur randomly. People who drop out of a study often differ from those who remain in ways that distort research findings. For example, researchers might lose some beginning-level EFL learners from their sample because they lose interest and drop out. This might leave the study not only with proportionally more participants of higher ability levels but with participants who have higher motivation. Moeller et al. (2012) reported that their study might have been affected by attrition. They clearly stated this:

With disaggregation of the data to represent solely students participating in all 4 years of consecutive levels of Spanish instruction, the sample size decreases significantly ($n = 24$). Conducting an analysis with such a small sample risks producing questionable results.

(p. 160)

The greatest improvement in goal setting occurred between the second and third levels of Spanish. This can be explained in part by the attrition of those students who discontinued their Spanish studies.

(p. 162)

The first statement warns us that we must question the results owing to attrition. The next statement tells us that attrition improved the results. What more can I say?

Sometimes researchers drop participants from groups to produce equal numbers in each group, often referred to as a *cell*. The reason they do this is that many statistical procedures are easier to interpret when there are equal cell sizes. However, you want to check whether participants are dropped randomly. If this is done, there is less chance that a bias may occur. Another caveat is that, when dealing with smaller numbers of participants, the loss of even one participant can have a significant impact on the results. The conclusion is that, when you read a research article, give attention to any irregularities in the sample. There should be clear documentation to show that the results of the study were not contaminated by any participant attrition.

Control Group Contamination

This one is important to consider when there is more than one group in a causal study. Many studies use control groups in their designs. Typically, a control group is one that does not receive the novel treatment which is the focus of the study. For instance, a new method for teaching vocabulary might be compared with a traditional method.[6]

However, this effect could better be referred to as *competing group contamination*. The reason is that some studies compare differences between groups, possibly without a control group. These studies have several competing treatment groups. In such studies the following discussion is still applicable.

Hung's (2015) study, discussed previously, is used in the following discussion as a platform for illustrating the four ways a competing group can affect the results of a study. Recall, she compared three conditions in her flip-the-classroom study: fully structured, semistructured, and a control group using traditional structured. She randomly assigned three intact classrooms to the three conditions. Remember that random assignment to groups does not mean the same things as random selection of participants for the sample. Competing group contamination can take four different directions. They are:

Competing Group Rivalry (the John Henry Effect)

When the behaviors of the competing groups differ because they are trying to outdo one another, you cannot be sure the results are due to the difference in treatments, i.e., the independent variable(s). This condition might occur if the competing group were explicitly labeled the *control group*. Not only might extra effort come from the participants in the group, but the person supervising the control group, such as a teacher, might apply extra effort to compete. The thing to look for is whether the researchers have specified what measures were taken to protect this from happening. Careful researchers will take precautions to keep the groups' identities a secret and report them in their study.

In Hung's (2015) study, the three classes came from the same institution. Though there was no mention of the possible *John Henry effect*, had the control group heard about what was going on in the other classes they may have been challenged to compete. This would have been a possible explanation had there been no difference between the experimental groups and the control group. However, the experimental groups outperformed the control group, so this was not a problem.

Experimental Treatment Diffusion (Compromise)

When the competing groups gain knowledge of the factors making up the differing treatment conditions and employ these factors in their own situations, the results might be corrupted. The extraneous variable here is *not* competition, as in the previous one, but rather the mixing up of the treatment factors in the competing groups due to knowledge about what is taking place in the other group(s). This often happens when the competing groups are in close proximity and have time to get to know what the other(s) is doing. Care should be taken to reduce the possibility of participants from the different groups discussing what the other(s) is doing.

Looking at Hung's (2015) study, we can conclude that this did not happen, although there might have been common awareness of what was happening in the experimental treatment. Similar to the John Henry effect, this problem might have been of concern if there had been no difference between the treatment and control groups, or if the control group outperformed the treatment group. However, the results for all three research questions revealed superiority for the fully flipped classroom treatment. Even the semiflipped classroom treatment outperformed the control group on a number of occasions.

Compensatory Equalization of Treatments

When attempts are made to give the competing group extra material or special treatment to make up for not receiving the experimental treatment, you no longer have a true control group. In fact, you would have a new treatment group.

The temptation to provide the control group with extra help arises when there is a possibility that the treatment group will have an advantage over the control group in some real-life situation. To illustrate, if researchers were comparing some new method of teaching grammar (treatment group) to the traditional way that grammar was being taught during a real language course (control group), they might be tempted to give the control group some extra material or help so that they would not be at an unfair disadvantage at the end of the course. However, in doing so, the differences between treatment and control could be distorted, making the results uninterpretable. Again, because the experimental group outperformed the control group in Hung's (2015) study, this most likely did not occur.

To prevent *compensatory equalization of treatments* from happening, researchers should use someone to supervise the control group who is unaware of the advantage the treatment group might have during the study. In addition, they should allow time after the experiment to help the control group catch up with those in the treatment group so that the control group is not unduly penalized. A well-written study will report how this problem was addressed.

Demoralization (Boycott) of the Control Group

This potential contaminator occurs when participants in the control group resent the special treatment given to the treatment group and lower their performance. This is the opposite of the John Henry effect. If participants in the control group, for example, learn that those in the treatment group have access to computers to help them increase their writing ability while they have to use paper and pencil, their envy might cause them to refuse to cooperate with their instructor. To prevent this, some strategy needs to be used to convince the control group that they are not being deprived.

Here Hung's (2015) study might have had a problem. Since the three intact classes used for both the treatment and the control groups were in the same institution, the control group might have become demoralized if they had news that they were not getting the new interesting classroom format. In turn, they might have given less effort to learn than normal.

This offers an alternative explanation for the inferior performance of the control group in comparison with the treatment group. Because Hung did not state whether she tried to prevent this, we are left with this alternative explanation regarding her findings.

Testing

This mine refers to ways in which measuring the dependent variable(s) can distort the results of a study. Under this heading, I list five sources to which the consumer of research needs to pay attention.

Instrumentation

The type of instrument used to measure performance on the dependent variable(s) can have an effect on the results. This can occur if two different types of instruments are used and the performances of the two are compared with each other. For example, if one test of English proficiency were used (e.g., a multiple-choice test) as a pretest and another test of English proficiency (e.g., an essay test) were used as a posttest, you would not know if any change in test scores was due to increase in ability or difference in the difficulty level between the two tests. Unless the two tests are parallel in all possible ways, the results between the two tests cannot be compared.

Measurement–Treatment Interaction

This is similar to instrumentation, but in this case the results are only found when using a particular type of measure. To illustrate, we might only be able to find certain effects of a novel method for teaching grammar in an EFL context with multiple-choice exams, but not with tests of written compositions. Any attempt to generalize results from only one type of measurement to all types would be groundless.

Almost every study using only one type of instrument to measure the dependent variables could be accused of having this problem. Derakhshan and Eslami (2015), for example, examined the effect of consciousness-raising video-driven prompts on the development of two speech acts, apology and request. They used a multiple-choice discourse completion instrument for their pretest both to check for preexisting differences between their three treatment groups and to set a baseline to measure change due to the treatment. They used the same instrument after the treatment after reordering the test items.

The discerning reader should ask whether the same results would have been found if other types of measures had been used. This is not to suggest, however, that the findings of this study are insignificant. They are important, but they are only part of the puzzle. To bolster their conclusions, this study should be replicated using other assessment formats to see if the findings are replicated. Derakhshan and Eslami (2015), in fact, commented that, if they had used a written discourse completion test along with the multiple-choice task and found the same results, their conclusions would have been stronger.

Pretest Effect

This is caused when a test given before the administration of the treatment interacts with the treatment by heightening participants' awareness of the importance of certain material. If this happens, the performance on the test given after the treatment (i.e., the *posttest*) would be higher if no pretest existed. The question here is whether the pretest alerts the participants to components in the treatment to which they would not normally pay much attention. The only way we would know if this occurred would be if we had another treatment group that did not take the pretest and compared their performance on the posttest with that of the pretest/treatment group. If there was no difference, then we could conclude that there was no pretest effect.

Derakhshan and Eslami's (2015) results might have been influenced by their pretest. They used the same test for assessing pragmatic awareness of requests and apologies in their pretest as they did for their posttest after the treatment.

Obviously, they were aware of this possible threat to the internal validity to their study. They tried to control for the effects of participants' memory of the test by reordering the items. However, had they used an additional group who did not take the pretest prior to the treatment, they could have tested whether there was any pretest effect. That is, if no difference between the two treatment groups (i.e., pretest with treatment vs treatment without pretest) on the posttest was found, they would have clear evidence that the pretest did not interact with the treatment.

Posttest Effect

The posttest can also have an effect on the treatment. Unwittingly, researchers might design their posttest so that it helps participants *make associations* between different concepts at the time of taking the test rather than during the time of treatment. Had another test been used, these associations might not have been made, and the conclusion would be that the treatment had had no effect.

Most likely you have experienced this effect when taking an exam sometime in the past, like most of us. It is known as the *click of comprehension* effect. As participants take the posttest, suddenly something in the test brings things together in a way that the participants had not thought of previously, but this effect was something that the treatment was supposed to have done prior to the posttest, not during it.

This effect might be seen when the posttest is an oral interview given after a treatment that tries to improve students' oral language ability. If interviewers are not careful, something that they say might actually teach the interviewee some correct form of spoken language that was not previously known. The interviewee then uses the newly learned form in answering the question, thus giving the impression that the treatment made the improvement. To avoid this, the interviewer must ensure that the target issues being assessed are not used inadvertently when asking questions.

Time of Measurement Effect

This relates to timing. Many studies apply whatever measurement they are using immediately after the completion of the treatment. To conclude that such results can be interpreted to mean that the treatment also has long-term effects would be misleading. For us to make such an inference, we would have to have an additional measurement with an appropriate time interval.

To control for the above effect, some studies administer the test a week or more later. Ekembe (2014) examined whether a large class size limited the use of a teacher-led interactive approach as compared to a traditional instructional approach when focusing on form. She used pretest, posttest, and delay posttest to study any differences. She noticed interesting increases from pretest to posttest, but the results changed after two weeks, when the delayed posttest was given. She provided a number of reasons for these findings, which I won't go into here. The important thing to note is that the results that a study finds immediately after treatment on a posttest might change over time.

Researcher Effect

Researchers can also be a source for data distortion, which in turn weakens the internal validity of the results. If the results are determined by who does the experiment or who does the interview, the results are questionable. This problem often occurs when researchers are the ones who are either administering the treatment or collecting data that depends on their judgments. Action research suffers from this potential effect almost by default. Remember from Chapter 4 that this type of research is often performed by a teacher within their own classroom. Calvert and Sheen (2015), for example, attempted to answer the question "How can a teacher who is inexperienced with tasks create ones that collectively engage learners, appropriately align to their level, and effectively meet shared learning goals?" (p. 227). A teacher (one of the authors) attempted to develop two tasks in an English for Occupational Purposes course for refugees. The question arises that, no matter what results are found, one does not know whether the results are due to the tasks or due to the person who is administering them, especially when the person administering the tasks is the researcher with vested interests. Had another person administered the treatment, would the results have been different? In the case of action research, this is not that important since the results are not expected to be generalized to larger populations but is only important to the situation in which the research is done.

Under the same heading, I include the *data gatherer effect*. Just the presence of a data gatherer can distort the way in which participants behave or think. The data gatherer may be a tape recorder or a video recorder, not just a human. Kim and Taguchi's (2015) study, entitled "Promoting Task-Based Pragmatics Instruction in EFL Classroom Contexts: The Role of Task Complexity," used recording devices to gather data. The participants were desensitized[7] to the presence of the equipment by the time the actual study took place. Had the researchers not planned this desensitization period prior to actual data collection, the results of the study would be suspect. However, one wonders whether the participants would have responded the same way had there been no recording device.

Consequently, you need to pay attention to who applies the treatment/ control and/or who does the data gathering. If the author(s) of the study is the one(s) applying the treatment, while another administers the control, the results are questionable. If the researcher is directly doing the data gathering, there should be at least one other person checking to make sure the data is objectively gathered. More is given about this in the next chapter.

Pygmalion Effect

This is a type of researcher effect that is caused by the change in the researchers' perception of the behavior of the participants caused by their expectations of the participants' performance. For instance, if the data collectors think that the participants they are observing are high-ability students, they might be more lenient (or demanding) in their observations than if they thought the participants were low ability. Any time participants have been divided into ability groups such as high/middle/low L2 language proficiency and the data collector is aware of this, there is a danger of this effect. The danger is even greater if the type of data collected requires any form of qualitative judgment on the part of the data collectors. Researchers need to take precautions that the data collectors are unaware of the ability level of the participants they are observing and clearly state what precautions they have taken in their report.

Hawthorne Effect

When participants behave differently because they know they are in a research study, distortions in their behavior can occur. In a normal class-room environment, the same results would not be found. This problem is usually dealt with by masking from the participants the fact that they are involved in a study.

Treatment Intervention

The results of a study can be affected in at least two undesirable ways: *novelty* and *disruption*. Some treatments are so new that their novelty affects the results on the dependent variable. For example, if a study is look-ing at the effects of using computers to teach L2 grammar in comparison with normal classroom teaching, the students in the computer group may be more motivated to do well because of the novelty of using computers. This novelty may wear off after sustained exposure to computers and their motivation drops. In this study, the improvement would not have been due to the effectiveness of computers but the motivation level of the students caused by something new in the classroom. To avoid this effect, a study needs to have a *cooling-off period*, where the novelty wears off before any measurements are made.

Not all things new are an advantage, however. Disruption in per-formance can be due to participants being unfamiliar with the new intervention being tried. Using the computer example above, many participants who have not acquired good keyboarding skills may perform more poorly than those using traditional paper and pencil. These results would mask any advantage the computer might have over traditional methods.

The Ekembe (2014) study, mentioned earlier, may have been influenced by some of these issues. The researcher recognized this problem in her discussion section by noting

> The majority of the learners in the interaction group responded timidly towards the communicative activities introduced in the class-room and always had to be led by the teacher. One major reason for this was their previous learning experience and culture. The learners had been brought up in a school culture where the teacher con-trolled the knowledge to be imparted to the learner. . . . As observed in the classroom, the learners saw a new way of doing things and

therefore needed more time and consistency to adapt to this learning style.

(p. 245)

The novelty of the new instruction method disrupted learning rather than facilitated it. I take my hat off to Ekembe for cautioning the reader by being candid about these matters.

Accumulative Treatment Effect

It is also known as the *multiple-treatment interference or order effect*. This is the result of the accumulative effect of the particular order in which treatments are presented. Some research designs administer several treatments to the same participants. When this happens, care needs to be taken that the particular order in which the treatments are given does not influence the results. The most common way to control for this effect is using what is called a *counterbalanced* design. This is a simple procedure whereby the order of the treatments is varied across participants so as to attenuate the effects of order.

A study that points out this issue was done by Moskovsky et al. (2013). Remember that they used 10 motivational strategies for their treatment to try to increase student motivation. Their results revealed that the treatment group performed higher than the control group. However, they presented the 10 strategies in one order. Could that particular order of presentation have produced these results? What if they had used another order? Maybe one particular order they did not use would have produced different results. To use a counterbalance design to test all the possible orders would have required them to divide their treatment participants into many different orders of strategies, which would have required a much larger sample. Testing whether their results remain over other orders of strategy presentation is something they can add to the list of other items for further research that they gave in their discussion section.

Treatment Fidelity

This issue has to do with whether the treatment was administered in the correct manner as defined by researchers (Gall et al., 1996). Studies that use people other than researchers as the treatment administrators are in danger of the treatment not being administered correctly. If the treatment is not properly given, the results cannot really answer the research question. However, if researchers do the implementation themselves the researcher effect could play a role. To ensure treatment fidelity and avoid researcher effect, researchers need to train treatment administrators other than themselves to the point where the treatment is administered at the appropriate level.

Moskovsky et al. (2013) realized this danger in their study so they instructed the teachers in the treatment group how to use an implementation guide for the 10 motivational strategies. They required teachers to review the implementation guide prior to every class and to try to use all the strategies in each lesson. One of the coauthors observed the classrooms over the experimental period to ensure that the treatment teachers followed the implementation guide and engaged in at least some of the designated behaviors. The control group was also observed to check if similar behaviors did not occur spontaneously. The research team was confident that their treatment had been administered correctly.

Treatment Strength—Time Interaction

Time is needed for the treatment to have any noticeable effect. Some treatments require more time than others. This potential problem especially relates to studies that deal with teaching methodology commonly found in applied linguistics. Time is needed for most innovative methods to take effect, which means that these studies need more than one or two weeks before testing whether an innovation works.

When the results find no effect for a new method being tried out, the reader needs to ask whether there was enough time in the research design to allow the treatment to work. This may have been a factor in the Moeller et al. (2012) study. Remember that they were studying the effects of goal-setting on students in Spanish over a five-year time period. In spite of their problem with a fluctuating sample, they noticed a consistent increase over time. However, they also noted that the program improved over time owing to development of the teachers. This suggests, and their data supported this, that improvement in achievement can take time, depending on the treatment.

As you can see from the above list of the many things that can cause differences in the dependent variable other than the independent variables, it is a wonder that anyone tries to answer the question "Why?" However, rather than turning you into a cynic, rejecting any research as a waste of time, I hope that you have come to appreciate the challenge researchers face when trying to tease out the answers to the Why question. Yes, you should have reservations, but in a healthy sort of way. You should take the results and interpretations of any one single study with a degree of caution, knowing that there is most likely a weakness or two. However, this should encourage you to find more studies that address the same question to find if the results agree. If you find a number of studies producing similar findings, you will have more confidence regarding any answers. In addition, when you find a study that is designed in such a way that it avoids all of the mines mentioned above, you will find yourself admiring the study as though it were a famous painting in the Louvre. Maybe that is taking it too far, but you will appreciate them more when you come across them.

In conclusion, there are many variations in the types of designs you will encounter in your readings. In many cases, you will even find combinations of the above designs included in one study. There is nothing to restrict researchers from using whatever they believe will best answer the research questions.

There has been a lot of material covered here, and you will probably not remember it all the first time through. I certainly did not. However, as you continue to read research you will want to review this chapter now and again to refresh your memory regarding the rationale for using certain techniques. As you do this, you will sharpen your skills at becoming a very effective discerning consumer.

However, before moving on to the next chapter, take the time to do the following exercise. It gives you an opportunity to find two studies that answer the Why question and apply what you have read. These should be easy to find because they often have terms in their titles that suggest causation between constructs. I have developed an instrument to help you catalog the information you will be looking for below, called the *internal validity evaluation inventory*.

Exercise 5.5

Find a recent study that answers a Why question using an experimental/ quasi-experimental design.

1. State the research question(s).
2. Identify the independent variable(s) and the dependent variable(s).
3. State any hypotheses and/or predictions made, if any.
4. Study the introduction and methodology section. In your own words, explain what procedures were used to determine the causal relationship.
5. Using the internal validity evaluation inventory (Table 5.1) rate the risk level of any one of the possible threats to internal validity. Summarize any precautions the researcher(s) took to prevent any of these effects.

Table 5.1 Internal Validity Evaluation Inventory

Risk	Risk Factor			Precautions Taken
	Low	Medium	High	
History				
Maturation				
Differential selection				
Statistical regression				
Subject attrition				
Competing group contamination				
a. Competing group rivalry: John Henry effect				
b. Experimental treatment diffusion (compromise)				
c. Compensatory equalization of treatments				
d. Demoralization (boycott) of the control group				
Testing				
a. Instrumentation				
b. Measurement–treatment interaction				
c. Pretest				
d. Posttest				
e. Time of measurement effects				
Researcher effect				
Pygmalion effect				
Hawthorne effect				
Novelty and disruption effect				
Accumulative treatment effect (multiple-treatment interference)				
Treatment fidelity				
Treatment strength/time interaction				

Key Terms and Concepts

accumulative treatment effect
action research
applied research
basic research
case study
causal-comparative design
compensatory equalization of treatments
confirmatory research
control group contamination
conversational analysis
correlational study
demoralization
differential selection
ethnography
experimental design
experimental treatment diffusion
exploratory research
external validity
grounded theory
Hawthorne effect
history
instrumentation
intact groups
internal validity
John Henry effect
longitudinal study
maturation
measurement–treatment interaction
posttest effect
pretest effect
Pygmalion effect
qualitative research
quantitative research
quasi-experimental design
random assignment
researcher effect
shotgun method
statistical regression
subject attrition
thick description
think-aloud technique
time of measurement effect

treatment fidelity
treatment intervention
treatment strength/time interaction
triangulation

Notes

1. There is no precise correct point to place these studies. We are only estimating their placement.
2. They have broadened this list in the third edition.
3. The combination of different sources for data to validate interpretations (see Chapter 7).
4. See Nunan (1992) for an interesting comparison between discourse analysis, interactive analysis, and conversational analysis.
5. I will discuss all statistical terminology in greater detail in Chapter 7.
6. Just a note of warning here. What constitutes a *traditional* method varies with each study. You should examine whether the traditional method is clearly defined so that you know exactly what is meant by *traditional*. By doing so, you will be able to understand to what the novel method is being compared (see *treatment fidelity* later in this chapter).
7. Desensitization occurs when the participants' behavior is no longer affected by the presence of the data-collection system, whether human or mechanical.

References

Agresti, A. (2012). *An introduction to categorical data analysis* (3rd ed.). New York, NY: Wiley.

Akbari, R., & Hosseini, K. (2008). Multiple intelligences and language learning strategies: investigating possible relations. *System, 36*, 141–155.

Bowles, M. A. (2010). *The think-aloud controversy in second language research.* New York, NY: Routledge.

Burns, A. (2010). *Doing action research in English language teaching: A guide for practitioners.* New York, NY: Routledge.

Calvert, M., & Sheen, Y. (2015). Task-based language learning and teaching: An action-research study. *Language Teaching Research, 19*(2), 226–244.

Creese, A. (2008). Linguistic ethnography. In K. A. King and N. H. Hornberger (Eds.), *Encyclopedia of language and education* (2nd ed., Vol. 10, *Research Methods In Language And Education*) (pp. 229–141). New York, NY: Springer Science.

Creswell, J. W. (2013). *Qualitative inquiry and research design.* Thousand Oaks, CA: SAGE.

Creswell, J. W., & Plano Clark, V. L. (2011). *Designing and conducting mixed methods research* (2nd ed.). Thousand Oaks, CA: SAGE.

Denzin, N. K., & Lincoln, Y. S. (Eds.). (2011). *Handbook of qualitative research* (4th ed.). Thousand Oaks, CA: SAGE.

Derakhshan, A., & Eslami, Z. (2015). The effect of consciousness-raising instruction on the pragmatic development of apology and request. *TESL-EJ, 18*(4), 1–24.

Ekembe, E. E. (2014). Interaction and uptake in large foreign language classrooms. *RELC Journal, 45*(3), 237–251.

Gabriel, C., & Kireva, E. (2014). Prosodic transfer in learner and contact varieties. *Studies in Second Language Acquisition, 36,* 257–281.

Gall, M. D., Borg, W. R., & Gall, J. P. (1996). *Educational research: An introduction* (6th ed.). White Plains, NY: Longman.

Gan, Z., Davison, C., & Hamp-Lyons, L. (2008). Topic negotiation in peer group oral assessment situations: A conversation analytic approach. *Applied Linguistics, 30,* 315–334.

Hung, H. (2015). Flipping the classroom for English language learners to foster active learning. *Computer Assisted Language Learning, 28*(1), 81–96.

Jacobs, G., & Slembrook, S. (2010). Notes on linguistic ethnography as a liminal activity. *Text & Talk, 30,* 235–244.

Johnson, D. C. (2010). The relationship between applied linguistic research and language policy for bilingual education. *Applied Linguistics, 31*(1), 72–93.

Kim, Y., & Taguchi, N. (2015). Promoting task-based pragmatics instruction in EFL classroom contexts: The role of task complexity. *The Modern Language Journal, 99*(4), 656–677.

Koyama, D., Sun, A., & Ockey, G. J. (2016). The effects of item preview on video-based multiple-choice listening assessments. *Language Learning & Technology, 20,* 148–165.

Kubanyiova, M. (2015). The role of teachers' future self guides in creating L2 development opportunities in teacher-led classroom discourse: Reclaiming the relevance of language teacher cognition. *The Modern Language Journal, 99*(3), 565–584.

Larsen-Freeman, D., & Long, M. H. (1991). *An introduction to second language acquisition research.* New York, NY: Longman.

Lazaraton, A. (2003). Evaluative criteria for qualitative research in applied linguistics: Whose criteria and whose research? *Modern Language Journal, 87,* 1–12.

Lee-Johnson, Y. L. (2015). A qualitative study of the out-of-class learning opportunities constructed by five ESL freshmen and their native speaking peers in a college town. *Journal of Ethnographic & Qualitative Research, 10,* 120–134.

Lee, C., Wong, K. C. K., Cheung, W., & Lee, F. S. L. (2009). Web-based essay critiquing system and EFL students' writing: a quantitative and qualitative investigation. *Computer Assisted Language Learning, 22,* 57–72.

Lin, G. H. C. (2008). Pedagogies proving Krashen's theory of affective filter. *Hwa Kang Journal of English Language & Literature, 19,* 113–131.

Machida, N., & Dalsky, D. J. (2014). The effect of concept mapping on L2 writing performance: Examining possible effects of trait-level writing anxiety. *English Language Teaching, 7*(9), 28–35.

MacIntyre, P. D., Baker, S. C., Clément, R., & Donovan, L. A. (2002). Sex and age effects on willingness to communicate, anxiety, perceived competence, and L2 motivation among junior high school French immersion students. *Language Learning, 52,* 537–564.

Martella, R.C., Nelson, J. R., Morgan, R. L., & Marchand-Martella, N. E. (2013). *Understanding and interpreting educational research.* New York, NY: Guilford.

Martin, F., Claydon, E., Morton, A., Binns, S., & Pratt, C. (2003). The development of orthographic and phonological strategies for the decoding of words in children. *Journal of Research in Reading, 26,* 191–204.

Miles, M. B., & Huberman, A. M. (1994). *Qualitative data analysis: An expanded sourcebook* (2nd ed.). Thousand Oaks, CA: SAGE.

Moeller, A. J., Theiler, J. M., & Wu, C. (2012). Goal setting and student achievement: A longitudinal study. *The Modern Language Journal, 96*(2), 153–169.

Moskovsky, C., Alrabai, F., Paolini, S., & Ratcheva, S. (2013). The effects of teachers' motivational strategies on learners' motivation: A controlled investigation of second language acquisition. *Language Learning, 63*(1), 34–62.

Nunan, D. (1992). *Research methods in language learning.* New York, NY: Cambridge University Press.

Ormrod, J. E. (1995). *Human learning* (2nd ed.). Englewood Cliffs, NJ: Merrill.

Ożanska-Ponikwia, K. (2016). The influence of immersion in the L2 culture on perception of the L1 culture-specific emotion of tęsknota. *International Journal of Bilingualism, 20,* 116–132.

Palmer, B. C., El-Ashry, F., Leclere, J. T., & Chang, S. (2007). Learning from Abdallah: A case study of an Arabic-speaking child in a U.S. school. *The Reading Teacher, 61*(1), 8–17.

Paltridge, B. (2006). *Discourse analysis: An introduction.* New York, NY: Continuum.

Perry, F. L., & Shwedel, A. (1979). Interaction of visual information, verbal information and linguistic competence in the preschool-aged child. *Journal of Psycholinguistic Research, 8,* 559–566.

Tashakkori, A., & Teddlie, C. (1998). *Mixed methodology.* Thousand Oaks, CA: SAGE.

Teddlie, C., & Tashakkori, A. (2009). *Integrating quantitative and qualitative approaches in the social and behavioral sciences.* Thousand Oaks, CA: SAGE.

Toyosaki, S. (2004). Ethnography of cross-cultural communication: Japanese international students' accounts of US-American culture and communication. *Journal of Intercultural Communication Research, 33,* 159–175.

Valeo, A. (2013). Language awareness in a content-based language programme. *Language Awareness, 22*(2), 126–145.

van Compernolle, R. A., & Henery, A. (2015). Learning to do concept-based pragmatics instruction: Teacher development and L2 pedagogical content knowledge. *Language Teaching Research, 19,* 351–372.

Venkatagiri, H. S., & Levis, J. M. (2007). Phonological awareness and speech comprehensibility: An exploratory study. *Language Awareness, 16*(4), 263–277.

Yang, J., & Kim, T. (2011). Sociocultural analysis of second language learner beliefs: A qualitative case study of two study-abroad ESL learners. *System, 39*(3), 325–334.

Chapter 6

Understanding Data Gathering

Chapter Overview

Once researchers determine the research design, they need to decide exactly how they will gather their data. A brief look at research articles in applied linguistics quickly reveals that there are many procedures used for collecting data. Some people argue that certain procedures are superior to others. However, I argue, along with others (e.g., Tashakkori & Teddlie, 2003), that the value of a data-gathering procedure depends on how well it provides answers to the research questions. As a consumer, you should become familiar with as many of these procedures as possible so that you will not be limited in your search for answers to your questions.

This chapter attempts to condense a body of information that could fill an entire course. For this reason, it is important for you to pause and complete each of the exercises which are presented at each major break. Similar to the sample subsection (see Chapter 4), the information typically provided about the strategy used for data collection in a research study does not occupy much space. However, the underlying issues in proper data collection can make or break the value of a study. As with Chapter 5, this chapter is one that you will want to review periodically as you read articles that use different procedures.

This chapter is divided into two sections. The first provides a survey of the different methods by which verbal data are collected and a discussion of the strengths and weaknesses of each. This is followed by a summary of how such data can be evaluated as dependable and credible. The second section examines methods that typically gather numerical data, followed by a discussion on how these data are judged as reliable and valid. These form the criteria that you, the consumer, need for evaluating whether the data-gathering procedures have been appropriately used.

Section 1: Collecting and Evaluating Verbal Data

This section summarizes a number of data-collection sources that are commonly used in applied linguistic research resulting in verbal data.

In Table 6.1, I group these under *observational* procedures along with the advantages and disadvantages of each procedure. In the following discussion, each of these procedures is expanded and illustrations from published research are given.

Observational Procedures

The procedures under this heading involve capturing data through visual observation. The use of human observers as data collectors is as old as research itself. It has long been known that the main advantage of human observation of data, over some form of impersonal instrument, is that the former allows researchers flexibility when exploring what new, and sometimes unexpected, phenomena might be uncovered.

On the other hand, some believe that observational procedures suffer from three disadvantages. The first is that they generally take more time than instrumental procedures. Consequently, they are usually more costly. Second, they are more limited in the numbers of participants/objects that are used for data gathering. Third, they allow for varying degrees of *subjectivity*. That is, the influence of factors such as attitude, temporary emotional and physical states, etc. can distort the perception of the observer. However, others believe that these three weaknesses are, in fact, strengths of this category of procedures. The fact that it takes more

Table 6.1 Verbal Data-Collection Procedures

Method	Potential Strengths	Potential Weaknesses
Observational	Discover new phenomena, flexible	Time consuming, observer effects
Self	Firsthand information, inner thoughts	Possible bias
Introspection	Immediate access, accesses inner states	Intrusive, difficult to validate
Retrospection	Not intrusive	Memory loss
Outside Observer		
Full-participant	Elicits natural behavior, not intrusive	Possible bias, deceptive, memory loss
Partial-participant	Not deceptive	Possible bias
Nonparticipant	Objective	Disruptive
Interviewer	Ability to probe, monitors comprehension, 100 percent feedback	Needs training, standardization, handling data

time, they argue, means that there is better chance to obtain quality information despite the cost. Using fewer subjects is not a problem if the purpose is to observe information-rich samples. Last, *subjectivity* is viewed as positive because researchers become personally involved with the data collection. In addition, if multiple observers are used and compared to one another for degree of agreement, subjectivity is controlled. When all is said and done, I believe that most everyone would agree that observational procedures are powerful means for gathering data.

Observational procedures have many different formats. First, the person(s) doing the observing can vary considerably. Observers can be researchers, people employed to make the observations, or participants observing themselves. Second, observers might be very involved with the purpose of the study or totally oblivious to why they are being asked to observe. Third, observers might be recording information that requires no interpretation of the observations or be required to give their own evaluative judgments as to what their observations mean. Fourth, the observation process may or may not be backed up with recording devices. Researchers often use recording devices (audio or video) to aid in further analysis.

In the following discussion, I will show how these different formats are used by surveying the most common observational techniques with their strengths and limitations. This section is based on the degree to which the observer is personally involved with who/what is being observed, beginning with the most involved observer, the self. It ends with the interviewer.

Self as Observer

Using participants as observers of their own behavior has become more common over the past years under the heading of *protocol analysis* (see Chapter 5). Although it was frequently used by psychologists before 1940 (Slezak, 2002), it is commonly found in applied linguistic research today (Bowles, 2010). This procedure requires participants to observe their own internal cognitive (or emotional) states and/or processing strategies either during an ongoing task, referred to as *introspection*, or after they have completed the task, known as *retrospection*.

Researchers usually record participants' thoughts on audiotape during a *think-aloud* task, as mentioned in Chapter 5. Remember Valeo (2013), who investigated whether focus-on-form (FF) instruction has any impact on language awareness in a content-based language program. She compared one group, who received both FF and meaning-focused instruction, with another, who got only meaning-focused instruction over a 10-week period. Valeo's data consisted of written retrospective think-aloud protocols, which she coded and analyzed.

The strength of the *introspection* technique is that it gets researchers as close as possible to the inner workings of the participants' mind. The problem, however, lies in validating whether the participants are providing accurate information. If the study is not done carefully, participants may simply tell the researchers what they think the researchers wants to hear. An even greater problem is that the very act of reporting what a participant is thinking can be disruptive. These intrusions can interfere with the natural cognitive processes, thus distorting the data and making them less authentic.

Another study using the *introspection* technique was done by Kubanyiova (2015). Remember, from Chapter 5, that she examined one teacher in depth to determine how the teacher's "cognitions were embodied in her descriptions of everyday experiences and events, including her reflections on specific lessons, teaching methods, students, relevant educational policies, past personal and professional experiences, and perceived future challenges and plans" (p. 569). Although Kubanyiova did not use the word "introspection," she required the teacher during extensive interviews to go within herself to reveal her inner thinking. I recommend you read Kubanyiova's study to see the care she took to make sure the data were as clean as possible.

As with any study using this approach, there are questions about the final data prior to analysis. First, did the teacher provide accurate descriptions of her cognitions? Second, did the presence of an interviewer asking questions influence what the teacher reported? However, let me add that the questions I have just raised should not be interpreted as criticisms. Rather, they should give us an appreciation for the complexity of trying to obtain data fresh out of the minds of participants. This is as close as we can get to authentic data. As Kubanyiova (2015) clearly understood, the introspection data, which she collected over one year, were just part of her study. She used a triangulation strategy where she brought in other data from videotapes and personal observation records. As we keep approaching our research questions from different angles (i.e. triangulation), we begin to form a picture of what is actually happening.

To eliminate the possible intrusive effect of the introversion technique that might have occurred in the above study, some researchers use retrospection. In this case, the participant is required to wait until after the task before reflecting on what they had done cognitively. However, as you might have realized, a different problem can potentially affect the data (i.e., loss of memory). If the task is complicated or takes a lot of time, the participant can forget some of the mental processes that occurred. The tendency found in the psychology of memory is that participants remember the first and last parts of the information and forget what is in between.

The study by Lee (2015) illustrates not only the use of thinking aloud, but also the use of two forms of retrospection: *introversion* and *retroversion*. Before discussing this study, however, I want to mention here that this is an interesting study for another reason. The researcher used a qualitative/exploratory/applied approach along with a quantitative/exploratory/applied study. They followed the normal pattern: qualitative results followed by a quantitative study. The reason is that qualitative methods of data collection often look for information-rich data to build theoretical categories. These categories are used for quantitative procedures to add data to support any hypotheses or theoretical explanations.

Lee (2015) used a mixed-method design to examine strategies used by Chinese-speaking graduate students when reading familiar versus unfamiliar topics in an English multiple-choice format reading comprehension test. All 36 participants of her study were given both the familiar and unfamiliar passages with attached tests. She extracted six general strategy categories from the verbal output using think-aloud protocols and semistructured interviews. Lee had her participants immediately think aloud right after each of two reading test. The think-aloud output was recorded producing protocols that were later analyzed for patterns. This was more retrospection than introspection, but it was as close to it as possible without interfering with the reading of the passages. It was also immediately after the reading to reduce memory effects.

Several concerns come to mind as I read this study. First, it was not clear whether the researcher was present during all of the think-aloud sessions. However, in light of the possibility of a researcher effect, the question must be asked whether the participants verbal output was not disturbed by the presence of the researcher to make sure all went according to plan. It looks like a case of "you're damned if you do and you're damned if you don't." If she had not been present with the participant, would she have obtained the same data?

Outside Observers

The more traditional form for observational procedures is found in research that uses people other than the participants to make observations. I refer to this type as *outside observers* (see Table 6.1). Whereas the self-observer is the best source to try to access the inner workings of the mind, the outside observer is better used for observing the outward behavior of the participants under study.

However, outside observers vary in how close (i.e., personally involved) they get to the people or events that they are observing and how aware the people being observed are that they are being observed. The closer observers get and/or more aware the observed person is, the more observers participate in who or what is being observed. Technically, the continuum ranges from full to nonparticipant observer (see Table 6.1).

The *full-participant observer* is one who is or becomes a full member of the group to which the participants/events being observed belong. This is a procedure commonly used to observe a group/event with someone who is either a member or pretending to be a member as an *informant* (i.e., a person who supplies the information). The group is usually unaware that they are being observed.

The obvious advantage of using a full-participant observer is that the other members of the group will behave naturally, thus providing a clear picture of the objective of the observation. The disadvantages are that 1) the observers may be so much a part of the group that they cannot remain objective in their observations, 2) the researchers are using deception to obtain the data, and 3) the observers may forget information if they have to wait until after the encounter with the group before recording the data. In the case of disadvantage, 1) limited and/or biased data may be reported by the observer, 2) the observers might become ostracized from the group when it is learned that they were informing on it, and 3) problems result in incomplete data.

I can imagine a study where researchers enlist the help of one of the foreign language students in the group being studied to find out what attitudes the group has toward the language program they are in. The student is the informant (i.e., a full-participant observer). Of course, the researchers could simply give an attitude survey to the group, which they may plan to do as well. To ensure that the members of the group do not paint a rosy picture on the survey to please the researchers, one of the students is asked to gather information predetermined by the researchers and unknown to the other members. By law in the United States, the other members of the group need to be informed that they were observed and their permission obtained before the data are used—especially if anonymity was not guaranteed. Depending on the sensitivity of the information, this could be threatening to full-participant observers, who then may not want to be totally honest in their reporting.

An example of the use of full-participant observers is found in Fang and Garland's (2014) ethnographic study, in which they examined teacher orientations to the new English curriculum and the forces influencing their orientations and practices. Fang, the first author, was the participant observer in the study since he had spent a year and half teaching in the program. Their participants were a maximum variation sample of five teachers, who represented the English department. They used a triangulation strategy that consisted of 138 classroom observations, 98 interviews, and field notes. As a result, the researchers believed that they were able to gain a rapport with the participants, an insider perspective on the practices, and discover phenomena that were unobtainable otherwise, such as "taken for granted" knowledge and "hidden activities" or sensitive events not open to outsiders.

Another example of a study that used participant observers was done by Pellerin (2014). She studied how mobile technologies (e.g., iPods and tablets) contribute to rethinking of approaches to language tasks for young learners in the classroom. She used 16 teachers in a French immersion program for participant observers in their own classrooms. She also used the students as participant observers, even referring to them as co-researchers. She added structured and semistructured interviews along with digital documentation to provide triangulation of data. To check for subjectivity creeping in to distort their data, she used a number of other methods for gathering data (i.e., triangulation).

At the other end of the degrees of participation continuum is the *nonparticipant observer*, who does not personally interact with the participants in any manner. The best use of this method is when the observer makes observations of participants' outward behavior. For example, an observer may measure the amount of time a teacher talks versus the amount of time students talk in a language classroom. In this case, the observer has no need to interact with either the teacher or the students to obtain these data.

The principal advantage of this strategy is that it is more *objective*[1] than the other participant methods. On the downside, the presence of an unknown observer, or any recording devices, may have a disruptive effect on the participants, causing them to deviate from their normal behavior. To avoid this, observers need to desensitize the participants to their presence before collecting the data to be used for the study. To do this, a common method is for the observer to attend the sessions long enough for the participants to disregard the observer's presence.

A study that used this nonparticipant method was done by Springer and Collins (2008), who tested the assumption that the type of oral interaction differs inside and outside the language classroom in the real world. They audio-recorded two adult students' interactions using personal microphones for the class and a tape recorder when they tutored outside of class for the duration of both programs. Springer was present during all recording sessions taking notes. They identified 26 situations where the two participants interacted. They transcribed and analyzed the verbal data. One wonders whether the recording devices had any effect on the quality of the interactions between the two participants. However, typically, people become desensitized to such equipment over time.

Somewhere between the full-participant and the nonparticipant observer lie varying degrees of partial-participant observation (see Table 6.1). There are several advantages of this over nonparticipant observation. First, access to less obvious data, such as attitudes or intentions, is more available. Second, the closer the participant feels the observer is to him-

or herself, the less the chance of falsifying the data. However, the closer the participant is to the observer the greater the possibility of bias on the part of the observer.

Partial-participant observers also have advantages over full-participant observers. First, there is less danger that these observers will become so involved with the participants that they lose objectivity. Second, the participants usually know that they are being observed, so there is no deception. However, partial-participant observers may be denied access to more private information that only full-participant observers would be able to access.

To illustrate the use of a partial-participant observer, Harklau (2000), in her classic study, used this strategy with an ethnographic case study to investigate how student identities change when moving from one language program to another. She observed three ESL students over a one-year period as they made the transition from a high school to a nearby community college. She collected data from several sources.

> In all, the data reflect over 50 formal interview sessions with students and instructors as well as over 25 other informal interviews with students' instructors, 10 days of high school classroom observations and over 50 hours of community college classroom observations, and over 5,000 pages of written materials collected from students and from the study sites over the course of the year in which the study took place.
>
> (p. 44)

Harklau (2000) was a partial-participant observer in that she met with students and teachers in lunch rooms and teacher lounges, where she held informal interviews. She most likely did this to establish personal rapport with her participants to ensure more authentic responses. I understand that she won the Newbury House 2000 Research Award for this study, which she no doubt deserves due to this giant undertaking.

One thing common to the Fang and Garland (2014), Pellerin (2014), Springer and Collins (2008), and Harklau (2000) studies is that the researchers did not limit themselves to only one procedure for gathering data. Rather, they all used a multiprocedural approach, as referred to previously, as *triangulation*. Researchers who want to protect their research from the weakness of only one approach, yet profit from the strengths of that approach, will build into their study several different data-collecting procedures. Researchers may use full, partial, or nonparticipant observers to gather data, but they should triangulate their findings with those of other procedures to increase the credibility of their findings.

The consumer of research may ask which of the above procedures is the most appropriate. As previously stated, the answer much depends on the research question and the nature of the data needed to best provide the answer. If the research question requires information that cannot be obtained by observing outward behavior, then a method needs to be used where the observer can get closer to the participants. Where easily observed outward behavior is sufficient, there is no need for closeness. Each approach has its strengths and weaknesses.

Regardless of what type of observer is used, observers need training to provide useful data. Of course, if researchers are doing the observing themselves there is no need of training because they know what they are looking for. In addition, to ensure that there is no bias, researchers should keep their observers *blind* to the purpose of the study, especially if any hypothesis is being tested. (This sounds like an oxymoron: keeping your observer blind.) If they fail to keep them blind, the observers might unconsciously see only what the researchers want to be seen. A well-written study will be very clear about whether training was given to the observers and whether the observers were aware of the ultimate purpose of the study.

The last set of studies we have looked at use researchers as observers. However, a study done by van Compernolle and Henery (2015) used video recordings to collect their data. They did a case study that examined one teacher's learning and the use of Vygotsky's *concept-based pragmatics* approach for teaching second language (L2) pragmatics. They examined a teacher's internalization and transformation of relevant pedagogical content knowledge. Their main data source was six 15- to 20-minute video recordings of the teacher's classroom and three 60-minute video recordings of mentoring meetings between the teacher and her collaborator. The data that they worked with were mainly verbal transcriptions of the video recordings. The videotaping made it possible for the researchers to review the participant's verbal behavior to decrease the chances that anything was missed. The one concern is whether the videotaping influenced the participants' behavior.

The Interviewer

As seen in the studies discussed above, interviews were used to obtain data as well (see Table 6.1). This method is a combination of observation under highly structured conditions and paper-and-pencil data recording. The difference between the observer and the interviewer is that the interviewer personally interacts with the participant through a series of questions to obtain data, whereas with the observer data is collected as it occurs without probing with questions. The difference between an interview and a questionnaire (which will be discussed under the instrument section) is that an interpersonal connection is formed between the interviewer and the interviewee. This connection allows for direct monitoring for comprehension of the questions and modification in the case of misunderstanding.

The quality of the data coming from an interviewer is determined by the care taken to ensure that the same procedures are used for each interviewee. Strict adherence to directions as to what questions are to be asked and in what order they are to be asked need to be observed. Otherwise the answers cannot be compared.

However, an interview can range from highly structured to semi-structured to open-structured. The *highly structured* interview follows a predetermined set of questions with no allowance for variation. The *semistructured* interview has a set of predetermined questions, but the interviewer is free to follow up a question with additional questions that probe further. The *open-structured* interview has a general interview plan but is not tied to predetermined questions. This allows the interviewer to explore whatever path seems appropriate at the time.

All of these techniques are commonly used in research. For example, Fang and Garland (2014) used 16 semistructured interviews with each participant to capture participants' experiences, views, and feelings. Harklau (2000) used what she referred to as *loosely structured* (i.e., semistructured) interviews to be free to generate more questions as the research progressed. Edwards and Roger (2015) investigated the change in L2 self-confidence in an adult advanced learner of English after arriving in Australia. They interviewed him twice, with a two-year gap between interviews. They stated that both interviews were semistructured. However, upon examining their study I noticed that the second interview consisted of open-ended questions guided by the responses from the first interview. This allowed for more relevant information to be gathered for their study.

When evaluating research studies that use one of the interview techniques, ask yourself these questions. Did the researcher pretest the interview questions with the interviewers? Were the interviewers trained and tested before they gave the interviews? Were the interviews audio- or videotaped to prevent the loss of information? Would the data be the same if another interviewer did the interview? If you answer yes to all of these questions, then the study followed sound interviewing procedures.

Evaluating the Dependability of Verbal Data Procedures

Verbal data cannot be taken simply at face value, and neither can numerical data. Researchers should provide evidence that the data they have used in their study are dependable enough to analyze. Researchers have at least five types of evidence to support the dependability of their data. They are as follows.

Representativeness

This is not referring specifically to whether the sample is representative of the population (i.e., external validity), as discussed in Chapter 4, although this is related. Representativeness is more to do with whether the veracity of the information is being influenced by the choice of respondents or events (i.e., internal validity or credibility). Related to the *possibe bias* mentioned above, information coming from one particular segment of a larger group of people can be misleading. Similar to the convenience sampling problem mentioned in Chapter 4, the most accessible and willing participants are not usually the best group to provide the most appropriate data.

In addition, researchers need to give evidence that the events on which generalizations are based are the most appropriate. They might not be present at all times for data collection. If not, consumers must ask about the proportion of time the researcher was present? If only some of the events were observed, were they typical of most events? The ultimate question for consumers is whether the researchers have provided evidence that data have come from observing an adequate number of events to ensure that subsequent inferences and conclusions were not based on the luck of the draw.

Prolonged Engagement and Persistent Observation

Researchers need enough time for interacting with the respondents and/or the event to gather accurate data. This allows time to gain personal access

Table 6.2 Methods for Determining Dependability of Verbal Data Procedures

Evidence
1. Representativeness
Respondents
Events
2. Prolonged engagement and persistent observation
3. Clarifying researcher bias
4. Check for researcher effects
Researcher on persons/events
Persons/events on researcher
5. Weighting the evidence
Informants access and proximity
Circumstances:
behavior observed firsthand
adequate exposure
informal settings
trusted fieldworkers
Continuous vigilance in checking for various biases

to the information being targeted. However, if too much time is spent on the research site, there is the possibility that one of the *researcher effects* discussed in point four of Table 6.2 might set in.

Clarifying Researcher Bias

Every researcher has his or her own set of biases. Because the analysis of data in a qualitative study begins and continues during the collection of data, knowing the researcher's particular biases can help the consumer discern why the data are being gathered and interpreted in a certain way. Therefore, researchers should disclose any biases that might have an impact on the approach used and any interpretations made on the data. This helps consumers determine how the researchers arrived at their conclusions.

Researcher Effects

These were discussed in Chapter 5 under threats to internal validity. In that chapter the influence was mainly looking at the unidirectional effect of the researcher on the behavior of the persons from whom data were being collected. However, Miles and Huberman (1994) point out that there is a reciprocal relationship between researchers and the persons/ events being observed. In one direction, researchers' presence or actions influence the behavior being observed (Chapter 5). In qualitative work, for example, respondents might change their behavior in the presence of the data gatherer to meet perceived expectations and/or hide sensitive information. Miles and Huberman warn that researchers "must assume that people will try to be misleading and must shift into a more investigative mode" (p. 265). To avoid this, they suggested such strategies as: researchers spending as much time as possible on site to become unnoticed, using unobtrusive methods, having an informant who monitors the impact the researcher is making, and using informal settings for some data gathering.

In the other direction of the reciprocal relationship, the persons/ events being observed can impact researchers. This can happen when researchers spend too much time with the people being researched, and the researchers *go native* by no longer being able to keep their own thinking separate from that of the respondents. This leads to a quandary because, to avoid the first problem of researcher-on-respondent impact mentioned above, the possibility of the respondents impacting the researchers increases. To avoid the respondent-on-researcher effect, Miles and Huberman (1994) proposed tactics such as using a variety of respondents, including people outside of the group being observed, controlling site visits, using an informant to monitor events when not present, using triangulation, using peers to critique the work, and so on.

When evaluating the data collected in qualitative research, consumers should look for ways for researchers to try to control for or be aware of the effect they might have had on the people or the situation and vice versa. This does not simply mean the effect on the *product*, in the form of the data, but also on the analysis *process*. If such care is taken and reported, the researchers deserve kudos and the credibility of findings has been enhanced.

Weighting the Evidence

Miles and Huberman (1994) pointed out that some data are stronger (or more valid) than others. They laid down three principles for determining the strength of data. I have summarized them here in the form of questions that the consumer can use to evaluate the strength of the data:

1. What information does the researcher provide about the access and proximity of the informants to the targeted data? The closer to the data, the stronger the observations.
2. To what extent do the data consist of actual behavior, observed firsthand, after adequate exposure, in informal settings, by trusted fieldworkers? The more the stronger.
3. What effort did the data gatherer(s) make toward checking for various biases (as outlined above) during the data-gathering process? The greater the stronger.

I use Harklau's (2000) study to illustrate how a researcher provides evidence for the dependability of verbal data. Remember that she did an ethnographic case study in which she examined how the identities of ESL students change as a result of the *representation* (i.e., stereotype) of different institutional programs. She followed three ESL students over a one-year period as they moved from their senior year of high school to their first year at a nearby two-year community college. Information used for the evaluation is listed in the following Box 6.1.

Harklau (2000) used five types of evidence from the list given in Table 6.2. Regarding how *representative* her data were, she provided detailed information about the three student participants: one Turk and two Southeast Asians, who were selected by their ESL teacher (see Box 6.1). The issue here is whether these three subjects are representative of other US immigrant seniors in high school who go to community colleges after matriculation.

In addition, Harklau (2000) gave a clear description of the two institutions (see Box 6.1), which would help any consumer to compare

BOX 6.1 Summary of Harklau's (2000) Study

Variable of concern: Institutional representations of ESL learners

Participants
  One Turk
  Two Southeast Asians
  Upper-level/college-bound students
  Lived in the U.S. for 6 to 10 years
  A teacher chose the student participants
  Teachers: no information given

Data Sources
  30 to 50-minute taped interviews
  50 formal interviews with students and instructors
  25 informal interviews with instructors
  Informal visits with students
  10 days of high school classroom observations
  50 hours of community college classroom observations
  5,000 pages of written materials collected over the year

Institutions
  The high school
  Ethnically mixed (60 percent black, 30 percent white, 10 percent
    other)
  45 out of 950 were in ESL program (predominantly Southeast
    Asian)

  The two-year community college
  State-sponsored
  Commuter campus
  Student body of over 13,000
  ESL program 250 international students (predominantly South-
    east Asian and Eastern European)
  Mainly coming from socially and educationally privileged
    backgrounds
  Mostly new arrivals to the States
  Course content: language plus acculturation

other institutional environments for possible transference of her findings. The high school had a majority of African-American students with an ESL program for 45 students, predominantly Southeast Asians. It was an upper-level program in an inner-city school.

However, it would have been helpful if Harklau (2000) had provided a more detailed description of the teachers used to provide data. Because teacher participants were as important as student participants regarding the nature of the data, a report of their personal characteristics would help the consumer understand how transferrable the teacher data are.

The next evidence type listed in Table 6.2 to support the dependability of data is *prolonged engagement and persistent observation* (point two). Harklau (2000) clearly reported that she had ample opportunity to engage the participants over an extended length of time. She collected her data over a one-year period as a partial-participant observer.

Regarding point 3, *clarifying the researcher's bias*, Harklau (2000) supplied details about her own philosophical and research biases in the study. She stated that her research disposition was derived from "critical theory, social practice, and poststructuralist approaches" (p. 37). She added that her premise was that personal identities are "locally understood and constantly remade in social relationships" (p. 37). To her credit, she declared, "like any researcher, I am a positioned subject who is 'prepared to know certain things and not others' (Rosaldo, 1989, p. 8)" (p. 45). The consumer needs to keep this type of information in mind when evaluating data from such studies.

For point 4, *checking for researcher effects*, Harklau (2000) did not discuss whether she monitored any effects she may have had on the participants, nor how the participants affected her. However, owing to long-term contact she had with her three student participants and the teachers prior to college, the possibility for either *researcher on persons/events* or *persons/events on researcher* effects could have occurred. One possibility was that she became so close to the student respondents that her perceptions were influenced by a feeling that the three students were being abused. Had she begun her study at the college level, and evaluated these students as they came into the program, I wonder if she would have made the same observations. These are not to be understood as negative comments. One of the positive points that qualitative researchers make is that they *become* part of the study. They too are participants in the study.

Under point 5 of Table 6.2, *weighting the evidence*, Harklau (2000) provided evidence that gives weight to the quality of her data. Regarding *informants' access and proximity* to data, she used three students and teachers from one high school to identify high school representation. She used the same students in addition to college teachers to assess the college representation. Certainly, these participants had good access and proximity to data. The *circumstances* under which Harklau gathered the data also added to the weight. The data were all gathered firsthand over many occasions in both formal and informal settings.

Before moving on to nonpersonal data-gathering methods, I suggest you do the following exercise to help instantiate what we have covered in the first part of section one. The following provides an outline of what to look for.

Exercise 6.1

Find a recent qualitative study that used at least one of the observational procedures listed in Table 6.1 that resulted in verbal data.

1. Summarize the research question(s).
2. Describe the type of data that is being gathered.
3. Briefly summarize the procedure used in the study.
4. Describe what was done to avoid the potential weaknesses discussed in Table 6.1.
5. Summarize what the research stated to show the dependability of the data from Table 6.2.

Section 2: Collecting and Evaluating Numerical Data

The second form that data come in is numbers—lots and lots of numbers. These numbers can be frequencies, test scores, numbers representing rank order, and so on. Numbers come from two main sources: human judgment and/or some form of impersonal instrument. First, I describe the procedures used to gather these numbers, and then I explain how these procedures are evaluated for reliability and validity. I discuss procedures in the following for obtaining these types of data (see Table 6.3).

The Judge/Rater

A major method for collecting numerical data in applied linguistics research is the use of judges/raters. (From now on, I will refer to both as judges. In the first edition of this book, I placed this information under the verbal data section. However, since judges provide their evaluations in the form of numbers—typically rating scales—I have moved it here.) Judges observe the outward behavior of the participant(s) and make evaluative judgments regarding the behavior. They do this by using some form of rating scale that ranges from low to high, poor to excellent, etc. and is usually expressed by some number.

Judges can vary considerably in their ratings for reasons other than quality of performance, as was seen from the 2002 Winter Olympics figure

Table 6.3 Numerical Data-Collection Procedures

Procedures	Potential Strengths	Potential Weaknesses
Judges/raters	Expert opinion	Subjectivity, fatigue, halo effect, ambiguous rubrics
Instrumental	Large coverage, time efficient	Inflexible
Questionnaires/ surveys		
Closed-form	Objective, broad coverage, easy to interpret	Restrictive, low returns
Open-ended	Information revealing	Subjective
Tests		
Discrete-item	Objective scoring, broad coverage, easy to score	Guessing, difficult to construct
Constructed response	Allows for individuality, limits guessing	Limited coverage, subjective scoring, training of scorers
Meta-analysis	Compares quantitative and qualitative results across published studies	Missing critical studies

skating scandal, where one judge was pressured for political reasons. However, in applied linguistics research judges are used to rate such things as writing or the oral proficiency of participants, or the distortion of meaning caused by the strength of a participant's accent, much less high-stakes than a gold medal. So, there should be no reason to allow such things as vote swapping for nationalistic reasons to influence one's rating.

However, the challenge with using judges in research continues to be _subjectivity_, which is defined here as the influence of judges' particular preferences and beliefs that differ from the criteria that they are supposed to use when judging. For example, some of my colleagues and I examined what criteria judges used when rating the writing ability of people trying to enter our university based on a half-hour essay test. We found that some judges used grammar as their main criterion while others used the quality of _organization_. There were a few others who were heavily influenced by _writing mechanics_. Obviously, the rating of four by one judge did not mean the same thing as a rating of four by another owing to using different criteria. The assumption should hold that judges use the same criteria when rating. If this is not the case then any interpretation of the data is uninterpretable.

To control for subjectivity, three precautions need to be taken: a well-defined _rubric_, _training_, and _multiple judges_. First, the rubric of the rating scale needs to be clearly defined. A well-written rubric clearly defines what each level of the scale means. The quality of these definitions helps judges apply the rubric in a consistent and meaningful way.

One of the most well-known rubrics used today was developed by the American Council on the Teaching of Foreign Languages (ACTFL). You can access their website (www.actfl.org) to see their rubrics for writing and speaking. Their most recent version is a four-level scale: superior, advanced, intermediate, and novice. For each of these levels, a short paragraph is provided that defines what a speaker or writer should be able to do in relation to several language abilities (e.g., grammar, vocabulary, etc.).

Related to having a good rubric, another method for controlling subjectivity in a judge's decision is training in the use of the rubric. The judge has to keep in mind each level of the rubric with its definition while rating participants. This is a formidable task and needs training to produce consistent results. The validity of the ratings will only be as good as the mastery of the rubric by the judges. A well-planned study will report how the judges were trained on the rubric.

Third, at least two judges need to be used when making judgments. By having multiple judges, researchers are able to check whether the judges are using the same criteria. In addition, the judges can be checked for the *severity* of their judgments. If one judge is consistently rating participants higher than other judges, then leniency could be the problem. If the judge rates the participants consistently lower than the others, then the problem might be severity. If there were only one judge rating the performance, researchers could not interpret the results.

The degree to which judges agree is measured by either the percentage of agreement or by statistically correlating their ratings with one another. When they agree from the high 80 percents onward, or correlate from .80 or higher, the judges are considered to be in agreement. This is referred to as inter-rater reliability (see Table 6.4 and the accompanied material later in the chapter).

A study that sheds light on the three precautions outlined above when using judges was done by Hijikata-Someya, Ono, and Yamanishi (2015). They examined whether three native English speakers (NES) differed from three non-native English speakers (NNES) when rating L2 students' summary writing. Their first research question addressed inter-rater reliability, using the well-known ETS holistic rubric. They found that the NES had higher internal agreement than the NNES group. Their second research question examined whether the two groups of raters differed on what components of writing they focused on. Their results revealed differences. They used an analytical scale rather than the holistic scale for this one. As mentioned in the previous discussion, the raters were focusing on different components of writing, which was not revealed by the holistic scale. They concluded that more training and experience is needed for the raters. They also concluded that the holistic scale was inappropriate for classroom use because it did not reveal the complex interaction of the various components of summary writing.

Besides subjectivity, there are two other obstacles that the research needs to attend to when using judges: *fatigue* and *halo effect*. Regarding the first, judges will become tired if they have to evaluate too many participants at any given time. The judgments made in the early part of rating a large number of participants may be very different from those made later due to judges simply becoming tired. The study by Hijikata-Someya et al. (2015) controlled for this problem. Each judge rated 102 summaries with the holistic scale and then another set of summaries two weeks later using a seven-point analytic scale. To control for the fatigue effects, they counterbalanced the order of presentation of the summaries for each judge. This does not illuminate this problem but it randomly distributes the effect throughout the data, reducing possible bias in the data.

The other obstacle, *halo effect*, is caused by the carryover effect of judging the work of one participant onto the work of the following participant. When judging the quality of writing, for instance, exposure to a well-written (or poorly written) passage may have a positive (or negative) influence on the judgment of the following passage. This is usually controlled for by making sure that the people or things being rated are not in the same order for the two raters. As you can imagine, Hijikata-Someya et al. (2015) controlled for this by counterbalancing the order of presentation. If any precautions are taken, the researchers should mention them to help the reader to rule out such effects. These researchers did precisely this.

Instrumental Procedures

The other general source from which to collect numerical data is some form of impersonal instrument that requires participants to supply data to the researcher. Table 6.3 lists two general instrument types, which encompass a wide range of devices used to collect data: *questionnaires* and *tests*.

The advantage of using instrumental procedures over observational ones is that researchers can gain access to many more participants in a timely and economical way. However, the main disadvantage is that, once they are put into print, they cease to be flexible during the data-collection process. Any new thoughts researchers might have will have to wait until the next study.

Questionnaires/Surveys (Q/S)

These types of instruments consist of various types of surveys that can capture a lot of information in a short amount of time. They consist of lists of questions and/or statements presented on paper or through some other media such as computers. Q/S are considered instrumental equivalents to interviews. They have two main advantages over interviews. First, they are useful for collecting data from larger numbers of people in fairly short amounts of time. Second, they are more economical to use than interviews because they do not take as much time or require trained interviewers to administer. As mentioned previously, the main disadvantage is that Q/S are not flexible in comparison to interviews in that the items (i.e., questions/statements) cannot be modified once they have been given to the respondent, nor can the Q/S probe the respondent for further information.

The items in a Q/S can be closed-form or open-form. *Closed-form* items provide a set of alternative answers to each item from which the respondent must select at least one. For example, an item might require a participant to choose either *yes* or *no*, *agree* or *disagree*. Or a statement might be given requiring participants to indicate by measuring their level of agreement on a five-point scale. This scale is often referred to as a Likert-type scale, named after R. A. Likert (1932), who used it for measuring attitude. The main advantage of using the closed form is that the data elicited are easy to record and analyze with statistical procedures.

On the other hand, *open-form* items allow participants to give their own answers without restrictions. This type works best when there could be a wide variety of answers that participants might give to a question, such as "How old are you?" Another common use is when researchers explore what possible answers might be given, as when asking participants what they think is good about the language program they have just completed.

Typically, most Q/S contain both open- and closed-form items. Demographic information about the respondent (e.g., gender, nationality, etc.) and the program (e.g., course level, etc.) use both formats. Even when the rest of the items in the Q/S are closed-form, the last item is almost always an open form to capture any other comment by the respondent.

A well-prepared Q/S should be *pilot-tested* before being administered in the main study. That is, it is tried out on a group of people similar to the target group who will eventually get it. The resulting feedback can provide useful information to make sure that all the items are clearly understood and that the entire Q/S is user-friendly.

One of the challenges in using Q/S is getting them back from potential respondents. *Response rate* is important because losing respondents is a form of attrition of the sample which can result in a biased sample.

Typically, the response rate is much less than the number of people who received the instrument. Trying to chase after people to return it is almost impossible because, to ensure anonymity, Q/S usually do not require respondents to identify themselves.

The rule of thumb is that researchers should get a response rate of at least 70 percent before the data are considered representative of a target population.[2] However, if the number of Q/S sent out is small, the return rate needs to be higher to maintain representativeness. A well-written study should report the number of Q/S sent out and the return rate to aid the reader in applying this criterion.

An example of the proper use of Q/S is found in Yihong, Yuan, Ying, and Yan's (2007) study. They examined how the relationship between motivation types and self-identity changes English learners in universities in China. They used a stratified sample consisted of 2,278 undergraduates from 30 universities in 29 regions with the aim to represent undergraduate university students of China. The instrument was a questionnaire consisting of motivation-type items and self-identity items, all in a five-point Likert scale format. They did five pilot studies during the development of the questionnaire to identify the best items and gain internal reliability. They obtained an impressive return rate of 92.1 percent of the questionnaires. As far as I can see, they did not control for *automatic response patterns*, which might occur when a respondent selects only one choice throughout the questionnaire, such as all 4s. This can be controlled by omitting the neutral option (e.g., 3) in the choices and by changing the order of the options for different versions of the questionnaire. Anyone not paying attention would have been detected and discarded from the data. To ensure complete understanding of the items, the questionnaire was given in the students' first language. As an added bonus, Yihong et al. provided a copy of the questionnaire at the end of the article for us to see.

Tests

The other main type of instrumentation commonly used in research is under this heading, also popularly referred to as *assessments*. Although I am sure that no one needs to be told what a test is due to years of experience taking them, I simply state that a *test* is an instrument that is designed to assess what participants can remember, do physically, and/or mentally. Because a single test can do all three, depending on the test items that make up the test, I use the term *test items*, rather than simply *tests* or *assessments*.

Test items come in all formats and modalities. They can be administered via paper or computer, or face to face with an examiner. They can assess language abilities through observing outward behavior, as when testing oral proficiency via an oral interview, or can assess cognitive outcomes through responses on paper or a computer screen.

Test items differ by making different cognitive demands on participants. Some items require participants to *recall* information. Such items as fill-in-the-blank and completion serve this purpose. Other items require participants to recall and integrate information, such as a test of writing ability in which they must compose an essay. Such items are also referred to as *open-ended* or *constructed response*. Other test items require participants to *recognize* from a set of alternatives the most appropriate answer. Items such as multiple-choice, matching, and alternative-choice are commonly used for this purpose.

Some people have preferences regarding item type. Yet, as with everything else we have discussed so far, the type of test item used in research should be determined by the question being asked. If a research question inquires whether participants can identify the meaning of a sentence or written passage, then recognition-type items are quite appropriate. However, if researchers seek to know whether the target information has been stored in such a way that participants can access the information easily, then a recall-type item would be better. If researchers are trying to assess whether participants can integrate information, then an essay format would be more appropriate.

Accordingly, there are some practical considerations researchers usually address when choosing item types. Two that are very much related are *time* and *cost*. Some item types take longer to administer than others and usually require trained judges to analyze the responses. For example, the open-ended essay prompt that requires a one- to two- page response from each participant when assessing writing ability can take one or more minutes to score, depending on the scoring technique. Not just anyone can evaluate these responses. As with training judges, raters of written compositions also need training. All of this takes time, and whatever takes time usually means greater costs. However, recognition-type items can be given to larger numbers of participants and scored by untrained personnel or even by optical-mark scanning machines in a minimal amount of time.

When evaluating the proper choice of item type, we need to ask ourselves whether the responses from the item type of choice are directly related to answering the research question. To illustrate, if writing ability is being investigated then multiple-choice items would probably not be appropriate. In contrast, if reading comprehension is the focus of the question, then multiple-choice items could be used effectively. If one's oral proficiency is being assessed, then some form of oral interview would probably be the best approach. Later in this chapter it will become apparent why choice of item type is important.

There are other terms you might encounter when reading the instrument section of a study. One common term is standardized test. The word *standardized* means that the test has been designed to be given under strict guidelines for administration and scoring. That is, the same instructions are to be given to the respondents at every administration of the instrument. The amount of time that is allowed to finish the test is also held constant for everyone, and the scoring procedure is the same for everyone. Standardization is important for producing data that can be compared. Research has shown that a change in such things as the instructions given by the test administrator can cause changes in the responses to the tests.

Two examples of standardized tests of English ability used around the world are the Test of English as a Foreign Language (TOEFL),[3] which is produced by the Educational Testing Service in Princeton, New Jersey, and the International English Language Testing System (IELTS),[4] developed by the University of Cambridge. Wherever the paper-and-pencil version of these tests is administered throughout the world, each is given on the same day, with the same instructions, allowing for the same amount of time for completion, and strictly scored according to specific guidelines (independent of one another, of course). Any changes in these procedures can render the data useless.

Commercially produced (CP) standardized tests, such as the two mentioned above, are usually developed for large-scale assessment and not specifically designed for individual research studies. However, some CP tests are occasionally used by researchers because they are assumed to have been carefully constructed to ensure reliability and validity—issues that are discussed in greater detail later in this chapter.

Crowther, Trofimovich, Isaacs, and Saito (2015) investigated whether the type of speaking task affects second language comprehensibility. They used two CP standardized tests to produce speech: IELTS long-turn task and the TOEFL iBT integrated task. The TOEFL iBT is considered to be more complicated than the IELTS because it is more cognitively challenging and does not have a live interlocutor. They used 60 participants to produce speech samples and 10 L1 experienced raters who rated 10 different categories. The raters had high inter-rater reliability for both types of tasks. The results showed that comprehensibility was higher for the IELTS task than the TOEFL iBT task. This illustrates that one has to be careful to interpret a measure of some language ability according to the particular instrument used. Just because an assessment instrument has popular notoriety, such as these two instruments, we cannot conclude that related scores reflect absolute abilities apart from the context from which they were gathered.

Although it is convenient to use an off-the-shelf CP standardized instrument, it might not be the best instrument to use in a particular research study. The reason is that these tests are designed for specific purposes that often do not match the need of the study. If researchers use the TOEFL exam to measure the effect of a new teaching method on improving English ability over one semester, for example, the results would probably not show any noticeable improvement. However, this lack of improvement may not be due to the ineffectiveness of the new method but instead to insensitivity of the TOEFL due to its global nature. That is, the limited learning outcomes that are targeted in a relatively short period of treatment are lost in the measurement of the multiple areas of the TOEFL. Nevertheless, the TOEFL would be appropriate for identifying various ability groupings in the English language of the participants to be used for research purposes.

In contrast to using CP standardized tests, many researchers design their own instruments for gathering data. The advantage is that they can streamline the instruments specifically to the needs of the study. However, this does not mean that the instruments should not be standardized. When they are given to more than one group of participants, they should follow strict standardization guidelines, such as giving the same time to finish the test to all groups, or else the data might vary between the groups.

Heras and Lasagabaster (2015), for example, looked at the impact of *content and language integrated learning* on motivation and self-esteem along with gender differences on vocabulary acquisition. They developed a Likert-type questionnaire to measure the affective variables and a 50-item vocabulary test for vocabulary acquisition. The instruments were administered on three occasions: pretest, immediate posttest, and delayed posttest. Heras and Lasagabaster piloted the instruments to refine them prior to implementation. They reported reliability information for the questionnaire (Cronbach alpha) but failed to do so for the vocabulary test. Since the instruments were designed specifically for their study, they would be most likely valid for detecting any changes due to the treatments. Differences between the times of testing confirmed this.

In addition to the term *standardization*, you will come into contact with two other terms in some instrument sections of various studies: *norm-referenced* and *criterion-referenced* tests. Both terms relate to how test scores are interpreted. *Norm-referenced* means that scores on the test are given meaning when compared with some norming group. A *norming group* is a body of people that is supposed to represent the population of all those who might take the test. On the basis of the statistics generated on the norming group, a person's score is interpreted in relation to the degree to which it is above or below the average of the norming group.

When using a norm-referenced test in a research study, it is important that the sample to which the test is given comes from a similar pool of participants as the norming group. Otherwise, the measurements cannot be interpreted by referring to the norming group. An example of a study that illustrates this was done by Kök and Canbay (2011), who adapted two CP tests to examine whether *Vocational Consolidation Strategy Training* has any effect on vocabulary learning and the use of vocabulary consolidation strategies. They constructed their instrument from two well-known standardized tests: Paul Nation's vocabulary levels test and Fan's vocabulary consolidation strategy inventory. They reported taking 37 items from the 60 in Fan's original inventory and testing them for internal reliability. However, it seems that they used Nation's vocabulary test as is. There is no information given as to whether they checked out this test's items with the participant population regarding internal reliability. They were not, and should not have been, concerned with comparing their data to any norming group outside of their study.

However, a *criterion-referenced* test does not use a norming group to establish guidelines for interpreting test results. Instead, one or more criteria are used to decide how well the examinee has done. These criteria are predetermined before administering the test and are used to establish cut-points. A *cut-point* is a point on the test score scale used to classify people into different categories such as high, middle, or low ability. For instance, all respondents scoring over 80 percent correct might be considered high ability, those scoring between 50 percent and 80 percent average ability, and those scoring below 50 percent below average.

Some people confuse the two terms *norm-referenced* with *standardized*, but they are not synonymous. The first term, *standardized*, relates to the conditions under which the test is given, while *norm-referenced* has to do with how the scores are interpreted. This confusion is most likely due to the fact that most standardized tests are also norm-referenced, such as the TOEFL or the IELTS.

As with a lot of research, Kök and Canbay (2011) did not use norm-referenced or criterion-referenced interpretations for their vocabulary tests. This is because they were not trying to make decisions about individual respondents. They were looking at the overall effect on the participants as groups who received the different treatments. This meant that they compared the averages of the two groups against one another, rather than looking at individual scores.

Meta-analysis

More commonly now you will see studies with meta-analysis in their titles in applied linguistics. At first glance, they look like literature reviews. But, in fact, they are primary research studies that use other studies as their data. The main purpose of a meta-analysis is to compare the results of a group of studies that address research questions raised by the authors. A meta-analysis has all the features of a regular research study: introduction, research question, samples, methodology, analysis, results, and discussion sections. One of the main things they compare across studies is *effect size*, which is basically the measure of the strength of a statistical finding. More will be said about this in Chapter 7 (cf. Oswald & Plonsky (2010)).

Lin's (2015) study provides a good example of a metasynthesis on the effectiveness of computer-mediated communication (CMC) in second language learning. She began, as most primary studies do, by arguing why her meta-analysis needed to be done. She then provided three research questions: one concerning the overall effect of CMC on L2 acquisition, the second asking if CMC's effectiveness differed depending on language skills, and the third concerning the effects of five learner and methodology features on CMC effectiveness. Besides CMC (the independent variable) and language acquisition (the dependent variable), being the main two variables, Lin listed a number of possible moderating variables. In her methods section, she informed us how she carefully selected the sample of primary studies that she included in her meta-analysis. She listed seven criteria for deciding which studies to include for her data. She ended with 59 studies, which were published between 2000 and 2012. Lin began her analysis by determining the effect size of each study. It is this piece of data that is the focus of a meta-analysis and is used to answer the research questions. More will be said about this in Chapter 7.

In concluding this section, procedures that are commonly used in gathering numerical data in research were reviewed. However, there are a number of criteria the consumer needs to understand to determine whether the data are of sufficient quality. These criteria are covered in the next section of this chapter. However, to help establish a foundation for understanding the next section, I suggest that you take the opportunity to complete the following exercise.

Exercise 6.2

Find a recent study that used one of the instrumental techniques listed in Table 6.3.

1. Describe the purpose of the study.
2. State the research question.
3. State any hypotheses, predictions, or even expectations if they are present.
4. Briefly summarize the data-gathering procedure in no more than a paragraph.
5. Describe what was done to avoid any of the weaknesses listed in Table 6.3.
6. Evaluate whether you think the procedures used provided the necessary data to answer the research question and/or to test any hypotheses.

Evaluating the Qualities of Numerical Data-Gathering Procedures

When many people think of research, they imagine numbers and statistics. However, the numbers that are gathered are based on various data-gathering methods as outlined in the previous section of this chapter. The quality of the data is determined by the caliber of the data-gathering strategy. To sharpen our ability to discern between weak and strong research, we must give attention to this aspect of research when evaluating the worth of a study. The purpose of this section is to provide an overview of these qualities and give examples of how they have been applied in research. My goal is for you to be able to use these criteria to evaluate the quality of a research study in a discerning manner.

Of any data-collection technique, the two most important qualities that have traditionally been considered essential are *reliability* and *validity*. The strong consensus in the research community is that the level of confidence we put into the findings of any given research is directly proportional to the degree to which data-gathering procedures produce reliable and valid data. I begin by discussing reliability, followed by validity. Some research methodology books place their section on validity before reliability; however, because validity relies heavily on reliability I will discuss reliability first.

Reliability

Reliability has to do with the *consistency of the data results*. If we measure or observe something, we want the method used to give the same results no matter who or what takes the measurement or observations. Researchers who use two or more observers would want those observers to see the same things and give the same or very similar judgments on what they observe or rate. Likewise, researchers utilizing instruments would expect them to give consistent results, regardless of time of administration or the particular set of test items making up those instruments.

The most common indicator used for reporting the reliability of a human or instrumental source is some form of *correlation coefficient*. A *coefficient* is simply a number that represents the amount of some attribute. A *correlation coefficient* is a number that quantifies the degree to which two variables relate to one another. Correlation coefficients that are used to indicate reliability are referred to as *reliability coefficients*.

I do not go into the mathematics of this particular statistic, but I want to give enough information to help in understanding the following discussion. Reliability coefficients range between 0.00 and +1.00. A coefficient of 0.00 means that there is no reliability in the observation or measurement. That is, if we were to make multiple observations/

measurements of a particular variable, a reliability coefficient of 0.00 would mean that the observations/measurements were totally inconsistent. Conversely, a reliability coefficient of 1.00 indicates that there is perfect consistency. This means that the observation/measurement procedure gives the same results regardless of whom or what makes the observation/ measurement.

Seldom, if ever, do reliability coefficients occur at the extreme ends of the continuum (i.e., 0.00 or 1.00). So, you might ask, "What is an adequate reliability coefficient?" The rule of thumb is the higher the better (wow, that was a no-brainer!), but *better* depends on the nature of the measurement procedure being used. Researchers using judges are very happy with reliability coefficients anywhere from .80 upward. Yet instruments measuring achievement or aptitude should have reliabilities in the 90s. Other instruments such as interest inventories and attitude scales tend to be lower than achievement tests or aptitude tests. Generally speaking, reliabilities falling below .60 are considered low, no matter what type of procedure is being used (Nitko, 2001).

There are a number of different types of reliability coefficients used in research. The reason is that each one reveals a different kind of consistency. Different measurement procedures require different kinds of consistency. Table 6.4 lists the different types of reliability coefficients, what kind of consistency is needed, and the corresponding measurement procedure.

The first one listed, *inter-rater* reliability, is required anytime different judges are used to rate participants' behavior. Typically, this type of

Table 6.4 Reliability Coefficients Used in Research

Type of Coefficient	For the Purpose of Consistency Over	Measurement Procedure	Statistic Used
Inter-rater	Different judges/ raters	Observation of performance	Correlation, percentage
Intra-rater	Different times for same judge/rater	Same as above	Same as above
Test–retest	Different times of testing same test	Standardized tests and inventories	Correlation
Alternate-form	Different sets of test items and different times of testing	Multiple forms of the same instrument	Correlation
Split-half (odd/even), Kuder–Richardson 20 and 21, Cronbach alpha	Internal consistency of items within a test	All forms of discrete-item instruments	Correlation, Spearman–Brown, alpha, KR-20, KR-21

reliability is determined by either computing a correlation coefficient or calculating a percentage of agreement between the judges. The study I previously discussed in Chapter 5 by Moeller, Theiler, and Wu (2012) looked at the relationship between goal-setting and language achievement. They developed the LinguaFolio goal-setting process rubric for rating student output through an elaborate process. The three researchers were the raters for the 10 students' sets of 30 scores each. The end product had inter-rater agreement of 90 percent, which gave the researcher confidence that raters were on the same page.

Also related to the use of observers/judges is *intra-rater* reliability. The type of consistency this addresses relates to observers/judges giving the same results if they were given the opportunity to observe/rate participants on more than one occasion. We would expect high agreement within the same person doing the observing/rating over time if the attribute being observed were stable and the observer/judge understood the task. However, if observers/judges are not clear about what they are supposed to observe/rate, there will be different results, and correlations or percentages of agreement will be low. Although this is an important issue, I have not seen many recent studies report this type of reliability.

Valeo's (2013) study, previously mentioned, used both inter- and intra-rater reliability. She used recall protocols to determine any relationship between learner attention and language outcomes. She subjected the scoring and coding of part of her data to inter-rater and intra-rater reliability analysis to weed out any problematic items. It would have been informative if she had included what the final ratings were in percentages and who exactly were the raters.

The remainder of the other types of reliabilities in Table 6.4 are used with paper-and-pencil or computer-administered instruments, whether questionnaires or tests. *Test–retest* reliability is used to measure the stability of the same instrument over time. The instrument is given at least twice and a correlation coefficient is computed on the scores. However, this procedure can only work if the trait (i.e., construct) being measured can be assumed to remain stable over the time between the two measurements. For example, if researchers are assessing participants' L2 pronunciation abilities, administering the instrument two weeks later should produce very similar results if it is reliable. However, if there is a month or two between testing sessions, any training on pronunciation may create differences between the two sets of scores that would depress the reliability coefficient. Nevertheless, if the time between the two administrations is too little, memory of the test from the first session could help the participants give the same responses, which would inflate the reliability coefficient.

A study that reported test–retest reliability was the study by Moskovsky, Alrabai, Paolini, and Ratcheva (2013), previously mentioned in Chapter 5.

They examined whether teachers' motivation strategies affected learners' motivation. They reported the internal consistency of their motivational indices using Cronbach alpha coefficients and test–retest reliability with correlations between the pre- and posttests.

Another type of reliability estimate typically used when a test has several different forms is the *alternate-form* procedure. Most standardized tests have multiple forms to test the same attribute. The forms are different in that the items are not the same, but they are similar in form and content. To ensure that each form is testing the same trait, pairs of different forms are given to the same individuals with several days or more between administrations. The results are then correlated. If the different forms are testing the same attribute, the correlations should be fairly high. Not only does this procedure test the stability of results over time, it also tests whether the items in the different forms represent the same general attribute being tested.

For example, if researchers were to use the Cambridge Certificate in Advanced English (CAE) test battery[5] in a research study, they would need assurance from the test publisher that, no matter what form was used, the results would reveal a similar measure of English language proficiency. Again, researchers should report the alternate-form reliability coefficient provided by the test publisher in his or her research report. The assumption cannot be made by researchers that those who read the study will know that a particular standardized test is reliable, even if it is well known. No matter what test is used, the reliability should be reported in any study where applicable.

A practice that you will no doubt see in your perusal of research is that of borrowing parts of commercially produced standardized tests to construct other tests. It seems that researchers doing this are under the assumption that, because items come from an instrument that has good reliability estimates, any test consisting of a subset of borrowed items will inherit the same reliability. This cannot be taken for granted. Test items often behave differently when put into other configurations. For this reason, subtests consisting of test items coming from such larger, proven instruments should be reevaluated for reliability before using them in a study.

Heras and Lasagabaster (2015), mentioned earlier, developed their own vocabulary test to measure vocabulary production and comprehension. They controlled for test–retest effects (memory) by using alternative pictures between pretest, posttest, and delayed posttest. They also alternated item types between testing events. Although they reported the Cronbach alpha coefficients for their questionnaire, I failed to find any correlational information that would have demonstrated alternative-form reliability. The Cronbach alpha shows the internal consistency of a test (see the following), but alternative-form reliability is needed to show that each form is testing the same thing. Without knowing this type of reliability, there is no way of knowing if results are comparable across the forms.

The last four methods of estimating the reliability of an instrument are concerned with the *internal* consistency of the items within the instrument itself (see Table 6.4). In other words, do all the items in an instrument measure the same general attribute? This is important because the responses for the items are normally added up to make a total score. If the items are measuring different traits, then a total score would not make much sense. To illustrate, if researchers try to measure participant attitudes toward a second language, do all of the items in the survey[6] contribute to reflecting their attitude? If some items are measuring grammar ability, then combining their results with those of the attitude items would confound the measure of attitude.

The first of these four methods presented is known as *split-half (odd/even)* reliability. It is the easiest of the four to compute. As the name suggests, the items in the test are divided in half. Responses on each half are added up to make a subtotal for each half. This can be done by simply splitting the test in half, which is appropriate if the items in the second half are not different in difficulty level, or if the test is not too long. The reason that length is a factor is that respondents might become tired in the latter half of the test, which would make their responses different from those of the first half of the test. To get around these problems, the test can be divided by comparing the odd items with the even items. The responses on the items for each respondent are divided into two subtotals, odd and even. That is, the odd items (e.g., items one, three, five, etc.) are summed and compared with the sum of the even items (e.g., items two, four, six, etc.). The odd/even method is preferred because it is not influenced by the qualitative change in items that often occur in different sections of the instrument, such as difficulty of item or fatigue. Whatever the halving method, the two subtotals are then correlated together to produce the reliability coefficient to measure internal consistency.

The next three methods of computing a coefficient of internal consistency, Kuder–Richardson 20 and 21 and Cronbach alpha, are mathematically related and sometimes symbolized with the Greek letter α (alpha). The first two, Kuder–Richardson 20 and 21, are really two related formulas symbolized as KR-20 and KR-21, respectively. Both are used with items that are scored dichotomously—also referred to as discrete-point items—that is, correct/incorrect, true/false, yes/no, and so on. Formula KR-21 is a simpler version of KR-20. In laymen's terms, these formulas correlate the responses on each item with each of the other items and then average all the correlations. Derakhshan and Eslami (2015), mentioned in Chapter 5, used the Kuder–Richardson 20 formula (KR-20) to check the internal reliability (i.e., consistency) of their discrete-point (correct/incorrect) items for their multiple-choice discourse completion test. For tests that are dichotomously scored (i.e., correct/incorrect), both tests had good reliabilities.

The Cronbach alpha (also known as coefficient alpha, reported previously) does the same thing as the KR formulas except that it is used when the items are scored with more than two possibilities. One use of this method is on rating scales where participants are asked to indicate on a multi-point scale—also referred to as Likert-type scale—the degree to which they agree or disagree. As with the KR formulas, the resulting reliability coefficient is an overall average of the correlations between all possible pairs of items. As previously mentioned, Heras and Lasagabaster (2015) used Cronbach alpha coefficients to test the internal consistency of the items within the five cluster of items in their questionnaire.

Both the Cronbach alpha and the KR-20/KR-21 are conservative estimations of internal consistency. The term *conservative* is used because they take into consideration all the relationships between items which usually produce lower coefficients than the split-half method—it has nothing to do with politics. For this reason, producers of all standardized instruments typically report this type to demonstrate internal consistency. Again, a well-written study will include this information in the data-collecting procedure section. But you will be surprised by studies that fail to report this information.

Factors that affect reliability are numerous. One of the major factors is the degree to which the instrument or procedure is affected by the *subjectivity* of the people doing the rating or scoring. The more a procedure is vulnerable to perceptual bias, lack of awareness, fatigue, or anything else that influences the ability to observe or rate what is happening, the lower the reliability.

Other factors that affect reliability are especially related to discrete-point item[7] instruments for collecting data. One of these is *instrument length,* which can affect reliability in two different ways. The first involves not having enough items. Instruments with fewer items will automatically produce smaller reliability coefficients. This is not necessarily due to the items being inconsistent, but rather is a simple mathematical limitation inherent to correlation coefficients. However, there is a correction formula available known as the *Spearman–Brown prophecy formula* (Nitko and Brookhart, 2011). This is used to project what the reliability estimate would be if the test had more items. When researchers use the split-half reliability coefficient (see Table 6.4), they usually report the Spearman–Brown coefficient because the test has been cut into halves which create two short tests. (No, it won't work on predicting your future.)

Garcia and Asencion (2001) followed this procedure in their study, which looked at the effects of group interaction on language development. They used two tasks for collecting data: a text reconstruction test and a test of listening comprehension. The first test was scored using two raters who were looking at the correct use of three grammar rules. They reported inter-rater reliability with a correlation coefficient of .98 (very high). For the listening test, which only consisted of 10 items, they used the split-half method along with the Spearman–Brown adjustment for a short test (0.73). This appears to be moderate reliability, but remember that it was a short test, so, in fact, the correlation is not bad.

The second way that the length of an instrument can affect reliability is when it is too long. Responses to items that are in the later part of the instrument can be affected by fatigue. Respondents who are tired will not produce consistent responses, which will lower reliability coefficients. When building an English-language test battery for placing students at the university where I teach, my development team and I noticed that the reliability of the reading component was lower than expected. This component was the last test in the battery. Upon further investigation, we found that a number of items in the last part of the test were not being answered. Our conclusion was that the test-takers were running out of time or energy and were not able to finish the last items. We corrected the problem and the reliability of this component increased to the level we felt appropriate. This is also a problem with very long surveys.

The final factor that I will mention is the *item quality* used in an instrument. Ambiguous test items will produce inconsistent results and lower reliability. Participants will guess at poorly written items, and this will not give an accurate measure of the attribute under observation. Items that have more than one correct answer or are written to trick the participant will have similar negative effects. Koyama, Sun, and Ockey (2016), mentioned in Chapter 5, initially developed 44 items in a video-based recognition test when looking at the effects of item preview on multiple-choice listening tests. After pretesting, they dropped two items due to ambiguity and one because it was too easy. They were content with the 41 items left. Had they left these three items in the test, the internal reliability would have decreased.

There are other factors that influence reliability coefficients, but they relate to correlation coefficients in general. I raise these issues in the next chapter when discussing correlation coefficients in greater detail.

However, to emphasize how important knowing what the reliability of an instrument is, I introduce you to the *standard error of measurement* (SEM; Hughes, 2003; Nitko and Brookhart, 2011). (Don't let this term make you nervous; it is not as bad as it looks. I will attempt to explain this in a nonmathematical way.) The reliability coefficient is also used to estimate how much error there is in the measurement procedure—*error* is a statistical term that means any variation in the instrument results due to factors other than what is being measured. By performing some simple math procedures on the reliability coefficient, an estimate of the amount of error is calculated, referred to as the SEM. If there is perfect reliability (i.e., 1.00), there is no error in the measurement; that is, there is perfect consistency. This means that any difference in scores on the instrument can be interpreted as true differences between participants. However, if there is no reliability (i.e., 0.00), then no difference between participant scores can be interpreted as true difference on the trait being measured. To illustrate, if I used a procedure for measuring language proficiency that had no reliability, although I might get a set of scores differing across individuals, I could not conclude that one person who scored higher than another had a higher proficiency. All differences would be attributed to error from a variety of unknown sources.

What about the real world, where reliabilities are somewhere between 0.00 and 1.00? A rule of thumb that I give to my students is that a measurement procedure that has a reliability coefficient even as high as .75 has a sizable amount of error. With this reliability coefficient, half of the average variation in measurement (see discussion on standard deviation in Chapter 7) between individuals can be attributed to error. For instance, if one person scores 55 on an instrument measuring proficiency in grammar and another person scored 60 with a SEM of 5.0, we cannot conclude with much confidence that the second person truly has higher grammar ability. I will come back to this in the next chapter when I discuss descriptive statistics. I might add here that very few studies, if any, report SEMs, although you might see it if you are reading a study about language testing. However, by using the simple reference point of a reliability equaling .75, which means that half of the variation between people being measured is due to error, you will be able to judge how stable the results of a study are. Knowing this will help in deciding how much weight you put on a study to answer your questions.

Validity

As with reliability, the quality of validity is more complex than initially appears. On the surface, people use it to refer to the ability of an instrument or observational procedure to accurately capture data needed to answer a research question. Unfortunately, many research methodology textbooks continue to use outdated terminology by distinguishing among a number of types of validity, such as *content validity, predictive validity, face validity, construct validity*, etc. (e.g., Brown, 1988; Gall, Borg, & Gall, 1996; Hatch & Lazaraton, 1991). These different types have led to some confusion (search Google using these terms and see that they are still alive and kicking). For instance, I have heard some people accuse certain data-gathering procedures of being invalid, while others claim that the same procedures are valid. However, when their arguments are examined more closely one realizes that the two sides of the debate are using different definitions of validity.

There is further confusion between validity of data-collecting sources and internal validity, which was discussed in Chapter 5. They are not the same. The former is concerned with whether the correct source was used for the purpose of the research. The latter has to do with whether the results of the study are due to the effect of the treatment. However, there is a place where the two intersect one another. If the data-gathering procedure is not (or is only weakly) valid, then the effect of the treatment will not be reflected in the data—thus weak or no internal validity.

Since the early 1990s, the above notions of validity have been subsumed under the heading of *construct validity* (Bachman, 1990; Messick, 1989). Rather than having a set of mini-validities, they are now referred to as different *facets* of a more global validity and are summarized in the upper half of Table 6.5.

In the upper half of Table 6.5, in the left column, validity is shown to be comprised of two main facets: trait accuracy and utility. *Trait accuracy,* which corresponds with the former *construct validity*, addresses the question of how accurately the procedure measures the trait (i.e., construct) under investigation. However, accuracy depends on the definition of the construct being measured or observed. Language proficiency, for example, is a trait that is often measured in research. Nevertheless, how this trait is measured should be determined by how it is defined. If language proficiency is defined as the summation of grammar and vocabulary

Table 6.5 Multiple Facets of Construct Validity

		Criterion-Related		Content Coverage	Face Appearance
Facets	Trait accuracy	Capacity to succeed	Current characteristics	Cognitive/ behavioral/ affective change	Consumer satisfaction
	Utility	Predictive	Diagnostic, placement	Achievement of objectives	Public relations
Procedures		Correlate with criterion	Correlate with other instruments, expert opinion	Correspond with learning targets	Surface impression
Types of instruments		Aptitude tests	Personality inventories, language proficiency tests, attitude scales, etc.	Tests, quizzes, performance assessments	All above
Examples		MLAT	TOEFL, IELTS	Exercises to test treatment effects	All above

knowledge, plus reading and listening comprehension, then an approach needs to be used that measures all of these components to accurately measure the trait as defined. On the other hand, if other researchers define language proficiency as oral and writing proficiency, then they would have to use procedures to directly assess speaking and writing ability. In other words, the degree to which a procedure is valid for *trait accuracy* is determined by the degree to which the procedure corresponds to the definition of the trait.

When reading a research article, the traits need to be clearly defined to know whether the measurements used are valid as regards the accuracy facet of validity. These definitions should appear in either the introduction or the methodology section of the article. To illustrate, Machida and Dalsky (2014), discussed in Chapter 5, focused on the effect of concept mapping on writing proficiency with writing anxiety as a moderating variable. They defined writing anxiety as "the fear of apprehension an individual may feel about the act of composing written materials (Daly, 1991)" (p. 28). They operationally defined writing anxiety by scores on a modified version of the *Daly–Miller Writing Apprehension Scale*. This practice of defining traits by using already existing instruments is common among researchers. In effect, the instrument provides the operational definition of the trait. To establish trait accuracy, researchers need to provide support that the instrument they used actually measures the definition of the construct. Often this is done by using expert opinion.

Regarding the second main facet of validity, *utility* is concerned with whether measurement/observational procedures are used for the right purpose. If a procedure is not used for what it was originally intended, there might be a question as to whether it is a valid procedure for obtaining the data needed in a particular study. If it is used for something other than what it was originally designed to do, then researchers must provide additional evidence that the procedure is valid for the purpose of his and her study. For example, if you wanted to use the results from the TOEFL to measure the effects of a treatment over a two-week training period, this would be invalid. To reiterate, the reason is that the TOEFL was designed to measure language proficiency which develops over long periods of time. It was not designed to measure the specific outcomes that the treatment was targeting.

Note in Table 6.5 that trait accuracy and utility are subdivided into three components: *criterion-related, content coverage*, and *face appearance*. These used to be referred to as separate validities: criterion-related validity, content validity, and face validity (e.g., Brown, 1988). However, within the current global concept of validity, these dimensions further refine the complex nature of validity.

Criterion-related simply means that the procedure is validated by being compared to some external criterion. It is subdivided into two different types of trait accuracy: *capacity to succeed* and *current characteristics.* *Capacity to succeed* relates to a person having the necessary wherewithal or *aptitude* to succeed in some other endeavor. Typically, this involves carefully defining the aptitude being measured and then constructing or finding an instrument or observational procedure that would accurately obtain the needed data. The *utility* of identifying people's *capacity to succeed* for this type is usually for prediction purposes. For instance, if researchers want to predict people's ability to master a foreign language, they would administer a procedure that would assess whether the examinees had the necessary aptitude to succeed. Predictive utility is determined by correlating the measurements from the procedures with measurements of the criterion that is being predicted. I will not go into further detail about how this is done; suffice it here to say that you can find more about this from any book on assessment (e.g., Nitko and Brookhart, 2011).

A number of measures have been used over the years to predict the success of students in acquiring a second language. One of the most well-known standardized instruments that has been around for many years is the Modern Language Aptitude Test, developed by Carroll and Sapon (1959). They developed this test for the purpose of predicting whether people have an aptitude for learning languages. Sasaki (2012) presented evidence in her review of this test that it was still valid for making predictions.

Others have also been involved in developing systems for predicting language learning aptitude more recently. One of the most comprehensive studies on this matter was done by Gardner, Tremblay, and Margoret (1997). They analyzed the predictive power of various combinations of 32 different attributes on second language achievement in French. They used various instruments to measure these attributes: language aptitude, attitudes, motivation, learning styles, learning strategies, and self-confidence in comparison with two measures of language achievement. The instruments varied from Likert-type rating scales, fill-in-the-blanks, multiple-choice, to essay. In most cases, the researchers clearly reported the reliability coefficient for each method. Some estimates of reliability were high (e.g., self-confidence, $\alpha = .91$), and some were low (e.g., the learning strategy of compensating for missing knowledge, $\alpha = .43$). The results showed that the five traits used in different combinations predicted achievement: self-confidence with motivation, language learning strategies with motivation, motivation with positive attitude, language aptitude along with learning style, and orientation to learn French. From these data, the researchers provided evidence for the validity of the combined use of five out of 32 traits to predict L2 achievement in French.

The second type of criterion-related trait accuracy that is validated against an external criterion is *current characteristics* (see Table 6.5). Such things as language proficiency, language anxiety, and motivation are considered as characteristics that individuals currently possess. Procedures that measure these attributes are used for (i.e., their utility is) diagnosing people for placement into different categories such as different language proficiency levels. For instance, Weigle (2010), investigated the criterion-related validity of the TOEFL iBT test for writing. She argued that this test is a writing proficiency test and not an aptitude test, meaning that the former is more sensitive to instruction and may change more rapidly than writing aptitude. To determine criterion-related trait accuracy, she compared the e-rater with human ratings for 51 Japanese EFL university students. The raters were three native English speakers and three non-native English speakers. A high correlation would suggest that using machine scoring with an e-rater would be a valid method for assessing writing proficiency.

One method commonly used for providing evidence for being able to validly identify *current characteristics* is determining whether the diagnoses of the procedure match expert opinion. Kobayashi (2002), for example, took care to use experts to judge the suitability of the passages for her reading comprehension test as well as for the test items. By doing so, she supplied evidence that her instrument was measuring what she intended to measure.

Another common method for showing the above facet of validity is to correlate the results of the procedure with performance on another instrument that has previously been accepted by the research community as a good criterion. Often, performance on instruments designed for a particular study is correlated with students' performance on a recognized standardized test such as the TOEFL to estimate validity. Douglas (2015), for instance, sought to determine the concurrent validity of the standardized lexical frequency profiling measure by comparing it with rater judgments of overall performance on the speaker and writing modules of the Canadian English Language Proficiency Index Program's general test. He reported a significant correlation, which provided validity evidence for using this instrument for determining speaking and writing ability.

The second component in Table 6.5 is *content coverage*. The general traits being assessed here are *cognitive, behavioral,* or *affective* change. In *experimental* research, the main question looks at cause-and-effect relationships in the form of treatment effects. Often the objective of the treatment is to increase learning or change the participants' behavior or attitudes. This same objective needs to be used when planning the measurement procedure because its main utility is to assess whether the treatment objective has been achieved. Thus, the validity of the measurement procedure is determined by how well its content aligns with the treatment objectives. In this case, validity is not assessed by computing a correlation coefficient, as with other validity procedures, but by matching various components of the measurement procedure with the treatment objectives.

To illustrate, Fitzgerald, Stenner, Sanford-Moore, Koons, Bowen, and Kim (2015) studied the relationship between age and years of EFL exposure with English reading ability. They used the E-LQ English reading comprehension assessment to measure Korean participants' English reading comprehension. This test was designed to assess reading ability at the beginning of the fifth and sixth grades and to be sensitive to growth over time. The researchers outlined the content of the test, demonstrating that the test was suitable for the grade levels (i.e., content validity).

The third component in Table 6.5 that defines trait accuracy and utility is *face appearance*, which some refer to as *face validity*. Related to accuracy, the key issue is whether a measurement procedure appears to the public eye to measure what it is supposed to measure. The closer it looks like it is gathering the correct data, the more valid it looks. In regards to utility, face appearance is important for public relations with examinees as well as with the outside community. Examinees who do not feel that the procedure is measuring what they think it should measure might not be motivated to do their best. This, in turn, will affect the results of the study. People outside a study might not see the relevance of a particular measurement technique and, therefore, not consider the results from such measurement useful for answering the researchers' question (i.e., the consumer). Although this aspect of validity is of lesser theoretical importance from a research perspective, it is the one that many practitioners in foreign language teaching give most attention to. This has led some people to make incorrect conclusions about the validity of data that result from some measurement procedures.

To show how easy it is to allow the facet of *face appearance* to overshadow other aspects of validity, I relate this somewhat bizarre, but true, story. One of my former professors once said something like this.

> If I were to tell you that I found a correlation of +0.95 (a very high correlation) between shoe size and success in learning a foreign language, and that I have found this high correlation in a number of studies with different groups of participants, would you use shoe size as a test to predict future success entrants into your foreign language program?

Most likely, you answer with an emphatic "No way!" However, I asked, "Why not?" His answer was "The test is not valid." If you agree with him, what aspect of validity do you have in mind? Most likely, you would be considering face appearance as he was. I, in contrast, argued that the test is valid on the basis of its predictive utility. Anything, no matter what it looks like, that correlates with something else as high as .95 is a powerful predictor. I certainly agree that shoe size does not appear at face value to relate to the ability to learn a language. For prediction purposes, however, face appearance is not necessary, although it is desirable. Understanding why something can predict something else does not have to be clear either, although we would certainly try to find out the reason. I would argue that, if my data are correct, we should use shoe size as an entrance test because it has been shown to have high predictive utility. Certainly, it would be the cheapest and quickest test to administer, although not very popular with people whose foot size predicted failure.

Before concluding this section of the chapter, I need to point out a very important principle. The relationship between validity and reliability is unidirectional. There are two aspects to this: 1) reliability does not depend on validity, but 2) validity depends on reliability. Regarding the first, reliability does not require or depend on validity, an instrument or observational procedure can be reliable (i.e., consistent) when measuring something, but not measuring the right thing. To illustrate, if we measure a person's height with a measuring tape, the results will be consistent (i.e., reliable) every time. No matter how many times we measure that person's height, we will get the same results. Yet if we claim that our measurement is an accurate assessment of a person's weight, our procedure is not very valid. Notice that I said *not very* and refrained from using *invalid*. The reason is that height is related to weight: Tall people are usually heavier than short people. Although related, height would not be a valid direct measurement of weight. In other words, a measurement procedure can be reliable but not equally valid.

However, the opposite is not true. We cannot have a valid instrument that is not reliable, aspect (2). Accuracy implies consistency but not vice versa. Obviously, if we cannot depend on a procedure to give us consistent (i.e., reliable) results, accuracy will also fluctuate. In fact, the validity of a procedure will never exceed its reliability. If a measurement procedure has low reliability, its validity will be low as well regardless of how valid the developer wishes it might be. To return to Gardner et al.'s (1997) study, mentioned previously, the researchers did not comment about the relatively low reliability of the instrument measuring the learning strategy of compensating for missing knowledge ($\alpha = .43$). With such a low reliability coefficient, I would be suspicious about the validity of the data coming from this instrument. On the other hand, a high reliability coefficient does not automatically mean that the instrument is also highly valid. Therefore, reliability is necessary, but not sufficient for defining validity. Once the instrument is determined reliable, researchers must then show with separate information that it is valid.

Do not lose focus from the above discussion. Validity is much more than reliability. It is more fluid than reliability. It is not a static concept.

Because it is tied very much to the facet of *utility*, it changes with every research design (cf. Chapelle, Enright, & Jamieson 2011).

In summary, when you read or hear the term *validity* being used, refer to Table 6.5 and try to determine what aspect of validity is being considered. Then ask yourself if the term is being used correctly. Remember that if a measurement has low reliability, regardless of its face appearance, it also has low validity. However, too few studies report how the validity of the procedures used was determined. Yet the results of a study depend heavily on whether the measurement procedures are valid. The weaker the validity, the less we can depend on the results.

In conclusion, the last section of this chapter has introduced the two principal qualities of numerical data-gathering procedures: reliability and validity. Regardless of what procedure researchers use, they need to report to the reader evidence that the procedure used provides reliable and valid data. If not, there is no way the reader will know whether the conclusions made based on the data have any credibility. With this basic information in hand, you should now be able to read the section about data gathering with understanding. In addition, you should have enough confidence to evaluate whether the procedure a researcher used provided reliable and valid information.

You are now ready to grapple with how data are evaluated. This is the subject of the next chapter. However, before you leave this chapter, try the following exercise so that you can gain firsthand experience in evaluating the data-gathering procedures used in a study of your choice.

Exercise 6.3

Task: Find a research study of interest in a recent journal related to applied linguistics. Do the following:

1. List the research question(s).
2. Look at the data-collection procedure used (i.e., tests, surveys, raters, observers, etc.). Does the procedure seem appropriate for answering the research question(s)?
3. What information was given relating to reliability?
   a. Type?
   b. Amount?
   c. How reliable was the procedure being used?
4. What facet of validity was examined?
5. In your opinion, how well did the procedure correspond to identifying the trait being measured?
6. Did statements about validity correspond to evidence of reliability?

Key Terms and Concepts

Collecting and Evaluating
Verbal Data

automatic response patterns
closed-form questionnaire items
full-participant observer
halo effect
highly structured interviews
informant
instrumental procedures
introspection
judge/rater
nonparticipant observer
objective
observational procedure
open-form questionnaire items
open-structured interviews
partial-participant observer
participant observers
retrospection
rubric
semistructured interviews
subjectivity
think-aloud procedure
triangulation

Collecting and Evaluating
Numerical Data

alternate-form reliability
coefficient
construct validity
constructed response items
content coverage
criterion-referenced tests
criterion-related
Cronbach alpha
discrete-point items
face appearance
internal consistency
inter-rater reliability
intra-rater reliability
item quality
Kuder–Richardson 20 and 21
norm-referenced test
predictive utility
reliability
reliability coefficient
Spearman–Brown prophecy formula
split-half (odd/even) reliability
standard error of measurement (SEM)
standardized test
test–retest reliability
trait accuracy
utility
validity

Notes

1. *Objective* is at the other end of the continuum from *subjective*, in that the observer's observations are not influenced by bias due to attitude, temporary emotional states, etc. In actual fact, there is no 100 percent purely objective or subjective observation.
2. Go to http://nces.ed.gov/statprog/2002 and search for Survey response rate parameters.
3. See www.toefl.org for more information.
4. See www.ielts.org for more information.
5. See www.cambridge-efl.org/exam/general/bg_cae.htm for more information.
6. Attitude surveys require the same internal consistency measures as tests.
7. This item tests only one thing and is scored as correct or incorrect.

References

Bachman, L. F. (1990). *Fundamental considerations in language testing*. New York, NY: Oxford University Press.

Bowles, M. A. (2010). *The think-aloud controversy in second language research*. New York, NY: Routledge.

Brown, J. D. (1988). *Understanding research in second language learning*. Cambridge: Cambridge University Press.

Carroll, J. B., & Sapon, S. M. (1959). *Modern Language Aptitude Test and Manual (MLAT)*. San Antonio, TX: Psychological Corporation.

Chapelle, C. A., Enright, M. K., & Jamieson, J. M. (2011). Test score interpretation and use. In C. A. Chapelle, M. K. Enright, & J. M. Jamieson (Eds.), *Building a validity argument for the Test of English as a Foreign Language* (pp. 1–25). New York, NY: Routledge.

Crowther, D., Trofimovich, P., Isaacs, T., & Saito, K. (2015). Does a speaking task affect second language comprehensibility? *Modern Language Journal, 99*(1), 80–95.

Derakhshan, A., & Eslami, Z. (2015). The effect of consciousness-raising instruction on the pragmatic development of apology and request. *TESL-EJ, 18*(4), 1–24.

Douglas, S. R. (2015). The relationship between lexical frequency profiling measures and rater judgements of spoken and written general English language proficiency on the CELPIP-general test. *TESL CANADA Journal/Revue TESL du CANADA, 32*(9), 43–64.

Edwards, E., & Roger, P. S. (2015). Seeking out challenges to develop L2 self-confidence: A language learner's journey to proficiency. *TESL-EJ, 18*(4), 1–24.

Fang, X., & Garland, P. (2014). Teacher orientations to ELT curriculum reform: An ethnographic study in a Chinese secondary school. *Asia-Pacific Educational Researcher, 3*(2), 311–319.

Fitzgerald, J., Stenner, A. J., Sanford-Moore, E. E., Koons, H., Bowen, K., & Kim, K. H. (2015). The relationship of Korean students' age and years of English-as-a-foreign-language exposure with English-reading ability: A cross-age study. *Reading Psychology, 36*, 173–202.

Gall, M. D., Borg, W. R., & Gall, J. P. (1996). *Educational research: An introduction* (6th ed.). White Plains, NY: Longman.

Garcia, P., & Asencion, Y. (2001). Interlanguage development of Spanish learners: Comprehension, production, and interaction. *The Canadian Modern Language Review, 57*, 37–401.

Gardner, R. C., Tremblay, P. F., & Masgoret, A. (1997). Towards a full model of second language learning: An empirical investigation. *The Modern Language Journal, 81*, 34–36.

Harklau, L. (2000). "Good Kids" to the "Worst": Representations of English language learners across educational settings. *TESOL Quarterly, 34*, 5–67.

Hatch, E., & Lazaraton, A. (1991). *The research manual: Design and statistics for applied linguistics*. New York, NY: Newbury House.

Heras, A., & Lasagabaster, D. (2015). The impact of CLIL on affective factors and vocabulary learning. *Language Teaching Research, 19*(1), 70–88.

Hijikata-Someya, Y., Ono, M., & Yamanishi, H. (2015). Evaluation by native and non-native English teacher-raters of Japanese students' summaries. *English Language Teaching, 8*(7), 1–12.

Hughes, A. (2003). *Testing for language teachers* (2nd ed.). Cambridge: Cambridge University Press.

Kobayashi, M. (2002). Method effects on reading comprehension test performance: Text organization and response format. *Language Testing, 19*, 193–220.

Kök. I., & Canbay, O. (2011). An experimental study on the vocabulary level and vocabulary consolidation strategies. *Procedia Social and Behavioral Sciences, 15*, 891–894.

Koyama, D., Sun, A., & Ockey, G. J. (2016). The effects of item preview on video-based multiple-choice listening assessments. *Language Learning & Technology, 20*, 148–165.

Kubanyiova, M. (2015). The role of teachers' future self-guides in creating L2 development opportunities in teacher-led classroom discourse: Reclaiming the relevance of language teacher cognition. *The Modern Language Journal, 99*(3), 565–584.

Lee, J. (2015). Language learner strategy by Chinese-speaking EFL readers when comprehending familiar and unfamiliar texts. *Reading in a Foreign Language, 27*(1), 71–95.

Likert, R. A. (1932). A technique for the measurement of attitudes. *Archives of Psychology, 140*.

Lin, H. (2015). A meta-synthesis of empirical research on the effectiveness of computer-mediated communication (CMC) in SLA. *Language Learning & Technology, 19*(2), 85–117.

Machida, N. & Dalsky, D. J. (2014). The effect of concept mapping on L2 writing performance: Examining possible effects of trait-level writing anxiety. *English Language Teaching, 7*(9), 28–35.

Messick, S. (1989). Validity. In R. Linn (Ed.), *Educational measurement* (3rd ed.) (pp. 13–103). Washington, DC: American Council on Education/Macmillan

Miles, M. B., & Huberman, A. M. (1994). *Qualitative data analysis: An expanded sourcebook* (2nd ed.). Thousand Oaks, CA: SAGE.

Moeller, A. J., Theiler, J. M., & Wu, C. (2012). Goal setting and student achievement: A longitudinal study. *The Modern Language Journal, 96*(2), 153–169.

Moskovsky, C., Alrabai, F., Paolini, S., & Ratcheva, S. (2013). The effects of teachers' motivational strategies on learners' motivation: A controlled investigation of second language acquisition. *Language Learning, 63*(1), 34–62.

Nitko, A. J. (2001). *Educational assessment of students* (3rd ed.). Upper Saddle River, NJ: Prentice Hall.

Nitko, A. J., & Brookhart, S. M. (2011). *Educational assessment of students* (6th ed.). Upper Saddle River, NJ: Prentice Hall.

Oswald, F. L., & Plonsky, L. (2010). Meta-analysis in second language research: Choices and challenges. *Annual Review of Applied Linguistics, 30*, 85–110.

Pellerin, M. (2014). Language tasks using touch screen and mobile technologies: Reconceptualizing task-based CALL for young language learners. *Canadian Journal of Learning and Technology, 40*(1), 1–23.

Sasaki, M. (2012). Test review: The Modern Language Aptitude Test (paper-and-pencil version). *Language Testing*, 29(2), 315–321.

Slezak, P. (2002). Thinking about thinking: Language, thought, and introspection. *Language & Communication*, 22, 373–394.

Springer, S., & Collins, L. (2008). Interaction inside and outside of the language classroom. *Language Teaching Research*, 12, 39–60.

Tashakkori, A., & Teddlie, C. (2003). *Handbook on mixed methods in social and behavior science*. Thousand Oaks, CA: SAGE.

Valeo, A. (2013). Language awareness in a content-based language programme. *Language Awareness*, 22(2), 126–145.

van Compernolle, R. A., & Henery, A. (2015). Learning to do concept-based pragmatics instruction: Teacher development and L2 pedagogical content knowledge. *Language Teaching Research*, 19, 351–372.

Weigle, S. C. (2010). Validation of automated scores of TOEFL iBT tasks against non-test indicators of writing ability. *Language Testing*, 27(3), 335–353.

Yihong, G., Yuan, Z., Ying, C., & Yan, Z. (2007). Relationship between English learning motivation types and self-identity changes among Chinese students. *TESOL Quarterly*, 41(1), 133–155.

Chapter 7

Understanding Research Results

Chapter Overview

Once researchers have collected their data, they must determine whether the results answer their research questions. If they are "What" questions, the answers will be in the form of information that 1) describes what variables are important, 2) identifies the context in which certain phenomena occur, and/or 3) uncovers important relationships between phenomena. If the questions are "Why" types, then the results will attempt to explain the cause behind certain phenomena. In either case, the analysis of the data will be presented verbally, numerically, or by a combination of the two.

In this chapter, various types of data and data analysis procedures that appear in results sections of research studies are discussed. Following a short introduction to data analysis, there are two main sections; the first relates to how verbal data are presented and analyzed, and the second introduces how numerical data are presented and analyzed. Although somewhat technical, this latter section does not require a background in math. It furnishes you with the concepts needed to understand the statistical procedures found in many results sections.

By the end of this chapter, my goal is for you to be able to read results sections of research articles with enough confidence to critically evaluate whether appropriate procedures have been used and correct interpretations have been made.

Introduction to Data Analysis

Numerical Versus Verbal Data

Some people think that numerical data are more scientific—and therefore more important—than verbal data because of the statistical analyses that can be performed on numerical data. However, this is a false conclusion. We must not forget that numbers are only as good as the constructs they represent. In other words, when we use statistics we have basically transferred verbally defined constructs into numbers so that we can analyze the data more easily. We must not forget that these statistical results must again be transferred back into terminology that represents these verbal constructs to make any sense. Consider the following statement by Miles and Huberman (1994) as an argument for the importance of verbal data:

> We argue that although words may be more unwieldy than numbers, they render more meaning than numbers alone and should be hung on to throughout data analysis. Converting words into numbers and then tossing away the words get a researcher into all kinds of mischief. You thus are assuming that the chief property of the words is that there are more of some than of others. Focusing solely on numbers shifts attention from substance to arithmetic, throwing out the whole notion of "qualities" or "essential characteristics."
>
> (p. 56)

Nevertheless, be careful not to swing to the other side of the pendulum, thinking that verbal data are superior to numerical data. Both types of data have their place and are equally important. Miles and Huberman provide a very powerful discussion on how the two types of data complement each other. This concurs with my position presented in Chapter 5 of this book.

Common Practice

In almost all studies, all of the data that have been gathered are not presented in the research report. Whether verbal or numerical, the data presented have gone through some form of selection and reduction. The reason is that verbal and numerical data are both typically voluminous in their rawest forms. What you see reported in a research journal are results of the raw data having been boiled down into manageable units for display to the public. Verbal data commonly appear as selections of excerpts, narrative vignettes, quotations from interviews, etc., whereas numerical data are often condensed into tables of frequencies, averages, and so on. There are some interesting differences, however, which I describe in the following two sections.

Section 1: Analysis of Verbal Data

Most of the credit in recent years for developing criteria for presenting and analyzing verbal data must go to researchers who have emphasized the use of qualitative research strategies. However, because of the variety of qualitative approaches used, there are differing opinions about the analytical steps that should be followed when analyzing verbal data. For instance, Creswell (1998) identified only three out of 13 general analysis strategies common to three different authors of qualitative research methods (Bogdan & Biklen, 1992; Miles & Huberman, 1994; Wolcott, 1994). This makes it difficult to set standards for evaluating the results section of a qualitative research article. Lazaraton (2003) was even more pessimistic. She stated, "Can any one set of criteria be used to judge any or all forms of qualitative research? My thesis, in answering this last question, is that they cannot" (p. 2).

In addition, unlike work with numerical data, presentation of verbal data and their analyses appear very much intertwined together in results sections of research reports. Numerical data, in contrast, are presented in some type of summarized form (e.g., tables of descriptive statistics) and followed with an analysis in the form of inferential statistics (see Section 2 of this chapter)

Consequently, the analyses of verbal data are not quite as straightforward as analyzing numerical data. The reason is that analysis of verbal data is initiated at the beginning of the data-collection process and continues throughout the study. This process involves the researcher interacting with the data in a symbiotic fashion. Literally, the researcher becomes the "main 'measurement device'" (Miles & Huberman, 1994, p. 7). Creswell (1998, pp. 142, 143) likened data analysis to a "contour" in the form of a "data analysis spiral," where the researcher engages with the data, reflects, makes notes, re-engages with the data, organizes, codes, reduces the data, looks for relationships and themes, makes checks on the credibility of the emerging system, and eventually draws conclusions.

However, when we read published qualitative research, we are seldom given a clear description of how this *data analysis spiral* transpired. In Miles and Huberman's (1994) words, "We rarely see data displays—only the conclusions. In most cases we don't see a procedural account of the analysis, explaining just how the researcher got from 500 pages of field notes to the main conclusions drawn" (p. 262).

If the researcher is working alone during the data analysis spiral, serious questions arise concerning the credibility of any conclusions made. First, there is the problem mentioned in Chapter 6 regarding possible bias when gathering data through observation and other noninstrumental procedures. However, because analysis begins during the data-collection stage in qualitative research, *analytical biases* become a possible threat to the credibility of conclusions. Miles and Huberman (1994) identified three archetypical ones: *the holistic fallacy, elite bias,* and *going native.* The first has to do with seeing patterns and themes that are not really there. The second is concerned with giving too much weight to informants who are more articulate and better informed, making the data unrepresentative. The third, *going native*, occurs when researchers get so close to the respondents that they are "co-opted into [their] perceptions and explanations" (p. 264).

So how are we, the consumers of qualitative research, supposed to determine whether the information in the results section is credible? Miles and Huberman (1994) list 13 tactics for enhancing credibility. Four of these tactics relate to the quality of data, which I included in Table 6.2. I place triangulation (point 1 in Table 7.1) under patterns and themes based on Creswell's (1998) use of the term, although Miles and Huberman included it with data quality. I list three[1] (points 2, 3, and 4) to evaluate patterns and/or themes proposed by the researchers, and five (points 6, 7, 8, 9, and 10) for appraising their explanations and conclusions.

Creswell (1998) provided eight verification procedures that he and a colleague extrapolated from a number of differing types of qualitative studies. Three of these overlapd with Miles and Huberman's (1994) list—triangulation, negative evidence, and member checks (i.e., informant feedback)—leaving five. Three of the remaining procedures relate to evaluating data quality, so I put them in Table 6.2 and discussed them there. The third, *peer review* (point 5 in Table 7.1), is useful for checking whether the perceived patterns are credible, although also useful for evaluating explanations. The last two, rich/thick descriptions (point 11) and external audits (point 12), are powerful tactics for evaluating explanations. Each of these tactics is further explained below.

Few studies will use all 12 of these tactics to enhance credibility. However, the more a study has in each category, the more evidence is put forward for strengthening the credibility of the results. There should be at least one tactic used in each of the two general categories in Table 7.1.

Table 7.1 Methods for Evaluating Credibility of Patterns and Explanations Drawn from Verbal Data

Evidence for . . .	Tactic
Patterns/themes	1. Triangulation
	2. Outliers and extreme cases
	3. Surprises
	4. Negative evidence
	5. Peer review
Explanations/conclusions	6. Spurious relationships
	7. If–then tests
	8. Rival explanations
	9. Replicating findings
	10. Informant feedback
	11. Rich/thick description
	12. External audits

Evaluating Patterns and Themes

One of the main goals of most qualitative studies is to extrapolate patterns and themes from the verbal data. The question for the consumer is whether these patterns are plausible based on the data. The first five tactics listed in Table 7.1 can be used to support patterns proposed by researchers (cf. Creswell, 1998, 2013; Miles & Huberman, 1994). The first, *triangulation*, shows how the same patterns are seen in data from different sources. The next three involve atypical data that might not fit the patterns or themes being proposed by the researcher. The temptation is to avoid these *hiccups* in the data by what quantitative analysis refers to as *data smoothing*. However, for the qualitative researcher, these exceptions are excellent means to test the perceived patterns or themes being formulated. The last tactic, *peer review*, involves getting a second opinion, which corresponds to criterion-related validity discussed in Chapter 6.

Triangulation

I have already mentioned studies in Chapters 5 and 6 that have used this procedure. It involves using data from multiple sources to converge on themes and patterns. For the purpose of adding credibility to an argument, the more evidence coming from independent sources the better. As in the law courts, one witness is not enough. The more independent witnesses the stronger the case. The same holds true for qualitative research: the more data coming from a variety of sources the better. This, of course, assumes that data from each source can stand the test of the other data quality criteria discussed in Chapter 6.

Some qualitative methods, such as conversational analysis (CA; see Chapter 5), that focus on one set of data coming from one source might have difficulty here. Basically, CA uses one source of data, normally in the form of transcripts form audiotapes (Lazaraton, 2003). Researchers repeatedly process the transcripts until constructs and relationships are perceived. They continually test and retest, typically using the *spiral* technique, until they are satisfied with their conclusions. Of course, more conversational data collected from the same source at different times and settings adds to support the interpretations. However, CA studies can use triangulation to support their conclusions, if so desired.

Simply stating, however, that triangulation of different data sources was used in a study does not necessarily increase credibility of the conclusions. Researchers need to inform us how and why triangulation was used. Questions such as the following need to be answered: How do data from each source contribute to the convergence of a perceived pattern or theme? In what way do the researchers believe that this particular combination of data adds to the overall credibility of the conclusions? These are questions researchers are obligated to answer to add weight to the overall credibility. Lee-Johnson (2015), mentioned in Chapter 4, did just this when discussing how she used triangulation of five sources of data to provide internal validity and credibility for the conclusions of her qualitative study.

Outliers and Extreme Cases

Examining such data seems to be counterintuitive to the tactic of checking for representativeness at the top of the list (see Table 7.1). However, it is a very effective way to check whether the patterns and themes perceived by the research are not due to some form of bias. Most qualitative studies limit themselves when it comes to how many people or situations are studied. Because of this, the perceived patterns and themes may be unique to the sample being used. However, once these patterns and themes have been formulated from the original sample, comparing them with samples of people or events that considerably differ is an excellent way to check credibility.

In some studies, the opposite might be true. Researchers deliberately use extreme cases compared to the original sample. The reason is that such samples are information-rich (see Chapter 4). However, once the patterns and themes have been extrapolated, it seems imperative that researchers would want to compare their findings with a sample that is less extreme. If the patterns and themes hold for the more general sample, they are made more credible. Scott and Huntington's study (2007) provides an example of using extreme cases to bolster the credibility of the patterns they had previously seen. Based on a previous qualitative study, they used a conversational analysis approach (cf. Chapter 6) to compare novice language learners' interpretative processing of a literary text, and whether they differed between a teacher-moderated classroom and a small group discussion employing L1. They reported differences that provided new information by using novice learners.

Surprises

Another tactic for promoting the credibility of perceived patterns and themes is examining unexpected findings. Reporting unexpected findings gives some confirmation that researchers are not so focused on what they want to find that they cannot recognize any anomalies. Of course, once the surprise has been noted by the researchers, they need to explain how it confirms or forces adjustment to the proposed pattern or theme. One example is Kraemer's (2006) qualitative study, which tested four hypotheses regarding the language use of English in the classroom by native and non-native teaching assistants. She used observations, interviews, and a questionnaire to collect her data. She added credibility to her conclusions when she reported that some of their data failed to support the research hypotheses. She found that teaching assistants used much less English in German-language classrooms than expected, thus going against two research hypotheses.

Negative Evidence

Here researchers actively seek evidence that will go against their patterns or themes. One would not think that researchers would want to find evidence contradicting their proposals. It certainly is not something that happens automatically as the data are being analyzed by researchers. They would have to make a planned effort to do this after beginning to formulate any patterns or themes. Just the fact that researchers made this effort would be impressive. However, it is not sufficient to simply report that negative evidence was found. Researchers need to identify the evidence and discuss the implications. This type of information reported by researchers in a published report adds more weight to the findings of the study. Rott's (2005) qualitative study examined the effects of two vocabulary learning interventions (two types of glosses) for word learning. She gathered data from several sources (triangulation), which strengthened her data set. To add credibility, she revealed data that did not support some of patterns she extrapolated from the data.

Peer Review

A *peer* is someone on the same level of the researcher "who keeps the researcher honest; asks the hard questions about methods, meanings, and interpretations" (Creswell, 1998, p. 202). The researcher, especially if doing the study alone, needs someone, such as a colleague, to evaluate proposed patterns as well as themes to prevent influences from such analytical biases as *holistic fallacy*, mentioned previously. Lee and Schallert (2007) did a qualitative study on the relationship between a teacher's writing feedback and two students' responses in their revisions. They used multiple methods on multiple sources to collect their data guaranteeing prolonged engagement and persistent observation (cf. Table 6.2). To add to the credibility of their findings, they used both triangulation and peer review.

Evaluating Explanations and Conclusions

The last phase of evaluating a qualitative study is examining the explanations and conclusions of the study. Table 7.1 presents seven tactics that researchers can use to bolster credibility, five from Miles and Huberman

(1994) and two from Creswell (1998). These are useful for consumers of qualitative research for evaluation as well. However, the burden of proof is on the researcher, not the consumer. The more tactics used by the researcher, the more weight is given to the credibility of the interpretations of the findings.

Spurious Relationships

Not all things that appear to be related are directly related. For example, lung cancer and the number of ashtrays a person owns are related. However, this relationship is spurious (i.e., misleading). Another variable directly related to each of these—the number of cigarettes smoked—produces an indirect relationship between ashtray and lung cancer. So, when researchers propose a direct relationship between constructs, they should provide a convincing argument that there are no other variables producing this relationship. Tomiyama's (2009) case study provides an interesting example. She studied the relationship of age and proficiency with L2 attrition. To do this she used two siblings, which automatically controlled for social background and language environment. The two siblings were about three years apart in age. Data was collected on seven occasions over a two-year period. She argued that cognitive maturity might have been the intervening variable behind the relationship between age and language attrition, thus making the relationship spurious.

If–Then Tests

These tests "are the workhorses of qualitative data analysis" (Miles & Huberman, 1994, p. 271). In the fuller version, an *if–then test* is a conditional sentence in the form of *if the hypothesis is true, then there should be a specific consequence*. Every explanation based on data is a type of hypothesis, usually in the form of relationships among variables, underlying principles, or processes. Researchers test their hypothesized explanations by predicting that some consequence would occur with a novel sample of people or set of events. This strategy is built into the grounded theory method discussed in Chapter 5. Yan and Horwitz (2008) studied how students' anxiety interacts with other variables in influencing language learning from the learners' perspectives. They used a three-staged grounded theory analysis method on the transcriptions of semi-structured interviews with purposefully selected participants representing high, medium, and low anxiety levels. Based on the analysis of their data, they developed a grounded theory model, which proposed an interesting relational structure between factors. In their discussion section, Yan and Horwitz proposed a number of *if–then* statements, which lead to a number of suppositions. However, they did not test any of these suppositions by applying them on new samples of participants from their sample pool to support them, which would have added credibility to such conclusions.

Rival Explanations

Eliminating competing explanations is a powerful way to add weight to a theoretical conclusion. The researcher formulates at least one plausible competing explanation and repeats the *if–then* test. The explanation that best explains the data is the most plausible. The researcher can then report how the weaker explanations could not compete.

However, the consumer must beware that the competing explanations offered are not *straw men*, that is, explanations that were not plausible in the first place and are easy to refute. This might occur if researchers are so bent on their own explanation that they do not address more plausible hypotheses but still want to give the appearance that they have used this technique to gain credibility.

Another caveat for consumers is to not conclude that, just because the competing explanations were not as robust as the one proposed by the researcher, the proposed one is the best one. There might still be a better explanation than the one proposed, but it has not been discovered yet. In other words, the last person standing may not be the strongest. On a more practical note, researchers must provide evidence that not only shows their explanation is better than the competition; they must also show that the explanations are also good in themselves. For example, Sneddon (2008) examined strategies, transfer of concepts, and the effect of learning to read in English and their L1 at home on bilingual children. In her discussion section, she was able to quickly dismiss a rival argument that children would choose the easier language when reading dual language texts in a multilingual environment. Her data supported the work of others in the field and uncovered explanations that need further research in a larger study.

Replicating Findings

This strategy is recognized by both qualitative and quantitative researchers as an excellent way to support hypotheses and theories. The more often the same findings occur despite different samples and conditions, the more confidence we can have in the conclusions. Hypothesized relationships that can only be supported by one sample of individuals in only one setting have little use in the practical world. Occasionally, researchers will report several replications of the study in the same report. It is a good way to provide evidence for the robustness of their explanations. Every study that has been cited in this book has used this strategy to add to the credibility of their conclusions by showing how their results were similar with previous published research.

Informant Feedback

This relates to the reactions that the informants have to the conclusions of the study. Such feedback can be used to check the plausibility of patterns perceived by the researcher. The researcher needs to take care here, however, owing to possible *researcher effects*. Respondents may simply agree with the researcher just to please the researcher, or the researcher may give the informant a final report that is too technical. This could result in agreement to hide the embarrassment of not understanding or produce a negative response based on misunderstanding. In either case, the researcher needs to inform the consumer of the report regarding the manner in which the feedback was obtained. The more effort the researcher reports to have made to facilitate the understanding of the informant, the more weight the consumer can give to the feedback. In her case study (cf. Chapter 4), Samimy (2008) showed Mark, her participant, a draft of her conclusions for his reactions, so as to add to the credibility of her interpretations.

Rich/Thick Description

This involves a detailed description of the participants, context, and all that goes on during the data-gathering and analysis stages. The purpose is to provide the reader of the study with enough information to decide whether the explanations and conclusions of the study are warranted. When this is done, you will notice that the researcher will provide excerpts from the data for each proposed explanation. The more excerpts, the more support—one excerpt does not establish a pattern or support an explanation. Be careful not to fall in the opposite trap, however, by mistaking quantity with quality. That is, the excerpts that are used to support an explanation need to be truly supportive. This strategy is so common that almost every study cited in this section provided many excerpts from their data pools to warrant their conclusions (cf. Pellerin, 2014, cited in Chapter 6).

External Audits

A seldom used, but powerful method (Creswell, 1998) to increase the credibility of the interpretations of a study is to hire an outsider to evaluate the study. A well-funded research project may employ such a person to add credibility to the findings and conclusions. Many studies have unpaid external reviewers critique them out of academic courtesy. One place where researchers recognize such people is in their acknowledgments at the end of the study. Kubanyiova (2015) thanked one specific and two anonymous people who reviewed the drafts of her study prior to publication (cited in Chapter 5). This is not exactly an external audit, which is very thorough, but it provides some level of evaluation for the reader.

Full Example

Harklau's (2000) study (see Chapter 6) illustrates how explanations coming from verbal data might be evaluated using the 12 tactics presented in Table 7.1. Remember that, in Chapter 6, we looked at Harklau's ethnographic case study, in which she examined how the representation (i.e., stereotype) of different institutional programs influenced ESL students' identities. A summary of the tactics I found in her study is presented in Table 7.2, followed by an expanded explanation.

Harklau (2000) made extensive use of triangulation to identify patterns in the data to formulate her constructs. She used data from different sources to provide evidence to support the identification of institutional representation. The high school representation, for example, was supported with data from sources such as excerpts from personal stories, classroom observation, and student and teacher interviews. For the college representation, she used, among other sources, interviews, classroom observation, and assignments.

Harklau (2000) did not report any *outliers* and *extreme cases* (tactic 2). However, she did use the *surprises* tactic (tactic 3) found in some of her data. In one incident, the high school teacher was shocked by one of the participants' behavior, which went against the proposed high school representation. Harklau also provided *negative evidence* (tactic 4) where the performance of one of the participants contradicted the high school representation of ESL students being hardworking. All of these contribute to the credibility of her construct of institutional representation that she was aiming to demonstrate.

Harklau's (2000) argument for the *believability* of her interpretations would have been enhanced had she reported a *peer review* (tactic 5) during her construct formation. Based on her article, she seemed to be the only one involved in the process—from data collection to final analysis. By using someone, such as a colleague, to check her interpretations of the data, she would have avoided the possibility of a number of biases, one being the *holistic fallacy* previously mentioned. However, Harklau did use the teacher participants to check whether her emerging themes had any validity. She reported meeting with them informally over the semester for this purpose. Although this is not exactly peer

Table 7.2 Evaluation Tactics for Verbal Data Applied to Harklau's Study (2000)

Checking for . . .	Tactics	Check
Patterns and themes	1. Triangulation	☺
	2. Outliers and extreme cases	
	3. Surprises	☺
	4. Negative evidence	☺
	5. Peer review	
Explanations and conclusions	6. Spurious relationships	
	7. If–then tests	
	8. Rival explanations	
	9. Replicating findings	
	10. Informant feedback	☺
	11. Rich/thick description	☺
	12. External audits	

☺ means that the tactic was effectively used

feedback, it is *informant feedback* (tactic 10), which is also a good tactic for supporting patterns and themes.

The final stage for evaluating verbal data analysis is *Explanations and conclusions* (see Table 7.1). There are seven tactics under this heading that a researcher can choose from for heightening credibility. Harklau (2000) used two of these in her study: *informant feedback* (tactic 10) and rich/thick description (tactic 11). Regarding the first, not only did she share her emerging data themes with teacher participants to get feedback; she also shared her conclusions with the student participants in final interviews along with providing them with a copy of the final report.

Harklau (2000) clearly used rich/thick description in her study. This is required if she hoped to back up her explanations regarding the impact of institutional stereotyping on student identity. For each of the conclusions that she made, she backed them up with rich and plentiful quotations from the different individuals she interviewed, along with quoting material from student journals and essays. She also summarized student classroom behavior that she observed. In many ways, this is similar to a lawyer arguing a case in a court of law.

Tactic 8, *rival explanations*, is one that few researchers have used but is a powerful addition to bolster the credibility of her conclusions. For Harklau's study, for example, one plausible explanation, in my opinion, might have been that the findings were not due to institutional representations but rather a misalignment of students' abilities with their programs. The college program was geared toward new foreign students who needed socialization as well as language training. The student participants of the study were mismatched with a program not meant for them. An alternative explanation could be that the particular US high school used in the study did not prepare their long-term resident ESL students with the study habits needed to compete at college level. Had Harklau proposed one or two competing explanations such as these and shown how her explanation was superior, she would have contributed greatly to her conclusions.

The example of Harklau's (2000) study shows how the 12 tactics drawn from combining the work of Miles and Huberman (1994) and Creswell (1998; see Table 7.1) are a reasonable way to evaluate the analysis of verbal data found in the results section of studies using qualitative approaches. As mentioned previously, not all of the tactics need to be used before the analysis is deemed credible by consumers. However, having some in each of the two categories certainly helps. Harklau (2000) clearly presented credibility evidence in both areas, which has definitely added to the main argument of her paper.

Exercise 7.1

Find a recent study of interest that used a qualitative research design that resulted in verbal data. Complete the following using these points.

1. Begin by stating what qualitative procedure was used by the researcher(s).
2. Describe the data that were the bases of any patterns or explanations.
3. Summarize any patterns/themes that the research found in the data.
4. Use Table 7.1 to describe the tactics used by the researcher to verify any proposed patterns or themes.
5. Summarize any explanations and conclusions the researcher proposed to explain the patterns/themes observed.
6. Use Table 7.1 to describe any strategies used to add credibility to any proposed explanations and conclusions made by the research.

Section 2: Analysis of Numerical Data

Many researchers try to answer their research questions by first converting their ideas and constructs into some form of numerical data before analysis. The main reason is that numerical data are generally easier to work with than verbal data. Not only are there a number of statistical procedures available to quickly identify patterns and relationships in large sets of data; these are also able to estimate whether the findings are greater than random chance. The purpose of this section is to introduce you to some of the most common procedures used to analyze numerical data and some of the basic concepts that underpin them.

However, before going any further, I want to address some of the reservations people have toward this topic. One word that seems to strike some trepidation in many of my students and some of my colleagues is *statistics*. One friend jokingly refers to it as *sadistics*. I have the strong impression that many avoid reading the results section of research studies because of the statistical terms that they might encounter. They see things like $p < .001$, df, Σ, r, t, and F and say to themselves, "No way; it's all Greek to me!"

Unfortunately, I find much of the reluctance toward statistics more a result of some traumatic experience people have had in their past with math. The result is that they have become *math-phobics*, which can develop into *stat-phobics*.

I believe that there are two things that turn a lot of people off about statistics: math formulas and a lot of technical jargon. Fortunately, understanding statistical formulas is not necessary for the consumer of research. Instead, the important things are to know why a certain statistical procedure was used for answering a research question and to have a basic understanding of what the results mean. After reading this section, I trust that you will have some degree of confidence in these areas.

The second hurdle that people must cross when dealing with statistics is the jargon that statisticians use. This is not as easy as it should be because different terms are used for the same thing depending on the discipline in which the statistician is working—as you will see later, alpha (α) does not always mean a Cronbach alpha. This section will give you a good grasp of the terminology as you see these terms applied in actual research situations.

Overview of Statistics

To understand the basic concept behind statistics, we need to review the concepts of *sample* and *population* discussed in Chapter 4. Recall that the population is the entire number of people to which researchers want to generalize their conclusions. The sample is a subgroup of that total number. Statistics are quantities (or numbers) gathered on a sample. They are estimates of what would be found if the whole population were used. Quantities that are gathered directly from the entire population are referred to as *parameters*. Parameters are the *true* values. They exactly describe the population. Because we are almost always dealing with samples, we use statistics rather than parameters.

However, when statistics (i.e., estimates) are used, we have to make inferences about what exists in the population. See Figure 7.1 to illustrate this process. As with any inference, mistakes can be made. Using statistics helps us understand what chance we are taking of making a mistake when inferring from the sample to the population. (Now, if you understand

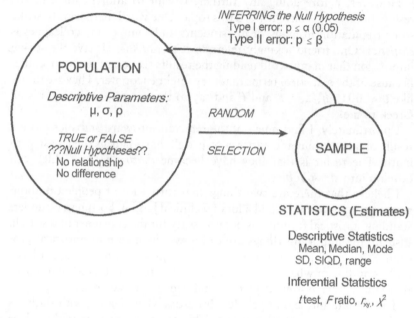

Figure 7.1 The Inferential Process from Sample to Population

what you have just read, you are well on your way to grasping a useful understanding of statistics.)

Statistics can be divided into two main categories: *descriptive* and *inferential*. As the name implies, *descriptive statistics* are those that describe a set of data. They are the fuel used by *inferential statistics* to generate answers to research questions. Inferential statistics not only produce answers in the form of numbers, they also provide information that determines whether researchers can generalize their findings to a target population.

The following subsections of this chapter expand these two general types of statistics. Obviously, they will not exhaust all that there is about these topics. In this regard, I see statistics like an onion; there are many layers (my students agree with the analogy as they shed some tears). This section will only deal with the outer layers at most. However, I have added another layer in Appendix B that takes you a little deeper into some of the more technical aspects of each of these statistical types if you want to gain some deeper insights. I also include in this appendix some more less-common procedures that you may want to continue with after mastering the following sections. The outer layers presented below give you enough information to be able to understand the majority of the studies that you will read. When you come across something in a research

Table 7.3 Three Important Areas in Descriptive Statistics

Shape of Data	Averageness	Variance
Symmetrical	Mean	Standard deviation
Skewness	Median	Interquartile range
Multimodal	Mode	Range

study not mentioned in the following, it most likely has been treated in Appendix B and my complementary website.

Understanding Descriptive Statistics

There are three basic concerns that should be addressed when using descriptive statistics to describe numerical data: the shape of the distribution, measures of average, and measures of variation (see Table 7.3).

The first is regarding the shape of the data. The concern is whether the data are symmetrically distributed and approximate a normal curve.[2] The importance of knowing this directly relates to researchers' choice of the statistics used in their study, both descriptive and inferential. This is seldom mentioned in most research articles, but it is important. Suffice it to state here that if a distribution of data is severely skewed (i.e., lopsided), rectangular (i.e., no curve at all), or multimodal (i.e., more than one cluster of data; see Table 7.3), certain statistics should not be used. Two common indicators are used to test this: the Kolomogorov–Smirnov (sounds like Russian vodka) and Shapiro–Wilk tests. If you want to go to the next level of the onion on this matter, see Appendix B.

Based on the shape of the data, the second concern is which statistic to use to describe *average*. There are three: mean, median, and mode (see Table 7.3). Briefly defined, the *mean* is computed by adding up all the scores and dividing by the total number of scores. The *median* is the middle point in the distribution of data, which divides the number of people in half. The *mode* is the most frequent score.

The reason that there are three measures used for average is discussed more fully in Appendix B. However, for research purposes, the mean is the most common estimate of average used by researchers for numerical data. However, on the occasion that the data distribution does not approximate a normal distribution, other indicators of average more accurately represent the data distribution.

The third concern also affected by the shape of the data is what statistic to use to indicate how much the data varies (i.e., the *variance*). There are also three different measures of variation (see Table 7.3): standard deviation, interquartile range, and range. The first, related to the mean, is the average deviation of scores from the mean. The second, related to the median, estimates where the middle 50 percent of the scores are located in the data distribution. The third is the distance from the lowest to the highest scores in the distribution. More detailed discussion is in Appendix B regarding how these three are used and relate to one another. However, because the standard deviation (*SD*) is the one most commonly used in research, it will get more treatment in the following discussions. Similar to the use of the mean, the *SD* is only appropriate for describing data if the distribution does not vary too much from normalcy.

Understanding Inferential Statistics

I began the section on statistics with the discussion about how researchers attempt to infer their findings to a population based on a sample of participants/objects (see Figure 7.1). This inferential process is where inferential statistics plays a crucial role. The main goal for the remainder of this chapter is to describe the various inferential statistical procedures that are commonly used, explain why they are used, and provide examples from published research in applied linguistics that have used these procedures. However, before going on to these various procedures, I must first discuss the meaning of the *null hypothesis, statistical significance, and effect size*. In my opinion, the need for the consumer to understand these two concepts is more important than remembering the names of the statistical procedures that will be described afterwards. In addition, I will discuss the assumptions that need to be met regarding data distributions, which determine what type of statistical procedures are used.

The Null Hypothesis

The notion of statistical significance directly relates to the testing of the null hypothesis. Therefore, I first discuss this famous hypothesis (although you may have never heard of it), which all studies test if they use inferential statistics, regardless of whether they explicitly say so. This is followed with a discussion of *statistical significance*, which is highly related.

   In essence, inferential statistical procedures can be boiled down to answering two types of questions: *are there relationships* between variables or *are there differences* between groups of data? The null hypothesis, as the word *null* suggests, assumes that there is either *no* relationship between variables or that there is *no* difference between groups. Regardless of whether there is a research hypothesis (also referred to as the alternative hypothesis), the null hypothesis is always there to be tested. In exploratory studies, for instance, where there are no stated hypotheses, behind every relationship being studied there is a null hypothesis that states there is no relationship to be found. For every study that explores whether there is a difference between groups of people, there is a null hypothesis that states that there is no real difference between the groups.

Few published studies in applied linguistics journals explicitly state their null hypotheses these days. Yet, whether stated or not, they are always inferred in the background. A good example of a study where a number of null hypotheses were clearly stated without any stated research hypothesis is one by Mekheimer and Aldosari (2013). They used a quasi-experimental longitudinal design to study the effectiveness of the integrated language skills instruction approach with EFL students. They stated four purposes for the study and five null hypotheses, for example "There are no statistical significant differences between post-test measures of reading comprehension and vocabulary development of experimental and control students" (p. 1266). If the statistical test used rejected any of these null hypotheses, the researchers could conclude that most probably there is a difference. The following will expand this.

Now why would someone want to state their hypothesis in the null form? Why not state the hypothesis in the positive: there will be a significant difference between programs? In practice, many researchers state their hypothesis in the positive. However, it is more accurate to state the hypothesis in the negative because it is this hypothesis that inferential statistics tests, not the positively stated hypotheses. Be that as it may, the answer to my question lies in making valid logical arguments. For those who would like to understand more about the logical argument that is the basis for using the null hypothesis, visit my companion website.

Statistical Significance

You will encounter the term *statistical significance* much more often than *null hypothesis* when reading the results section of an article; however, the two terms are very much interrelated. When researchers refer to some result as *statistically significant*, they are referring to the *null hypothesis*, regardless of whether they are aware of it.

Statistical significance has to do with the probability of a mistake being made when inferring that the results found in a sample reflect some truth about the target population (see Figure 7.1). This mistake (or error) is directly related to the null hypothesis. Figure 7.2 should help to illustrate this discussion. The heading over the columns of the 2 × 2 matrix[3] is labeled *reality* (i.e., what is true for the population). There are only two possibilities: either the null hypothesis is true (column one) or it is false (column two). That is, there is either no true relationship or difference between variables in the population (i.e., the null hypothesis is true) or there is a relationship or difference in the population (i.e., the null hypothesis is false). There is no middle ground.

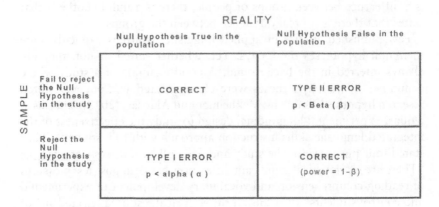

Figure 7.2 Testing the Null Hypothesis

However, in research using a sample it is impossible to know for sure whether the null hypothesis is true unless the research is done on the whole population. This means that the truth about the null hypothesis must be inferred from the sample to the population.

The heading for the rows of the matrix in Figure 7.2 is labeled *sample*. Again, there are only two possibilities: the results either *fail to reject* the null hypothesis or they *reject* the null hypothesis. If the results show that no relation or difference was found, then the findings fail to reject the null hypothesis (i.e., no statistical significance was found). In this case, no error was made (see Figure 7.2, column one, row one). However, if the null hypothesis is, in fact, false in the population (i.e., there is a true relationship or difference between variables), the results from the sample are misleading and an error has been made. This is known as a *Type II error* (Figure 7.2, column two, row one). That is, the results of the study failed to reveal that the null hypothesis was false in the population. Moving down to row two, the other possible finding from the sample is that the results reject the null hypothesis. Translated, this means that a statistically significant relationship or difference was found in the results. Yet, if in the population (i.e., reality) there was no relation or difference (column one), then to infer from the sample to the population that the null hypothesis was false would be erroneous. This is referred to as a *Type I error*. However, if the null hypothesis was truly false in the population (column two), it would be correct to infer that there was probably a relationship, or difference in the population based on the findings from the sample. (At this point, I suggest that you stop and ponder on all of this. Very few grasp the above in one reading.)

I am sure you did not fail to notice in column one/row two and column two/row one the $p <$ alpha $(\alpha)^4$ and $p <$ beta (β), respectively. These have to do with the probabilities of making a Type I and a Type II error. The most common one cited in results sections is the probability of making a Type I error ($p < \alpha$). Statistical significance is based on this estimate.

Statistical significance has been somewhat arbitrarily defined by statisticians (and probably some gamblers) as the probability of making a Type I error either equal to or less than 5 percent (i.e., $p \leq .05$). Translated, this means that there is a 5 percent chance or less that a mistake has been made when inferring that the null hypothesis (i.e., no relationship or no difference) is not true in the population (i.e., the null hypothesis is rejected). Sometimes you will see other probabilities such as $p < .01$ or $p < .001$. These, of course, are even smaller than $p < .05$, which means that the probability of making a Type I error is even less (1 percent or .1 percent, respectively). Mekheimer and Aldosari (2013), for example, found statistically significant differences between the treatment and control groups' posttests for all speaking and writing tasks at the $p < .01$ level. This does not mean that their findings were 99 percent true—a common misunderstanding of what statistical significance means. What it means is that they can have a lot of confidence that they did not make a Type I error.

Two other misconceptions are common regarding statistical significance. One is to think that, because something is statistically significant, there is a strong relationship between variables or a big difference between groups. This may not, in fact, be the case. It is not uncommon to see small relationships or small differences statistically significant. The reason is that statistical significance is directly related to the size of the sample. If the sample size is fairly large, then small relationships or small differences may come out to be statistically significant. When the sample size is smaller, the same statistical value found for a relationship or a difference will not be statistically significant.

Here is where the probability of making a Type II error becomes important. When the sample size is relatively small and the results were found not to be statistically significant (i.e., the null hypothesis failed to be rejected), the probability of making a Type II error is higher than when a larger sample is used. This means that, in reality, the null hypothesis may be false (i.e., there is a relationship or difference), but due to a small sample size the results failed to reveal this. Another way to say this is that researchers might have found a statistically significant relationship or difference had they used a larger sample. For more information on the Type II error and a discussion on the related topic of *power*, go to Appendix B.

The other common misunderstanding regarding statistical significance is to confuse it with *practical significance*. As mentioned above, a relationship may be weak but still statistically significant; or a difference between groups may be small but still statistically significant. Here is where we can be misled if we are not careful when reading statistics results. If a relationship is weak or a difference between groups is small, regardless of how statistically significant it is, there may be no practical use for the results. For example, who wants to spend money and time making curricular changes if students using a new method only increase by a few test points compared with those using a traditional method, even if the result was statistically significant. This point is illustrated in several research studies mentioned later in the chapter. Related to this is the concept of *effect size*, which many journals (e.g., *Language Learning*) require when reporting statistical significance.

Effect Size

Yes, size does matter when it comes to looking at the practical significance of statistical findings. In fact, meta-analysis research deals mainly with effect size and many consider it more important than statistical significance. Here is a brief explanation about what it is and does. It is mainly a measure of the magnitude of the difference between groups or the magnitude of a relationship. It is one thing to get statistical significance; it is another to realize the magnitude of the difference. When it comes to practical significance or usefulness of the findings, effect size is important to know.

There is a whole set of indices used today to show effect sizes. For correlations you will see eta-squared η^2, omega-squared ω^2, Cohen's f^2, and Cohen's q. For differences between groups you will encounter Cohen's d, Glass's Δ, Hedges's g, and more. If you want to go into more depth on these, go to https://en.wikipedia.org/wiki/Effect_size. Also check out Appendix B and my companion website.

Assumptions Regarding Data Distributions

There are two main assumptions that need to be met for deciding which statistical procedures will be used: normalcy of data and homogeneity of variance. The first has to do with whether the data approximates a normal distribution (see previous discussion under descriptive statistics). To use different sets of data that are not close to being the same shape or highly skewed will lead to faulty conclusions. Researchers use tests such as Kolomogorov–Smirnov and Shapiro–Wilk to determine whether there are violations. The second has to do with whether the variances between different sets of data are comparable enough (i.e., homogenous) to use for determining correlations or differences. To test this assumption, researchers use tests such as Hartley's Fmax, Cochran's, Levene's and Barlett's tests to determine any violations. Strangely, you will rarely see researchers reporting that they have tested this assumption about their data, although they often report testing for normalcy. As you will see later, if either of these assumptions is not met, nonparametric statistics will be used.

Although the previous discussion seems to be beyond what a consumer might need to understand in a results section, the issues discussed above are the foundation stones for building an understanding of the statistical procedures about to be outlined. However, before going on to the more interesting stuff, I suggest you do the following exercise to give yourself feedback on how well you have understood this last section. Rushing ahead without grasping what we have just read will hinder understanding the following section.

Exercise 7.2

Choose a study that uses numerical data.

1. Was the study looking for relationships or differences between groups?
2. Look for any mention of a null hypothesis.
3. Now examine the results section and look for values like $p < .05$, $p < .01$ or some index of effect size.
4. How does the researcher interpret these results?
5. What is the probability of the Type I error being made in this study?
6. Explain what this means in your own words.

Inferential Statistical Procedures

There seems to be no end to all the statistical procedures that are available for analyzing numerical data. To describe them all would take several large volumes. For this reason, I have selected the most common statistical procedures that are presented in the applied linguistic literature in this section. The procedures presented look at several more layers of the statistical onion, but there are others that lie deeper. For those who would like to go further than what is presented here, more issues and procedures are presented in Appendix B, along with a discussion on how they are used.

At the end of this current section, the consumer should be able to understand what some common statistical procedures are used for and what their results mean. There are no formulas to understand or to calculate, only definitions, applications, and interpretations. Examples from published research are given to show how these procedures have been applied.

Inferential statistics can be divided into two general categories: *nonparametric* and *parametric* statistics (see Figure 7.3). Nonparametric

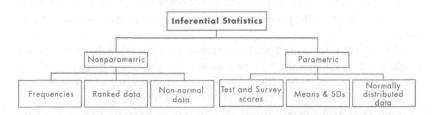

Figure 7.3 The Two Main Categories of Inferential Statistics with Corresponding Data Types

statistics are used for analyzing data in the form of frequencies, ranked data,[5] and data that do not approximate a normal distribution or homogeneity of variance. Parametric statistics are used for any data that do not stray too far from these two assumptions and typically involve the use of means and standard deviations. Scores on tests and surveys usually fit these criteria.

As previously mentioned, the objectives of most researchers are to find relationships between variables or differences between groups. Under each of these objectives there are both nonparametric and parametric procedures for analyzing data.

Relationships Between Variables

Figure 7.4 summarizes some of the more frequently used procedures according to the two types of statistical procedures: nonparametric and parametric.

Nonparametric Procedures

Under the *relationships/nonparametric* heading on the left side of Figure 7.4, there are two procedures that are frequently seen in published research: *chi-square* and *Spearman rank correlation (rho)*. There are several others, but they are less commonly used. All of them have to do with assessing whether a relationship exists between at least two variables.

The Pearson *chi-square* (pronounced ky-square and portrayed with the Greek symbol χ^2) is the procedure of preference when dealing with data in the form of frequencies (or relative frequencies in the form of percentages). In its simplest form, the chi-square procedure compares the observed frequency (or percentages) of the occurrences within each level of a variable with what would be expected if no relationship existed (i.e., the null hypothesis).

For example, if researchers ask the question "Is there a relationship between gender and success in learning English as a foreign language?"

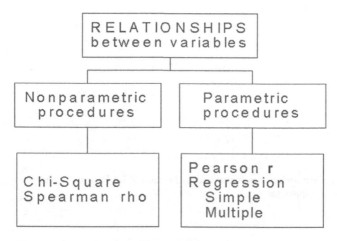

Figure 7.4 Statistical Procedures for Analyzing Relationships

they would compare a random sample of males and females on their success rate. Figure 7.5 illustrates what the data might look like if there were 40 females and 40 males sampled. Note that the null hypothesis would predict that there would be no difference between the number of males and females who pass or fail. If this were true, then the expected frequency should be 20/20 for each sex, which is indicated by the numbers in parentheses. However, in our fictional data the researcher found that 27 females and 17 males passed, and 13 females and 23 males failed. Can researchers conclude that there is a relationship? Although the frequencies appear to differ, do they differ from what would be expected if the null hypothesis were true? Rather than rely on an "eyeball" analysis, researchers could do a chi-square analysis. Out of curiosity, I did an analysis on this data and obtained a chi-square value of 5.05 which is statistically significant at p = .02. The null hypothesis is rejected with a 2 percent probability of making a Type I error. Researchers can therefore conclude that there is most probably a relationship between gender and success rate at learning ESL.

To illustrate with a real study, recall in Chapter 5 that Moskovsky, Alrabai, Paolini, and Ratcheva (2013) examined the effects of teachers' motivational strategies on the motivation of students. They divided participants into two groups (treatment and control). To eliminate any preexisting differences between the two groups, they matched participants on a number of demographic characteristics. They performed a chi-square analysis on the final placement matrix to ensure that there was no bias in the placement of participants. They found only one, region of origin, where there was a significant difference between treatment and control

	Passed	Failed	Total
Males	17 (20)	23 (20)	40
Females	27 (20)	13 (20)	40

Figure 7.5 Comparisons of Males Versus Females Who Passed and Failed in Frequencies

groups ($\chi^2 = 10.898$, $p < .005$). However, they reported that the effect size was small (Cramer's $V = .19$), so they did not expect any distortion of their results from this. (I threw these stats in here to expose the reader to the kinds of things you see in results sections.)

The second method for examining relationships under nonparametric statistics is the *Spearman rank-order* correlation coefficient, also known as the Spearman rho correlation coefficient. This procedure analyzes data in the form of ranks, and the correlation coefficient is symbolized by either r_s or ρ_{rank} (using the Greek symbol rho). This coefficient ranges from $\rho_{rank} = -1.0$ to $\rho_{rank} = +1.0$. The first value (-1.0) means that there is a perfect negative relationship: as ranking of one variable goes up, the other goes down in perfect order. The value of $+1.0$ is a perfect positive relationship, where both variables' rankings correspond perfectly in the same direction. A coefficient of 0.00 means that there is no relationship. As a coefficient increases between 0.00 and 1.00, despite whether it has a + or − sign in front of it, the relationship between the two variables increases: The + increases in a positive direction, and the − increases in a negative direction.

Moghtadi, Koosha, and Lofti (2014) used the Spearman rho procedure in their study to test whether L2 (Persian) proficiency correlates with L3. They gave two tests of proficiency (Persian and English) to Azari students and computed correlations with the Spearman rho procedure. They did not explain why they chose this nonparametric procedure, but one can assume that the data did not meet the assumptions for a parametric procedure. Moghtadi et al. reported a rho of .60 with a sample size of 100 ($N=100$), statistically significant at $p < .01$. They interpreted this as moderate positive correlation, which I would agree with. However, one needs to keep in mind that large samples can produce statistically significant correlation coefficients despite being small. The question becomes whether, despite the correlation being statistically significant, a correlation of this magnitude is of any practical use. More is stated about this under parametric procedures.

There are other nonparametric measures of relationships that you will occasionally see in research, such as the Cohen's Kappa, phi coefficient, Cramer's V, Somer's d, and so on (see Appendix B for more information). To give proper treatment of all of these procedures would require a separate book; however, if you are interested in knowing more about these other procedures you can do a search on your favorite web browser by entering *nonparametric statistics*, or enter the specific name of the procedure you are interested in.

Before moving over to some parametric procedures for relationships, I suggest you look at a study related to your interest that has used some form of nonparametric statistic to examine a relationship. The following exercise gives you steps to follow to guide you in this task. Enjoy!

Exercise 7.3

Find a study that looked for a relationship between two or more variables using either chi-square or the Spearman rho (or any of the other statistics listed above) in its statistical analysis.

1. What form (frequencies, percentages, ranks) are the data in?
2. What is the null hypothesis being tested (explicitly or implicitly)?
3. Are the results statistically significant? At what level? What does this mean regarding making inferences?

Parametric Procedures

One of the most common parametric statistics used to examine relationships between variables is the *Pearson product-moment correlation coefficient* (PPMC) (see Figure 7.4). With a name like this, it is no wonder people don't like to look at statistics. It is more commonly referred to the Pearson r, after Karl Pearson. You will also see it reported simply as r or r_{xy}. This coefficient, like the Spearman rho, is computed on two variables for every participant, such as measures of grammar ability and writing ability. The end product is an r that ranges from -1.00 to $+1.00$, indicating a perfect negative or perfect positive relationship, respectively. As with all coefficients of correlation, a 0.00 means no relationship. The null hypothesis usually states that the relationship is 0.00 in the population.

A study we looked at in Chapter 5 by Venkatagiri and Levis (2007) studied the relationship between phonological awareness and speech comprehensibility. They calculated Pearson correlations on all relationships between 17 measures for phonological awareness and phonological short-term memory tasks and intelligibility ratings. This resulted in 128 correlation coefficients, which they weeded through to find the relationships they were interested in. One of their findings was that a Pearson's correlation coefficient between comprehensibility scores and phonological awareness scores was statistically significant ($r = .491$, $p < .05$), which suggests a mild positive relationship. Interestingly, they did not discuss the negative correlation ($r = -.58$, $p < .05$) between two of their tasks, which was also statistically significant, although they reported non-significant relationships between other tasks.

Using the above results, I want to illustrate a misapplication of the correlation coefficient that occasionally appears in the literature (see Chapter 5)—correlation means causation. Although Venkatagiri and Levis (2007) clearly stated that their results cannot show causation, someone might think—and some people do—that greater phonological awareness causes greater comprehensibility. Although this might be the case, correlations do not directly show this. Why? Because correlations are bidirectional (i.e., symmetrical), which means that both of the following statements are correct: A correlates with B, and B correlates with A. In other words, Venkatagiri and Levis could have stated that greater comprehensibility positively correlates with phonological awareness. To show a causal relationship, they would have had to use an experimental design where a treatment was given to increase the participants' phonological awareness followed by some assessment of their pre- and postinstruction speech comprehension. In fact, Venkatagiri and Levis suggested just this. At most, a correlational analysis can find if there is a potential causal relationship before going to the more arduous task of doing a full-blown experiment. If there is no statistically significant correlation, a causal relationship can be ruled out right from the start.

A second important misuse of the correlation coefficient is assuming that, because a correlation coefficient is statistically significant, it means that it has important practical use. This is where a measure of the effect size would be helpful. Unfortunately, Venkatagiri and Levis (2007) do not report any effect sizes for the correlations they found. Is a correlation of $r = .27$ of any practical use, for example? This correlation would be statistically significant if the sample size were 100 participants. The answer is made clear when you square the correlation coefficient. This is signified by r^2 and is a measure of the *percentage of common variance* between the two variables. Another way to say this is that r^2 represents the amount of variation that the two variables have in common. This value is commonly used to determine the importance of the relationship. We can see clearly in this case that $r = .27$ becomes $r^2 = .07$, meaning that the two variables only have 7 percent variance in common—not much to warrant any practical significance. However, one of the correlations that Venkatagiri and Levis found (i.e., $r = .58$) with 17 participants shows more potential for practical use. The r^2 = .25, which indicates 25 percent common variance.

The issue of amount of common variance is important because some people may try to push their own agenda based on statistically significant correlations that are not strong enough to justify an agenda that costs time and money to implement—Venkatagiri and Levis (2007) did not do this, by the way. Therefore, when you want to make your own evaluation of the strength of a correlation coefficient, simply square the correlation and interpret the result as the strength of the relationship.

The next common parametric statistical procedure used to explore relationships is *regression analysis*. This is highly related to the Pearson *r* coefficient and r^2. Regression analysis is used to identify variables (referred to as *independent variables*) that either predict or explain another variable (the *dependent variable*). There are two forms of regression analysis: *simple* and *multiple*. In its *simple* form, there is only one independent variable and one dependent variable. The independent variable is the predictor or the variable that explains, and the dependent variable is the variable being predicted or explained. For example, if we want to find out whether we can predict success in university for foreign students defined by their grade point average (GPA) with their TOEFL results, we would use a simple regression procedure. The TOEFL scores would be the independent variable (i.e., the predictor) and students' GPA after their first semester or year at university. On the other hand, we might want to know how much students' scores on an essay exam (i.e., the DV) can be explained by their grammar ability (i.e., the IV). The first addresses a prediction question, the second an explanation question. It is important to note here that in neither case are we suggesting that the IVs are causing the variation in the DVs. See Venkatagiri and Levis (2007), cited above, who used this procedure and found that composite phonological awareness scores accounted for approximately 19 percent of the variance of rated comprehensibility scores.

In its *multiple* forms, regression analysis is used to determine which combination of independent variables best predicts or explains the variation in one dependent variable. For instance, we might want to know what combination of independent variables best predicts or explains success in university. Thus, multiple regression procedure will be the correct procedure.

The key statistic for regression analysis is R^2. It means the same thing as the Pearson r^2 mentioned previously. In fact, $R^2 = r^2$ when there is only one predictor variable. That is, R^2 is the percentage of variance in the dependent variable that is related to the combination of predictor (i.e., independent) variables and ranges from 0 percent to 100 percent. The first thing that is tested for statistical significance is the R^2. If it is found to be statistically significant, the null hypothesis, which states that no variance can be predicted (or explained) by the IVs, is rejected. When this happens, each predictor variable (IV) in the equation is tested individually for statistical significance to see if it contributes to the overall prediction (or explanation) of the dependent variable. A study using multiple regression for prediction purposes was done by Martinsen, Alvord, and Tanner (2014). Among other things, they asked whether level of instruction and/or motivational intensity could predict foreign accent rating. The first two were the independent variables with foreign accent rating the dependent variable. (Sidenote: based on an earlier discussion, IVs are usually considered variables that cause change in the DV, but in regression language this is not the case. In regression language, the IVs are the predictor variables and the DV is the predicted variable.) Martinsen et al. did a step-wise regression analysis where they first entered one IV, level of instruction, as a predictor into the equation (step one). They found this to be statistically significant ($R^2 = .669$, $p < .05$), which meant that level of instruction accounts for 67 percent of the variance of the rating for foreign accent. They then did step two by adding motivation intensity to the equation, making two predictors. This added another 1.5 percent to the variance accounted for, which is not much, although it was a statistically significant increase. The more variance of the DV, or predicted variable, that is accounted for by the predictors the better the prediction. The practical question that researchers must ask in a case like this is whether the cost (time and money) of adding variables that contribute very little to the prediction is worth gathering. This was not the purpose of this study but it does illustrate this point.

There are more complex methods using correlational procedures for dealing with more specialized questions that I will not cover here. So, when you come across terms like *factor analysis, discrimination analysis, latent trait analysis, structural equation modeling,* and so on, remember that these involve correlating variables with other variables for the purpose of identifying which variables share common variance. Not only that, but some of these procedures are actually used to detect cause-and-effect relationships. You might think I just contradicted myself after all that ranting and raving about correlation not meaning causation. Not really. When these procedures are used to determine cause-and-effect relationships, they are guided by specific theories that instruct the researcher where to place each variable in the equation to manipulate all the variances. If I go any further than this, you might close the book and run, so I will move on. More on this topic will be on the companion website.

Exercise 7.4

Find a study that looks for relationships between variables using either the Pearson *r* or one of the two regression procedures.

1. What are the variables? (In the case of regression, what are the IVs and the DV?)
2. Describe the data used in the analysis.
3. What is the null hypothesis being tested (explicitly or implicitly)?
4. Are the results statistically significant? At what level? What does this mean regarding making inferences?

Differences Between Groups of Data

The second type of research objective is to find whether groups of individuals differ from one another. As with relationships, both nonparametric and parametric procedures are used to analyze these differences (see Figure 7.6).

Nonparametric Procedures

Chi-square analysis is also used for finding differences between groups. It is used when data are in the form of frequencies (or relative frequencies in the form of percentages). Chatouphonexay and Intaraprasert (2014) compared beliefs about English language learning between EFL pre-service and in-service teachers in higher education institutions in Laos. Their data came from questionnaires adapted from a standardized instrument developed for this purpose. They used chi-square analysis to test the differences in frequency of choices on a five-point rating scale. The researchers combined *strongly disagree* and *disagree* into one disagreement category, and the *agree* and *strongly agree* into an agreement category, leaving the middle, uncertainty, category as is. This is done sometimes to

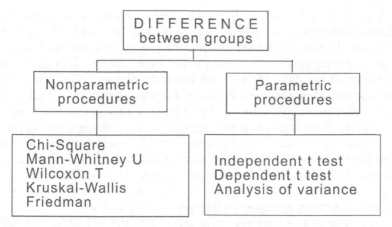

Figure 7.6 Statistical Procedures for Analyzing Differences Between Groups

bolster the cell frequencies to meet the conditions for doing a chi-square. They computed a chi-square for each questionnaire item, resulting in 11 out of 39 chi-squares being statistically significant. All but one of 11 χ^2s were statistically significant at the $p < .001$ level. Although Chatouphonexay and Intaraprasert did not adjust the probability level for committing a Type I error owing to many comparisons, they did report that the majority of their chi-squares were significant at $p < .001$.

By adjusting for the Type I error, I mean that for each comparison (i.e., χ^2 computed) there is a 5 percent probability of making a Type I error ($p < .05$). When multiple comparisons are made with the same level of 5 percent for each comparison, the probability of making a Type I error increases. For 10 comparisons, for instance, the overall probability increases to 40 percent (plug "familywise error rates" into Google for more information). Chatouphonexay and Intaraprasert (2014) would have been more precise to report what the probability level was for each of the chi-squares instead of lumping them all under $p < .05$. They would have been more accurate if they had limited the overall probability of making a Type I error to a much lower level, such as $p < .001$, for each comparison. Of course, this would have meant that the one statistically significant chi-square at the $p < .05$ level would not have been accepted as statistically significant.

When the data are other than frequencies and do not approximate a normal distribution, the difference between two independent samples[6] of participants on some dependent variable is typically analyzed using the *Mann–Whitney U test*. This procedure converts the data into ranks within each group for analysis. There are no means or SDs involved. The statistic computed is a *U* value, which, if statistically significant at the $p < .05$ level, means that the difference between the two groups is statistically significant.

A study done by Kim and Taguchi (2015) illustrates the use of the Mann–Whitney statistic. Remember that I cited this study in Chapter 5. Kim and Taguchi examined the role of task complexity on learning request-making expressions among junior high students. They tested for normalcy of the data distributions using the Shapiro–Wilk tests. This revealed that their data violated the assumption of normalcy needed for using a parametric procedure (discussed later), so they used nonparametric procedures. They stated that they set their familywise error rate (Type I error rate) at $p < .05$. For examining the differences between the two treatment groups (aka pair-wise comparisons), they used the Mann–Whitney *U* tests. Rather than reporting values for *U*, they reported *z* scores (e.g., $z = 3.04$, $p < .001$). This is often done because *z* scores, once you get to know them, are easier to interpret than *U* scores.

When two sets of data are not independent, the *Wilcoxon matched-pairs signed rank test* (also known as the *Wilcoxon T test*) is used to test any difference. This means that the two sets of data are *dependent* or *correlated* with one another in some way. This can occur in two different situations. The first is when the two sets of data are gathered from the same group of participants. The second occurs when two different groups of participants are compared on one variable while matched on some other variable. The first situation can occur, for instance, when data are gathered before some treatment is given on a pretest and compared with data from a similar measurement after the treatment on a posttest. Both measurements are made on the same participants. The second situation could occur when the researcher tries to control for (or eliminate) the effects of an extraneous variable, such as intelligence, on the dependent variable by pairing up participants from the two groups based on that extraneous variable.

An example of the first situation is found in Kim and Taguchi (2015), who used a pretest, posttest, and delayed posttest design to measure the effects of the reasoning condition on the two groups. It is clear that the same participants were measured three times: pre-, post-, and delayed posttest. They tested the four within-group differences using the Wilcoxon signed ranks test. This resulted in four tests: pre with post, pre with delayed post, and post with delayed posts. They reported their results again using z scores (e.g., $z = -3.87$, $p < .001$).

An example for the second situation occurs when researchers want to control for (i.e., eliminate) the effects of an extraneous variable while testing for differences between two groups. They would do this by using the Wilcoxon procedure on the dependent variable by *matching* participants in pairs from the two groups based on the extraneous variable. For this reason, the Wilcoxon procedure is sometimes referred to as the *Wilcoxon matched-pairs signed rank test*. Unfortunately, I have not been able to find an applied linguistics study that has used this matching procedure. However, a quick hypothetical example of using the matching procedure would be to measure attitudes of two different groups of participants (treatment vs control) toward learning a second language; we might want to make sure that our results are not due to differences in language proficiency between the two groups. Thus, we match participants before we begin the treatment by finding two participants with the same language proficiency, however measured, and put one participant into the treatment group and the other in the control group. We do this for the rest of the participants, producing matched pairs. Now we apply the treatment and compare the two groups on a measure of attitude. When using the Wilcoxon method, we would measure the difference in attitude for each matched pair of participants and then compute the Wilcoxon statistic based on those differences.

What happens if a researcher wants to compare more than two sets of data that do not fit the normalcy criterion? The *Kruskal–Wallis test* is typically used for this purpose and is either reported as an H or a χ^2. This method is an extension of the Mann–Whitney test. However, it compares more than two independent groups of participants using the same procedure of ranking data prior to analysis. The study by Kim and Taguchi (2015) also used this test in their study to test the differences between their three treatment conditions (complex, simple, and control groups). Because they had more than two independent groups (i.e., each group had different participants) they used this procedure rather than the Mann–Whitney test. They reported their findings using chi-squares (e.g., $\chi^2 = 35.29$, $p < .001$), even though this is not a chi-square test mentioned previously. (Don't let this put you off. The important thing is for you to know what a Kruskal–Wallis test is and why they used it.) However, Kim and Taguchi's work does not end here. When they found a statistically significant Kruskal–Wallis test, they then had to figure out where the differences exist because all that this test tells you is that somewhere there is a difference between the groups. They did this by using—guess what—the Mann–Whitney U test, where they did all the pair-wise comparisons between the groups. Their results showed that each of the treatment groups outperformed the control group for both types of posttests, but they did not differ from one another. The reason Kim and Taguchi did the Kruskal–Wallis first, rather than going straight to making pair-wise comparisons with the Mann–Whitney, was to control for the Type I error when making multiple comparisons. For each statistical test there is the probability of making a Type I error. So, if one uses the shotgun approach of making all possible pair-wise comparisons, the probability of making a Type I error increases rapidly. They avoided this problem by following the procedure they used.

There is also a nonparametric procedure for testing the difference between three or more sets of dependent data. The *Friedman test* does exactly this. It is very similar to the Wilcoxon T test, in that it tests the differences between different measures on the same set of participants, referred to as *repeated measures* or a *nested design* (see Appendix B).

An example of a study using this procedure was done by Munro, Derwing, and Thomson (2015), who did a two-year longitudinal study examining the segmental pronunciation difficulties between Mandarin and Slavic learners of English in Canada. They recognized that their data did not meet the assumption of normality, so they used nonparametric statistical analyses to test differences. They used the Kruskal–Wallis procedure to test the differences between the two language groups (note: they could have called it the Mann–Whitney U test because they only compared two independent groups). Munro et al. used the Friedman procedure to test any differences between the four times they gathered data over the two years because the measures were on the same participants within each language group. Munro et al. found one statistically significant

Friedman value. However, like the Kruskal–Wallis test of more than two groups, a significant Friedman finding should have been followed up with a series of pair-wise comparisons using the Wilcoxon T tests to determine where the differences lie. By looking at their Figure 1b, it is very possible that there were only one or two differences for the Mandarin group (i.e. the results for the second time of testing were greater than both the first time and third time that data were collected). If this is true, then their conclusion that the Friedman test showed a significant improvement over the two-year period would not have been supported. They were careful to warn the reader, however, that these analyses were only for descriptive purposes, whatever that might mean.

There is a lot more that could be included about nonparametric statistics. In fact, there are entire books that only address nonparametric statistics. However, I have introduced you to some commonly used procedures that you will come across in research. If there are others you see and want to know more about what they do, you can find needed information by searching the web. However, before moving on to parametric statistics, the following exercise provides you with an opportunity to find a study of your own to apply what you have read.

Exercise 7.5

Find a study that looked for differences between groups of data that uses one of the nonparametric procedures discussed above.

1. Describe the data and any reasons why the researcher used the procedure.
2. What are the independent and dependent variables?
3. What is the null hypothesis being tested (explicitly or implicitly)?
4. What statistical procedure is used?
5. Are the results statistically significant? At what level? What does this mean regarding making inferences?

Parametric Statistics

When the assumptions regarding the data distribution are met (normalcy and homogeneity of variance), parametric procedures can be used to analyze differences between groups. The statistical procedures discussed below are almost a mirror image of the ones discussed under the above nonparametric section. One difference is in the type of data that is analyzed, and another is that means and SDs are being compared.

The parametric equivalent to the Mann–Whitney and the Wilcoxon T tests is the t test. It is used to test the difference between two sets of measures on one dependent variable. (Just think of the song "Tea for Two" to help remember this.) Corresponding to the two nonparametric procedures above, the *t* test comes in two forms: *independent* and *dependent*. However, the *t* test requires that the distributions of data do not depart too much from normalcy or the variation in each set of data (i.e., *SD*s) does not differ too much.

The *independent t* test analyzes the difference between the averages (i.e., means) on one dependent variable for two independent groups. This is similar to the Mann–Whitney test on the nonparametric side, except that the *t* test deals with means and variances, not rankings. The two independent groups usually represent two levels of one independent variable, such as male and female for the variable of gender, and the measure used for comparison represents one dependent variable, such as the scores on a single reading test.

Hung's (2015) study, mentioned in Chapter 5, provides an example of this procedure. Remember that she examined the impact of flipping classroom lesson plans on English language learners' learning performance, attitudes, and participation using a quasi-experimental design. The independent variable was the flipped classroom condition: full, semi, and nonflipped control. The dependent variables related to this example were attitude and participation. As far as I see, she did not report testing her data sets for normalcy or homogeneity of variance. She did several independent *t* tests for two of the dependent variables (attitude and participation) using only two levels of the IV: full and semiflipped groups. Attitude was measured by four items in her questionnaire. Hung performed a *t* test on each of these items. Only one of the four was found to be statistically significant ($t = 5.92$, $p < .001$), with the fully flipped group more satisfied then the semiflipped group on that item. Later she concluded by saying that this finding supported previous research that students are more satisfied with flipped classrooms than traditional ones. However, since only three out of four of her questions showed no differences, I am not sure how she can make this conclusion. Maybe it would have been better to test the differences between the fully flipped condition with the nonflipped condition. Later, we will revisit this study under ANOVA.

The *dependent t* test (aka *correlated t test* or *paired t test*) assesses the difference between the means of two sets of scores for either the same group of participants or two groups whose participants have been matched in some way (cf. the Wilcoxon *T* test). An example of the first scenario would be when one group of participants have been given a pretest, followed by a treatment, and then given a posttest. The difference between the means of the two tests is tested using this procedure.

The second scenario would occur if two groups (e.g., males vs females) were being tested on reading achievement, but the participants were matched on some other variable such as intelligence. That is, one male is matched with a female based on an intelligence test and then placed in their corresponding group. By doing this, the researcher eliminates any difference between the two groups due to intelligence. The averages for the two groups are then analyzed for difference by the dependent t test. It is comparable to the Wilcoxon test discussed in the nonparametric section, except that means and variances are used.

Mekheimer and Aldosari (2013), mentioned previously, used a pretest, posttest, and control group design in a quasi-experimental study to examine the effectiveness of an integrated holistic teaching method. To test whether there was any gain between pretests and posttests for each of the groups (treatment and control), they performed a series of dependent (or paired) t tests. As far as I can figure out, they did not test for normalcy or homogeneity of variance of their data distributions before choosing what statistical procedure to use. One other concern I have for their study is that they did not inform the reader that they were doing dependent t tests when testing differences between pre- and posttests, although they reported when they used independent t tests when testing the differences between the experimental and control group. Though related, these are the not the same test. The first compares scores on two tests for the same people group; the second compares scores on the same test for two different people groups. Researchers need to be precise when discussing the procedures they use. Before moving on to a more complex procedure, use the following exercise to help you apply what you have just read.

Exercise 7.6

1. Find a study that looked for differences between two data sets that used some form of the parametric t test.
2. What are the independent and dependent variables?
3. What form are the data in?
4. What is the null hypothesis being tested (explicitly or implicitly)?
5. What statistical procedure(s) is used (dependent or independent t tests)?
6. Are the results statistically significant? At what level? What does this mean regarding making inferences?

Other than the t test, the statistic that is probably the most commonly used in the applied linguistics literature is *analysis of variance* (ANOVA). As the Kruskal–Wallis and the Friedman tests are to the Mann–Whitney and Wilcoxon T tests, respectively, the ANOVA is to the independent and dependent t test. Whereas the t test compares two sets of data, ANOVA is used to compare more than two sets.

The simplest form of ANOVA involves the use of one independent variable and one dependent variable. This is referred to as a *one-way ANOVA*. The IV may have three or more levels with one DV. The objective is to find whether the means for the groups on the dependent variable differ from one another. For instance, say that researchers want to study whether there is any difference on reading proficiency (DV) based on nationality (IV). Thus, they would take equal random samples from three or more nationalities, obtain measures of reading ability, and perform a one-way ANOVA. In effect, the researchers would compare the means between the groups with one another. The statistic reported is the *F ratio*, which is determined to be statistically significant by the same criterion for all inferential statistics ($p \leq .05$).

If the *F* ratio in the above example is statistically significant, it only indicates that somewhere there is at least one difference between the group means that is statistically significant. It does not identify where the differences are. The researcher must now find out where those differences are by performing pair-wise comparisons post hoc (after the fact). Two common ones that are used in the literature are the Tukey's HSD and Newman–Keuls[7] (sounds like a brand of cigarettes) tests. You can think of these tests like you would a series of *t* tests, only they are more stringent regarding making a Type I error for multiple comparisons. There is another procedure used if the researcher wants to combine several groups to compare with one other or with another combination of groups called the Scheffé test.

By now you should realize why we would not simply do a whole bunch of *t* tests. The reason is that the probability of making a Type I error increases with the number of statistical tests. If we do a lot of *t* tests at the $p < .05$ level, we multiply this probability by the number of tests made, as mentioned previously in several places. The ANOVA approach, along with subsequent pair-wise procedures, controls for this by keeping the overall probability of a Type I error at the 5 percent level or less. (There is a repeated measures ANOVA (cf. the Friedman test), which is discussed in Appendix B.)

An illustration of the use of a one-way ANOVA is the study by Hung (2015), previously mentioned. She tested the difference between the three treatment groups in her study: flipped, semiflipped, and control. She performed a one-way ANOVA on her data for each of the three lesson assignments and found a significant *F* value for lesson assessments II and III ($F = 12.56$, $p < .001$; $F = 12.24$, $p < .001$, respectively). As mentioned above, a significant *F* value only tells us that there is at least one difference. It does not tell us where the differences are between the three groups. To test for these differences, Hung used a post hoc Tukey HSD pair-wise procedure. For Lesson II, she found the following pattern: flipped > semiflipped > control (all statistically significant). However, for

Lesson III, she found the flipped group outperforming both the semiflipped and control groups, but the latter two did not differ from one another. As you can see, it is important that such post hoc tests are done.

A slightly more complicated form of ANOVA is the *two-way* ANOVA. This approach is used when a researcher wants to look at the effects of two independent variables on one dependent variable at the same time. Each of the independent variables can have two or more levels. For example, the first independent variable may be nationality, with four levels (e.g., French, Egyptian, Chinese, and Russian). The second independent variable may also have two or more levels, such as gender (male and female). If this study were found in the literature, the analysis would be referred to as a 4 × 2 ANOVA, meaning that it has two independent variables, with the first having four levels and the second having two levels.

The order of the independent variables is not important, although in the above study the nationality would come first and gender second. They can be switched around. Thus, in our example, we might have a 2 × 4 ANOVA (gender by nationality) rather than a nationality (4) by gender (2) ANOVA. However, with any type of ANOVA you can always assume that there is only one dependent variable (also referred to as univariate).

When a two-way ANOVA is performed on the data, there are three things that are being tested. The first is the main effect for the first IV. The second is the main effect for the second IV, and the third is the interaction between the two IVs. *Main effect* can be translated into the question "Are there any differences between the levels of an independent variable taken one at a time, ignoring all else?" In effect, it is like doing a one-way ANOVA on each independent variable. In our example above, the main effect for the IV, nationality, would test whether there are any differences on the dependent variable (e.g., test scores for reading ability) among the four nationalities. If there are, and there are more than two levels of the IV, some form of post hoc pair-wise comparison would need to be made to find out exactly where the differences lie. For each main effect there will be a separate F ratio and $p < \alpha$ for statistical significance.

The third thing to be tested is whether there is any interaction between the two IVs. The interaction is actually more informative than the main effects, although often they are treated as secondary. The interaction informs us whether the dependent variable behaves differently at the different meeting points of the two IVs. Again, using our nationality by gender example, it would be more informative to know if males and females of one nationality performed differently on reading ability tests than males and females do of other nationalities. A statistically significant interaction would suggest that they do. Figure 7.7 contains two graphs (a and b), which illustrate this. Figure 7.7a shows what data might look like when there is a main effect(s) but no interaction, and Figure 7.7b shows what a significant interaction might look like. In the top graph there is a significant main effect for gender but no significant interaction between gender and nationality. Note that the females outperform the males for all the four nationality groups by about the same difference. This graph shows that there is probably a statistically significant main effect for nationality as well. The French, in general, performed higher than the Russians and possibly higher than the Chinese.

In contrast, the lower graph illustrates what a significant interaction might look like. Observe that females outperformed males in the French group but not in the other nationalities, although they were still slightly superior. For illustration's sake, I have added information in the graph that would not normally appear in such a graph in a published article. A significant interaction would be determined by an F ratio, with $p \leq .05$ for the interaction effect, but this F ratio does not tell the researcher where the difference lies. To find this out, the researcher would have to compare the difference between female/male means for each nationality using some form of post hoc comparison. As you can see, finding this differential effect would be more informative then simply knowing that nationalities or genders differ on reading ability as a whole.

Koyama, Sun, and Ockey (2016) provided a good example of the use of a two-way ANOVA when they analyzed their data. Remember from Chapters 4 and 5 that they looked at the effects of previewing test items on multiple-choice listening tests. The first IV (factor) was test condition, with three groups: preview both question stem and answer options, preview stems only, and no preview. The second IV (factor) was listening proficiency level: high and low. The dependent variable was a video-based multiple-choice listening test. This is referred to as a 3 × 2 ANOVA. Prior to performing this analysis they tested the data distributions for normalcy and homogeneity of variance (Levine's test), both of which met the assumptions for ANOVA. Koyama et al.'s results revealed a main effect for test condition, $F(2, 132) = 71.8, p < .05, \eta^2 = .10$), which means that there is at least one significant difference among the three test condition groups. (Note that the 2, 132 refers to degrees of freedom, which will be discussed in Appendix B, and $\eta^2 = .10$ is the effect size discussed earlier). They also found a main effect for listening proficiency, which was not surprising because they deliberately made sure the two groups clearly differed prior to treatment. They did not find a statistically significant 3 × 2 interaction between the two IVs, which means that the pattern of results for the test conditions were the same for both listening proficiency levels. This last finding conflicted with findings of other studies.

For some reason, Koyama et al. did a one-way ANOVA on the test condition, which is redundant since the main effect they found for test condition in the two-way ANOVA was sufficient for testing difference on this factor. At any rate, they correctly followed up this main effect with a

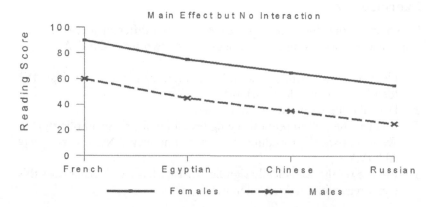

Figure 7.7a Illustration of a Main Effect Between Gender and Ethnic Group

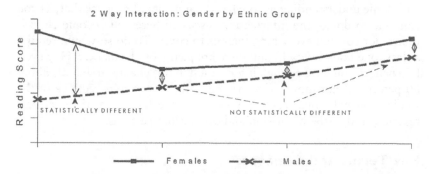

Figure 7.7b Illustration of an Interaction Between Gender and Ethnic Group

post hoc Tukey's HSD test to find out where the differences existed. They found that the Q-option group and the Q-only group outperformed the No-prev. group, but the Q-option and Q-only groups did not differ. They interpreted this to mean that previewing the question stem improved performance on the listening test.

There are many more permutations of ANOVA that will not be discussed here. However, in Appendix B, other more complex designs that can be found in applied linguistic research are presented. If you come across the terms three-way or four-way ANOVA, ANCOVA, MANOVA, or MANCOVA, look in Appendix B for brief explanations with some examples. However, before moving on to the last chapter, I suggest you find a study that has used some form of ANOVA and do the following exercise. In my opinion, there is nothing better than finding a study of one's own interest to see how these procedures work.

Exercise 7.7

Find a study that looks for differences between different levels of independent variables, using either a one-way, or two-way ANOVA.

1. Identify the independent variable(s). How many levels are in each IV? Identify the dependent variable.
2. Describe the nature of the data used.
3. What is the null hypothesis being tested (explicitly or implicitly)?
4. What statistical procedure(s) is used (one-way ANOVA, two-way ANOVA)?
5. Are the results statistically significant? At what level? What does this mean regarding making inferences?

I trust that you have been able to follow through this chapter and feel more confident that you can read through the results section of a study with some understanding as to what is happening. I promise that, as you continue to do so, the information discussed here will become clearer. I have not covered everything there is to cover. To do so would require at least one book by itself, and there are plenty on the market. However, I do believe you have enough information in this chapter to handle about 80 percent, if not more, of what you will see in results sections of the studies you will come across. Now on to the last piece of the typical research study—the discussion and conclusions sections.

Key Terms and Concepts

Analysis of Verbal Data	*Analysis of Numerical Data*
external audits	analysis of variance (ANOVA)
if–then tests	average
information feedback	chi-square
negative evidence	dependent *t* tests
outliers and extreme cases	descriptive statistics
peer review	*F* ratio
replicating findings	Friedman test
rich/thick descriptions	homogeneity of variance
rival explanations	independent *t* test
spurious relationships	inferential statistics
surprises	interquartile range
triangulation	Kruskal–Wallis test
	Mann–Whitney *U* test
	mean
	median
	mode

multiple regression
nonparametric statistical procedures
normal distribution
null hypothesis
one-way ANOVA
pair-wise comparisons
parameters
Pearson product-moment correlation
practical significance
range
regression analysis
skewed distribution
Spearman rank correlation (rho)
standard deviation
statistical significance
two-way ANOVA
Wilcoxon matched-pairs signed rank test
Wilcoxon T test

Notes

1. Miles and Huberman originally treated outliers and extreme cases as separate tactics. However, because they stated that the latter was a type of the former, I combined them into one.
2. This is a bell-shaped curve that has many properties used by research. There is a more detailed discussion in Appendix B.
3. Figure 7.2 is an adaptation of a similar matrix in Hopkins and Glass's (1978, p. 280) work.
4. This is not the Cronbach α, referred to in Chapter 6.
5. Ranked data is data that has been converted into ordinal numbers, i.e., first, second, third, etc.
6. By *independent samples*, it is meant that the participants in one group are different individuals than those in the other group.
7. See http://davidmlane.com/hyperstat/intro_ANOVA.html for more information.

References

Bogdan, R. C., & Biklen, S. K. (1992). *Qualitative research for education: An introduction to theory and methods*. Boston, MA: Allyn & Bacon.

Chatouphonexay, A., & Intaraprasert, C. (2014). Beliefs about English language learning held by EFL pre-service and in-service teachers in Lao People's Democratic Republic. *English Language Teaching*, 7(3), 1–12.

Creswell, J. W. (1998). *Qualitative inquiry and research design: Choosing among five traditions*. Thousand Oaks, CA: SAGE.

Creswell, J. W. (2013). *Qualitative inquiry and research design*. Thousand Oaks, CA: SAGE.

Harklau, L. (2000). "Good Kids" to the "Worst": Representations of English language learners across educational settings. *TESOL Quarterly*, 34, 5–67.

Hopkins, K. D., & Glass, G. V. (1978). *Basic Statistics for the Behavioral Sciences*. Englewood Cliffs, NJ: Prentice-Hall.

Hung, H. (2015). Flipping the classroom for English language learners to foster active learning. *Computer Assisted Language Learning*, 28(1), 81–96.

Kim, Y., & Taguchi, N. (2015). Promoting task-based pragmatics instruction in EFL classroom contexts: The role of task complexity. *The Modern Language Journal*, 99(4), 656–677.

Koyama, D., Sun, A., & Ockey, G. J. (2016). The effects of item preview on video-based multiple-choice listening assessments. Language Learning & Technology, 20(20), 148–165.

Kraemer, A. (2006). Teachers' use of English in communicative German language classrooms: A qualitative analysis. *Foreign Language Annals*, 39, 435–450.

Kubanyiova, M. (2015). The role of teachers' future self guides in creating L2 development opportunities in teacher-led classroom discourse: Reclaiming the relevance of language teacher cognition. *The Modern Language Journal*, 99(3), 565–584.

Lazaraton, A. (2003). Evaluative criteria for qualitative research in applied linguistics: Whose criteria and whose research? *Modern Language Journal*, 87, 1–12.

Lee, G., & Schallert, D. L. (2007). Meeting the margins: Effects of teacher-student relationship on revision processes of EFL students taking composition course. *Journal of Second Language Writing*, 17, 165–182.

Lee-Johnson, Y. L. (2015). A qualitative study of the out-of-class learning opportunities constructed by five ESL freshmen and their native speaking peers in a college town. *Journal of Ethnographic & Qualitative Research*, 10, 120–134.

Martinsen, R. A., Alvord, S. M., & Tanner, J. (2014). Perceived foreign accent: Extended stays abroad, level of instruction, and motivation. *Foreign Language Annals*, 47(1), 66–78.

Mekheimer, M. A., & Aldosari, H. S. (2013). Evaluating an integrated EFL teaching methodology in Saudi universities: A longitudinal study. *Journal of Language Teaching and Research*, 4(6), 1264–1276.

Miles, M. B., & Huberman, A. M. (1994). *Qualitative data analysis: An expanded sourcebook* (2nd ed.). Thousand Oaks, CA: SAGE.

Moghtadi, L., Koosha, M., & Lotfi, A. R. (2014). Second language grammatical proficiency and third language acquisition. *International Education Studies*, 7(11), 19–27.

Moskovsky, C., Alrabai, F., Paolini, S., & Ratcheva, S. (2013). The effects of teachers' motivational strategies on learners' motivation: A controlled investigation of second language acquisition. *Language Learning*, 63(1), 34–62.

Munro, M. J., Derwing T. M., & Thomson, R. I. (2015). Setting segmental priorities for English learners: Evidence from a longitudinal study. *International Review of Applied Linguistics in Language Teaching*, 53(1), 39–60.

Pellerin, M. (2014). Language tasks using touch screen and mobile technologies: Reconceptualizing task-based CALL for young language learners. *Canadian Journal of Learning and Technology*, 40(1), 1–23.

Rott, S. (2005). Processing glosses: A qualitative exploration of how form-meaning connections are established and strengthened. *Reading in a Foreign Language, 17,* 45–74.

Samimy, K. (2008). Achieving the advanced oral proficiency in Arabic: A case study. *Foreign Language Annals, 41,* 401–414.

Scott, V. M., & Huntington, J. A. (2007). Literature, the interpretive mode, and novice learners. *The Modern Language Journal, 91,* 3–14.

Sneddon, R. (2008). Young bilingual children learning to read with dual language books. *English Teaching: Practice and Critique, 7*(2), 71–84.

Tomiyama, M. (2009) Age and proficiency in L2 attrition: Data from two siblings. *Applied Linguistics, 30,* 253–275.

Venkatagiri, H. S., & Levis, J. M. (2007). Phonological awareness and speech comprehensibility: An exploratory study. *Language Awareness, 16*(4), 263–277.

Wolcott, H. F. (1994). *Transforming qualitative data: Description, analysis, and interpretation.* Thousand Oaks, CA: SAGE.

Yan, J. X., & Horwitz, E. K. (2008). Learners' perceptions of how anxiety interacts with personal and instructional factors to influence their achievement in English: A qualitative analysis of EFL learners in China. *Language Learning, 58,* 151–183.

Chapter 8

Discerning Discussions and Conclusions

Completing the Picture

Chapter Overview

The final section of a research article is the Discussion/Conclusions. This is where researchers interpret their findings, make practical applications, and try to fit them into the big picture to answer their research questions. No matter which research design was used, no matter which type of data (verbal or numerical) was gathered, no matter how the data were analyzed (looking for patterns or statistics), researchers arrive at the same place: they have to make sense of what they found. They have to interpret their results and provide explanations, draw conclusions, and make applications. For these reasons, after the abstract at the beginning of the study, this section is the most read part of the average study.

Many reasons are given as to why the stuff between the abstract and the discussion/conclusions section is jumped over. I often hear "Why bother with the rest? Let's just go to the conclusion and find out what we can use for our purposes." However, if this *lazy* route is taken, the consumer will never be able to evaluate whether proper conclusions have been made based on solid research, which in turn will lead to faulty applications. Such slothfulness has resulted in a lot of money and time being wasted based on conclusions that have been drawn from faulty research.

The purpose of this final chapter is to facilitate in developing the consumer's ability to discern whether researchers are making valid interpretations and conclusions based on their data and whether appropriate applications are being suggested. I first explain what the discussion/conclusions section is supposed to do, and then summarize a number of concerns to which the consumer should give attention. To illustrate these principles, I will close the chapter with two examples from two different types of research designs.

Six Needed Ingredients

Researchers vary in the format they use to wrap up their studies. Some will only have a discussion section. Others will have both discussion and conclusion sections. You might also see additional subheadings, such as "summary" and/or "implications." Some attach their discussion section to their results section, labeled something like "results and discussion," followed by a final conclusion. Almost all will have at least a paragraph on the limitations of their study. Regardless of the format they use, they usually include the following six ingredients in the discussion/conclusions section of their paper.

- *An overview of the study*: The purpose of the study should be restated, the questions under investigation summarized, and any propounded hypotheses reiterated.
- *Overview of the findings*: The findings should clearly be related to the research question(s) and/or shown how they support or fail to support any hypothesis being proposed.
- *Relation of findings*: The findings of the study should be related to previous research findings and theoretical thinking.
- *Attention to limitations*: The researchers should evaluate their own study and point out any weaknesses and/or limitations.
- *Possible applications*: The conclusions should contain how the results can be applied to practical situations.
- *Future possibilities*: Topics for future research should be proposed.

Seven Questions Every Consumer Should Ask

When evaluating the discussion/conclusions section of a study, there are questions that the consumer should address:

1. *Do the findings logically answer the research questions or support the research hypothesis?* Here is where the consumer must be wary. Many, if not all (except for me, of course—ha!), researchers have their biases and would love to find answers to their questions, or support their hypothesis from the results of their studies. Because this final section gives researchers the right to conjecture about what the findings mean, it is easy to unintentionally (or even intentionally) suggest things that the results do not support.
2. *Does the nature of the study remain consistent from beginning to end?* My students and I have noticed that some studies begin as exploratory studies but end up as confirmatory ones. In such cases, the introduction section has one or more research questions, with no specific hypothesis stated. However, in the discussion section we suddenly read "and so our hypothesis is confirmed by the results." Another variation of this is that some researchers generate hypotheses in the discussion section—which is their right—but then go on to suggest that their results now support the hypotheses. This is circular

reasoning. We cannot use the same data to support hypotheses from which they have been formulated. A new study must be made to test these hypotheses.

3. *Are the findings generalized to the correct population or situations?* Most studies, in fact, cannot be generalized to a broadly defined population. The reason is that most samples are not randomly selected, nor are they typically large enough to adequately represent a target population. Consequently, results of such studies are suggestive at most and need to be followed up with a number of replications. If the same findings are repeated using different samples from the target population, then we can have more assurance that we are on the right track. (This is where *meta-analysis* plays an important role—to be discussed in Appendix A.) A well-written discussion section will be careful to warn readers of this problem.

4. *Are the conclusions consistent with the type of research design used?* The main concern here is whether *causation* is being inferred from research designs that are not geared to demonstrate this effect. Having an idea of the type of design being used will help the consumer know whether this error is made when reading the discussion and conclusion section. Nonexperimental designs such as descriptive or correlational ones cannot be used to directly show causation. Yet, especially in the latter case, some researchers have slipped into suggesting that their findings indicate that one variable influences another. When researchers apply their findings, they are often tempted to recommend that people manipulate one variable to cause changes in another. Unless their research design warrants this application, they have made a logical error.

5. *Are the findings and conclusions related to theory or previous research?* To help contribute to the big picture, a well-written discussion/conclusions section should attempt to tie the findings and interpretations to any current theoretical thinking or previous research. This might be done through showing how the findings support what has gone before or by providing evidence to refute some theory or challenge previous research.

6. *Are any limitations of the study made clear?* There are very few, if any, *perfect* studies in the literature. Regardless of how good a study is, a conscientious researcher will mention what the limitations are to caution the reader from being overly confident about the results. Often they even dedicate a subheading to this.

7. *Is there consistency between the findings and the applications?* As previously mentioned, when inferential statistics was discussed, some researchers confuse statistical significance with practical significance. I repeat the warning here. Just because a finding is *statistically significant* does not mean that it has *practical significance*. I have seen

relatively small correlations, such as $r = .30$, interpreted as an important finding because it was statistically significant, or the difference of five points between a treatment and a control group given importance for the same reason. Yet, is either of these findings large enough to get excited about? Maybe, but much depends on the cost in time, human resources, and finance to make changes based on that .30 correlation or those extra five points owing to the treatment. The consumer needs to be on alert when a researcher advocates costly changes based on statistical significance. This is where *effect size* is applied, as mentioned in Chapter 7 and elaborated in Appendix B.

In the following, the discussion/conclusions sections of two studies have been evaluated using the above set of questions. The criteria I used for choosing these articles were that they were used previously in former chapters and they each represented a different type of research: qualitative and quantitative. The first is an example of a qualitative study using a microethnographic design and verbal data. The second is an example of a causal-comparative study using numerical data.

Qualitative Example

As mentioned in Chapter 5, Lee-Johnson (2015) did a (qualitative/exploratory/applied) study that looked at the effects of out-of-class social interactions between ESL learners and their native-speaking counterparts on their overall learning experiences. She had three research questions but no hypotheses. She concluded her study with discussion and limitations and future research sections.

The Six Ingredients in the Discussion/Conclusion Section

1. *An overview of the study*: Lee-Johnson did not restate the purpose of her study, but she outlined the discussion section with restatements of her three research questions.
2. *Overview of the findings*: Lee-Johnson clearly summarized her findings and how they related to the corresponding research questions. For example, she stated:

> The first research question in this study focused on out-of-class learning opportunities, which were available to the core participants. My findings showed that the tutorial sessions, on-campus jobs, lunch and dinner gatherings with friends, social gatherings at the dormitories, and other on-campus social events provided learning opportunities to the core participants.
>
> (p. 130)

3. *Relation of findings*: Lee-Johnson related all of her findings to previous research findings and theoretical thinking. For example, after the above summary of her findings, she stated "This corroborates Hull & Shultz's (2001) claim that the boundaries were often blurred between in-school and out-of-school events" (p. 130). Later she says that her findings corroborate Strong's (2007) observations.

4. *Attention to limitations*: Lee-Johnson created a clear section for this. However, she did not list any limitations of her study.

5. *Possible applications*: Lee-Johnson argued that the findings of her study filled a research gap by adding how naturalistic social interaction helps language learning beyond only learning linguistic features. She also proposed that out-of-class social literacy training needed to be stressed.

6. *Future possibilities*: Lee-Johnson proposed that longitudinal studies should be done, as well as investigating which domains are more responsive to learning.

Seven Questions for Evaluation:

1. *Do the findings logically answer the research questions or support the research hypothesis?* In my opinion, Lee-Johnson answered all three of her research questions. Her conjectures were consistent to the findings.

2. *Does the nature of the study remain consistent from beginning to end?* Yes.

3. *Are the findings generalized to the correct population or situations?* Lee-Johnson stated that the findings of her study might be transferable. However, she was clear that her findings cannot be generalized to other higher education institutions, especially in urban settings.

4. *Are the conclusions consistent with the type of research design used?* Lee-Johnson's study was exploratory with no stated hypothesis. Everything in her study was consistent with her design, and she did not claim her study supported any predictions.

5. *Are the findings and conclusions related to theory or previous research?* As stated under the ingredients section above, Lee-Johnson discussed how her study filled in a gap in the field of TESOL and added information to literacy studies. She also pointed out how her findings supported the claims of other researchers.

6. *Are any limitations of the study made clear?* I was surprised that Lee-Johnson did not report any limitations to her study. As mentioned previously, no study is without its limitations.

7. *Is there consistency between the findings and the applications?* Lee-Johnson used in-depth microethnographic discourse analysis to study her verbal data for patterns. She reported a sufficient amount

of verbal excerpts to support the patterns she was looking for. Her discussion regarding the applications of her findings were consistent with her findings.

In addition to the seven questions listed above, keep in mind the criteria listed in Chapter 7, Section 1, under Analysis of Verbal Data (see Table 7.1). They should also be taken into consideration when evaluating the final discussion and conclusion section of a qualitative study. However, because interpretations and conclusions are ongoing during the data-collection stages in a qualitative study, these criteria apply both then and in the final discussion.

Quantitative Example

Munro, Derwing, and Thomson (2015), did a two-year longitudinal, quasi-experimental study examining the segmental pronunciation difficulties between Mandarin and Slavic learners of English in Canada (see Chapter 7). They had four research questions but no hypothesis. They identified a separate section for each of the discussion and the conclusion.

The Six Ingredients in the Discussion/Conclusion Sections

1. *An overview of the study*: Munro et al. did not restate the purpose of their study, but they did repeat their four research questions.
2. *Overview of the findings*: Munro et al. followed each research question with a clear summary of their findings directly related to the question.
3. *Relation of findings*: They tied their findings to other studies under each of their research questions. In the conclusions section, they compared their study to one done by two of the authors.
4. *Attention to limitations*: In their conclusions section, Munro et al. pointed out two limitations. The first had to do with the use of only single-word elicitations for their targets. Second, they stated that speaker consistency between the different words with the same targets was not taken into account.
5. *Possible applications*: Munro et al. provided several applications for their findings. The main one related to computer-assisted pronunciation teaching (CAPT). They cited a number of papers that related to this topic and how their study might relate.
6. *Future possibilities*: Munro et al. pointed out several possibilities for future research. Under question two, for example, they suggested that further research needs to be done to examine why some segments require intervention and others do not.

Seven Questions for Evaluation

1. Do *the findings logically answer the research questions or support the research hypothesis?* I believe that Munro et al. provided data that answered their four questions.
2. *Does the nature of the study remain consistent from beginning to end?* Yes.
3. *Are the findings generalized to the correct population or situations?* Interestingly, in their conclusions section Munro et al. state "The most noteworthy outcome of this study is the evidence it provides of between-speaker variability in the production of consonants and consonant clusters, a finding that points to the need for individualized pronunciation instruction" (p. 55). However, they follow this in the next sentence with "Of course, it is important not to extrapolate too much from these results." They were careful not to fall into the trap of overgeneralization.
4. *Are the conclusions consistent with the type of research design used?* Munro et al.'s study was causal-comparative due to the lack of randomly sampled participants. However, they did not mention this, nor did they point this out in their limitations. This fact weakens their somewhat strongly stated conclusions.
5. *Are the findings and conclusions related to theory or previous research?* Munro et al. related their findings to several studies. However, they discussed them in great deal in relation to a number of citations having to do with CAPT.
6. *Are any limitations of the study made clear?* Munro et al. were very clear about their limitations in their last paragraph, when they stated

    > we considered only a small portion of the English inventory of consonants and consonant clusters, and we limited the study to two language groups. Moreover, we have not considered other aspects of pronunciation such as vowels and prosody, which are known to have an impact on intelligibility.
    >
    > (p. 55)

7. *Is there consistency between the findings and the applications?* Munro et al.'s conclusions were mainly applied to CAPT programming. Their findings added to this discussion, no doubt. They also pointed out several areas for further research that are important for the continuance of this discussion.

As you can see, the discussion/conclusions section of an article cannot be treated lightly. Yet, to discern its quality, you, the consumer, must be able to evaluate how the preceding sections of a research study logically develop to support the interpretations and conclusions a researcher makes.

Without understanding and evaluating each building block leading to the final result, it is impossible to evaluate the end product.

Hopefully, the above discussion has provided you with guidelines to help you determine whether the end product (i.e., the conclusions) is warranted. If it is, you are able to make your own conclusions regarding the worth of the study for answering your own questions. Therefore, the best recommendation at this point is to provide you with an exercise that will help you apply what you have just read.

Exercise 8.1

Use one of the recent studies you have used in previous exercises. Evaluate the discussion/conclusions section of the study by answering the following questions. Provide a quick rationale for each answer.

First, check for the six ingredients in the discussion/conclusions section mentioned above.

Second, answer the following seven questions for your evaluation.

1. Do the findings logically answer the research questions or support the research hypothesis?
2. Does the nature of the study remain consistent from beginning to end?
3. Are the findings generalized to the correct population?
4. Are the conclusions consistent to the type of research design?
5. Are the findings and conclusions related to theory for previous research?
6. Are any limitations made clear regarding the study?
7. Is there consistency between the findings and the applications?

Congratulations! You have come a long way. Welcome to the Consumers of Research in Applied Linguistics Association—*whenever we get around to starting such an organization*. Let me close with this analogy. Research is like scuba diving, which I love to do. Many people are afraid to learn how to scuba dive because they think that they will drown, or that they will be claustrophobic. I find that the opposite is true. When I am under water, it is one of the most relaxing experiences I have ever had. I get to see the underwater beauty of sea life from a perspective that many will never see. The only danger is not following the principles that I studied when I was training for certification. Studying research is similar. There are those who stand on the edge of the ocean of research afraid to jump in and experience for themselves the treasures that await them. Their excuses are fear of drowning in the sea of data and statistics. But, as with diving, if they follow the principles discussed in this book, not only will they find themselves discovering many important pieces of information but they will begin to enjoy swimming in the depths. Now it is your turn to jump into the ocean of research and begin finding the treasures of information that await you. Appendix A provides a set of guidelines for completing your own review of the research literature that will address any research question you might have. May you approach it with great confidence.

References

Lee-Johnson, Y. L. (2015). A qualitative study of the out-of-class learning opportunities constructed by five ESL freshmen and their native speaking peers in a college town. *Journal of Ethnographic & Qualitative Research, 10,* 120–134.
Munro, M. J., Derwing T. M., & Thomson, R. I. (2015). Setting segmental priorities for English learners: Evidence from a longitudinal study. *International Review of Applied Linguistics in Language Teaching, 53*(1), 39–60.

Constructing a Literature Review

Introduction

If you have grasped the content presented in the chapters of this book, you are now ready to complete a review of the research literature that focuses on some topic in which you are interested. Whether you are trying to answer a practical problem in the language classroom, prepare a paper on some topic for colleagues, or fulfill a requirement for a course assignment, the ability to do an effective research review is necessary.

There are three types of research reviews you will encounter. The first, and more common, is the section in the introduction of a published study that summarizes current thinking and research that is part of the rationale for the study—sometimes referred to as the literature review. This type is mentioned in Chapter 3. Suffice it to say here that such reviews are very selective in taking out material from each study to weave an argument for justifying the research project proposed in the introduction.

The second and third types of review are complete articles in themselves. The first of these is what I have referred to in Chapter 2 as a review of research. The second is referred to as a meta-analysis. The former type attempts to map out an extensive number of research articles on a given topic. The latter is in fact a research study that uses purposefully sampled sets of research studies as data for analysis. I summarized meta-analysis in Chapter 6. For this reason, I will only focus on the review of research that could be used for a chapter of a thesis or dissertation or for a separate publishable document.

Why Do a Review of Research?

The main benefit of doing a review of research is to provide the consumer with a mosaic of what is happening concerning a given topic. No single research study exhausts all there is to know about a given topic. However, when you can integrate various recent research articles into a meaningful picture, you will be able to discover a number of interesting things (see Norris & Ortega, 2006).

First, you will realize whether there are any plausible answers to your questions when you see the bigger picture. On first blush, your impression might be that there are no clear answers, and you might be tempted to give up your search. However, as you weave the studies together in an integrated review, you might find answers for practical use.

In addition, you might find conflicting results between studies. This might cause you to want to give up with the conclusion that no one can agree on anything. However, this is when being a discerning consumer will pay off. On careful scrutiny of the studies, you will begin to see why there are conflicting results. You might realize that the differences in the samples used in the studies produced the differing results. Or there might have been a difference in the procedures or the materials used in the treatment. You now have to decide which study best corresponds to the context surrounding your particular research question. The closer the correspondence, the more applicable the findings might be to your situation.

However, if you find that the same results are replicated over a variety of studies, you can have more confidence that you are on the right track. Here is where *external validity* comes into play. Regardless of the sample, procedures, materials, or type of tests used, if the same findings keep appearing, you can be quite confident that you have a workable answer for your question. Without a well-done review of research, you cannot have this assurance.

Occasionally, you will discover that there is little recent research on a particular question. When this happens, you should take this as a warning to proceed with caution. Maybe your research question is stated in such a way that your search accessed only a few studies. If this is the case, you will have to adjust the key concepts in your question to produce more rewarding searches. You might have to go back further in time to see if there was anything done earlier. Then again, your question may be so novel that there is little research available to date.

To illustrate, one of my students raised a question concerning the usefulness of the *critical period hypothesis*. However, when looking over a five-year period he could not find enough research to fill a short three-page review. He first asked whether this topic had been researched out— that is, had research gone as far as possible, whether by sufficiently answering the question or by being limited due to various constraints. Most probably, in my thinking, the latter might have been the case, i.e. the variables used to test this hypothesis were beyond capabilities to manipulate or measure. If this is the case, we cannot make strong conclusions about children's seemingly superior language learning abilities as compared with adults. Since that time, a current search over a five-year period on ERIC revealed 10 studies. Maybe some finding has shed more light on this topic.

Second, doing a research review is important if you plan to do a study yourself. Such a review will give you an overview of the different kinds of methodologies, instruments for collecting data, and ways in which to analyze data that have been commonly used in the research for a given area. This knowledge can help you decide whether your proposed study is even feasible given your time, material, and financial constraints. Many fledgling researchers could have saved themselves needless angst if they had realized that the study they were interested in doing required more time and resources than were available before launching into the task.

Where to Begin

As described in Chapter 2, the first place to begin is searching for studies using *preliminary* sources. These are used to find documents that report research studies or theoretical positions, and I suggest you review Chapter 2 regarding how to make the best use of these valuable tools. Most university libraries, as well as some public libraries, have such computerized search capabilities. Now that the Internet is available in most countries, you should be able to obtain a list of research studies pertinent to your questions even from your home computer.

Again, as mentioned in Chapter 2, your search will be as good as the *keywords* (or descriptors) you use. You might have to try different combinations of these words to obtain sufficient results for your review, or you might have to use a *thesaurus* from the preliminary source you are using to identify related keywords to guide your search.

Your goal is to access firsthand research studies (i.e., *primary studies*) that relate to your questions. How many studies you include will depend on the nature of your question(s). If you want to do an exhaustive literature review, you will want to cover as many studies as you can find. However, most people want to put some limitations on their literature review, such as time constraints and/or only journal articles, to confine their search to studies with only certain characteristics.

Figure A.1 illustrates the results of a search I made for research articles using the ERIC database on the Internet. I began with the very broad search only using the keyword *ESL*. Under **Publication Date** column on the left, I clicked on **Since 2012,** (note: the numerical year increase every year) which only looks at studies between 2012 and 2016. The result is 784 studies. I only wanted journal articles, so I scrolled down the left-hand column to **Publication Type** and clicked **Journal Articles**. This dropped the number of articles to 641. I then narrowed it down to articles dealing with *ESL* AND *writing*, resulting in 219 references. If my question of interest was something like "What does research say about writing in ESL?" I might have wanted to stop here and scan through all 219

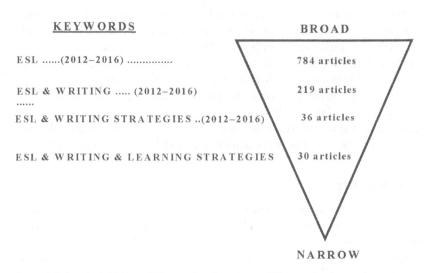

KEYWORDS   BROAD

ESL ......(2012–2016) ....   784 articles

ESL & WRITING ..... (2012–2016)   219 articles
......

ESL & WRITING STRATEGIES ..(2012–2016)   36 articles

ESL & WRITING & LEARNING STRATEGIES   30 articles

NARROW

Figure A.1 Results of Using Different Combinations of Keywords in a Literature
Search Using ERIC for Years 2012 to 2016

references. (Note that not all of these references will necessarily be primary research studies. Some could be position papers or reviews of research.)

Most likely, I would want to narrow my search even more. For instance, I am interested in finding research studies about strategies ESL people use when writing. So, I restated my search terms to be *ESL* and *writing strategies*. As shown in Figure A.1, this captured 38 journal articles.

I could have stopped there, but I wanted to make sure that the way I worded my keywords did not prevent me from seeing some study that might be using different terminology. I did one more search, adding *learning strategies* to my list of keywords. This reduced the search to 30 journal articles.

You might ask the question "How far back in time do you go in your search?" My recommendation is that you begin by looking at the last 10 years of research. Usually this will result in enough current research to provide viable information addressing your question(s). I then suggest that you begin with the most recent research and work backward in time. This way, you will stay abreast with the most recent issues and findings with which researchers are currently working. This can save time by not getting involved with outdated issues with which people in the discipline are no longer concerned.

Once you have identified the studies you want to consider for inclusion in your review, you face the challenge of getting your hands on the actual articles. Hopefully, you will be near a good library that can access the journals electronically so that you can have ready access to the studies.

If the library does not subscribe to a journal's online service, they may have a library loan agreement with other libraries that do have the journals. Many journals such as *Language Learning* and *Modern Language Journal* have electronic versions to which your library might have access. In such cases, you can download full articles for reviewing. See the companion website for a list of many journals and their URLs, which you can copy and paste into your search engine (e.g., Google). If all else fails, you can order journal articles from the journal publishers and they will send them to you electronically, usually at your expense.

Abstracting Primary Literature

In preparation for constructing your review of the research literature, you will need to formulate a systematic procedure for cataloging and storing your information for each study. Back in the Stone Age, we used to have to put our information on 5″ × 8″ (i.e., 12 cm × 20 cm) cards, which were awkward to handle. However, in our computerized day, there are a number of online information storage systems that make this task much easier. For example, check out web research tools such as Diigo.com and Zotero.org to help you build databases (see Chapter 2) and organize research information. Such online programs will revolutionize your research gathering endeavors. These programs allow you to highlight, attach sticky notes, store, sort, and aggregate various studies at the click of a mouse. Once you enter the information, which I discuss shortly, you will have created a database of studies from which you can draw information for your literature review.

When you set up your database of studies for your review, enter the following information in the format (e.g., APA, MLA) that you most commonly use. First, record accurately the last names and all initials for every author of each study. If you have only one author, it is useful to identify their gender as well, because you might want to use personal pronouns when summarizing his or her study rather than speaking in the formal "the researcher." Next, you record the exact title of the article. When doing this, use the style (e.g., APA or MLA) that you plan to use for your review. (Note that systems like Zotero do this automatically.) This will save you time when you prepare the table of references because you will not have to retype them. At most, you will only have to cut and paste with your word processing software. Following this you will need to record the year published, the exact title of the journal (in italics), the volume number (in italics), the issue number (in parentheses), and the page numbers from beginning to the very last page of the article.

If you have read a published review of research, you will have noticed that the author basically looks for 10 things when summarizing the main body of the study. They are as follows:

1. The focus of the study: what area and/or issue are being studied?
2. The research question(s) being asked.
3. The hypotheses being tested (if any).
4. The size of the sample and important characteristics such as age and gender. How the sample was chosen or assigned to the study, whether randomly or by some other procedure.
5. The variables in the study, such as:
   a. descriptive
   b. independent
   c. dependent
   d. moderating.
6. The procedures followed, including any materials, test instruments, or observational techniques.
7. The overall findings of the study.
8. The conclusion(s) that the researcher draws from the findings.
9. Any other observations they have made that pertain to their interests.
10. Any concerns they have with the study that they want to point out in their review.

Writing a Review of Research

The outline I recommend for writing a good review of research is one that I have adapted based on Chapter 6 of Cooper's classic book, *Synthesizing Research* (1998). This pattern seems to be the one followed by many reviewers of research published in journals (e.g., Dolean, 2015; Kleinsasser, 2013), although they don't use the headings as much as they used to.

I. Introduction
   A. The research question or purpose that your review addresses.
   B. The importance of the topic.
   C. Historical background of the topic (theory, methodological issues, previous reviews, etc.).
   D. The goal of your review: how you plan to add to the theory and information already available.
II. Method section: details regarding the makeup of the review.
   A. What years are covered?
   B. What preliminary sources were used to locate the studies?
   C. What key words guided your search?
   D. Criteria for deciding which studies to review.
      1. Description of the constraints that limited your selection.
      2. Rationale for choosing these constraints.
   E. What studies were excluded and why?
III. The results section: studies summarized.

    A. An overview of what studies will be discussed and their relation to one another and the review as a whole.

    B. At least a paragraph for each study, containing a summary of the following:

        1. The main point of the study.

        2. The question(s)/hypothesis being studied.

        3. Samples used and how they were chosen.

        4. Procedure(s) used.

        5. General findings (results).

        6. Author's interpretations/applications of the findings.

        7. Any concerns to which you might want to alert the reader.

IV. Discussion section.

    A. Give an overview of major results of your review.

    B. Compare/contrast the results between studies.

    C. Provide possible reasons for any differences.

    D. Relate results to any theoretical issues you mentioned in the introduction.

    E. Compare with past reviews if any exist.

    F. Explain any difference in findings with past reviews.

    G. Application of findings toward future research.

Whenever possible, I recommend that you construct tables to help summarize your findings. What you put in a table will depend on what you are trying to highlight in your review. The purpose of the table is to provide a visual aid that will work with your text in helping the reader understand all of the relationships that you are trying to point out (see also Feak & Swales, 2009).

Kleinsasser (2013) provided a good example of how to make good use of tables to summarize the information he extracted from 79 studies in his review. The purpose he stated for his review was to summarize articles in the journal *Teaching and Teacher Education* between the years 1985 and 2012. He used five tables in his review to help the reader summarize various issues. His first table summarized the descriptors (keywords) he used for his literature search, along with the number of articles he found for each descriptor. The second table showed the number of articles by country where they came from. I found the fourth table interesting. It summarized the focus of the article by country with references to the articles themselves. He narrowed the number of studies he reviewed to 12. Then he provided an overview in his fifth table, which supplied citations (author names and dates), country, participants, data source(s), and general themes. Kleinsasser used the themes in the fifth table as headings for the results section of his review, under which he summarized various articles. He titled his discussion and conclusion sections "Reflections, Comments, Discussion," in which he does exactly that. I recommend your perusal of this review as one example. However, there are many other well-written literature reviews available that will vary in style, which you may also want to use as a prototype.

Exercise A.1

The purpose of this exercise is for you to produce a review of research in an area of your own interest. You are to review whatever number of studies you find relevant in the space allowed. Next develop an overall picture of what is being studied in your chosen area.

Criteria for the main body of the text:

I.   Introduction: conceptual presentation
     A. What is the research question or purpose that motivates your review?
     B. Why is the review important to applied linguistics?
     C. What is the historical perspective behind your review?
II. Method section
     A. Details of the nature of your search.
         1. What years did you cover in your search?
         2. What preliminary sources did you use?
         3. What keywords guided your search?
     B. Criteria for deciding which studies to review.
         1. What criteria did you use for including a study?
         2. Why did you select these criteria?
         3. What studies did you exclude and why?
III. The results section.
     A. An organized summary of the studies: Each study should include the following in your own words:
         1. The main point of the study.
         2. The question(s)/hypothesis being studied.
         3. The sample used and how and why it was selected.
         4. The procedure(s) used for implementing the study.
         5. The general findings (results), in words not statistics.
         6. The researcher's interpretations/applications of the findings.
IV. Discussion section
     A. Summarize the major results of your review. (Use tables to provide visual aids in your summary if possible.)
         1. Compare/contrast the results between studies.
         2. Provide possible reasons for any differences.
     B. Compare with past reviews, if any exist.
     C. Explain any difference in your findings compared with past reviews.
     D. Apply your findings to answering your future research.

References

Cooper, H. M. (1998). *Synthesizing research: A guide for literature reviews* (3rd ed.). Thousand Oaks, CA: SAGE.

Dolean, D. D. (2015). How early can we efficiently start teaching a foreign language? *European Early Childhood Education Research Journal, 23*(5), 706–719.

Feak, C. B., & Swales, J. M. (2009). *Telling a research story: Writing a literature review.* Ann Arbor, MI: University of Michigan Press.

Kleinsasser, R. C. (2013). Language teachers: Research and studies in language(s) education, teaching, and learning in *Teaching and Teacher Education*, 1985–2012. *Teaching and Teacher Education, 29,* 86–96.

Norris, J. M., & Ortega, L. (Eds.). (2006). *Synthesizing research on language learning and teaching.* Philadelphia, PA: John Benjamins.

BEST WISHES ON YOUR ADVENTURE IN RESEARCH!

Going to the Next Level of Statistics

More About Descriptive Statistics

Types of Scales

Before looking at statistics in greater detail, you need to understand something about the type of numbers that are used as data. This is important because the type of descriptive or inferential statistic used is dependent on the nature of the data. Numerical data come in one of four forms, referred to as *scales*: *nominal, ordinal, interval,* and *ratio*. The word *nominal* for the nominal scale means that the levels of a variable are categories. The categories can be identified with words (e.g., female, male), or numbers (e.g., 1, 2). The numbers assigned would only be used to identify each level, without having any other meaning. That is, the value 2 for one of the sexes does not mean that sex had twice as much of gender than the other sex. It is just a numerical name. The frequency of individuals in each category is the data. The frequencies are sometimes converted to relative frequencies (i.e., percentages), but the results are the same. For example, a study may have 60 males and 80 females, or 43 percent males and 57 percent females.

Another example of the use of a nominal scale would be when a researcher is interested in knowing whether there are differences in the number of people representing three different nationalities. Nationality is the variable of the study, and the data are the frequency of people for each of the nationalities.

Data for the *ordinal scale* represent some form of ranking. As with the nominal scale, words or numbers can be used. However, in contrast with the nominal scale, the words or numbers have quantitative meaning. For example, the variable of language proficiency might be expressed verbally as low, average, or high ability. It could also be in the form of numbers: 3 = high ability, 2 = average ability and 1 = low ability.

A commonly used ordinal scale in applied linguistics is known as the *Likert scale*. One use is with measurements of attitude with the rankings: 5 = *strongly agree*, 4 = *agree*, 3 = *neutral*, 2 = *disagree* and 1 = *strongly disagree*. This scale has two important qualities: unequal distance between values, and no true zero. What is meant by the first quality is that the distance between a 2 and a 3 on a rating scale, for example, may not represent the same amount of difference in the trait (the attribute) being measured as the distance between the 1 and the 2. What is meant by *no true zero* is that, if a 0 were used, it would only represent a level of ability that was lower than the level 1. It would not mean that participants at level 0 were absolutely devoid of the trait being measured.

To illustrate, the following graph shows what the real distance between the numbers are in the amount of a trait being measured—which in reality we do not know. Note the unequal distances between the numbers. The amount of trait measured (or distance) between 1 and 2 differs from that between 2 and 3. The problem is, we do not usually know how much of the trait is being represented by the numbers. We only know that one level is more than the other.

Many ordinal scales are used in applied linguistic research. In fact, any rating scale is almost always an ordinal scale. Beside attitude scales mentioned previously, there are rating scales for writing and oral proficiency, anxiety, and so on. Back in Chapter 5, I cited Machida and Dalsky (2014), who examined the effect of concept mapping on L2 writing performance. They measured their variables, anxiety and writing proficiency using two different types of ordinal scales. To measure the anxiety level of students while writing in L2, they used an adapted version of the Daly–Miller Writing Apprehension Scale. This instrument consisted of 26 items that were in a five-point Likert scale format, with 1 = strongly disagree to 5 = strongly agree. They measured the second variable, writing proficiency, by using the TOEFL writing rubric, which is a 0 to 5 holistic scale that raters use to judge students' individual abilities. As you can see, a 0 on the TOEFL scale does not mean a student cannot write at all. The Educational Testing Service, which developed the TOEFL rubric, state that a 0 means that the writer copied words from the topic, produced words not related to the topic, etc., whereas the rubric defines a 1 as meaning that the writer has made serious flaws in organization, providing appropriate detail, and/or serious structure or usage errors. In such an ordinal scale, a 1 means that the writer has more writing ability than someone with a 0, based on how the rubric defines these numbers.

Measurement of a variable can also be in the form of an *interval scale*. Whereas the values used in the ordinal scale might represent unequal amounts of the variable being measured, the intervals between the values in an interval scale are *equal*, as illustrated below.

1____2____3____4____5____6____7____etc.

However, as with the ordinal scale, there is no *true zero*. A common example of an interval scale is the scale used to measure heat on a thermometer. The one-degree difference between 20° and a 21° Celsius in amount of heat is the same as the one-degree difference between 29° and 30°. In other words, the units of measurement mean the same in terms of the amount of the trait (heat, in this example) being measured no matter where it is on the scale. At the same time, there is no true zero. Zero degrees Celsius does not mean the total absence of heat. It is a *relative* zero in that it is used as a reference point determined by the freezing of water. And, as we all know, zero degrees Celsius is warmer than zero degrees Fahrenheit (0° C = 32° F).

Scores on aptitude or achievement tests are usually treated as if they are on interval scales. Each correct test item is considered as one unit of the trait being measured, so that a person scoring a 30 on the instrument is 10 units higher on the trait than one who scores 20. (In fact, in the measurement world, this is known not to be true, but that is for another book.) A zero on a test is not a true zero because it does not mean that the subject has absolutely no knowledge of what is being tested, although some teachers might think so. It simply means that the examinee did not answer any of the items correctly. All data that consist of the total of summed scores are usually treated as interval scales.

Finally, there is the *ratio scale*, which is seldom ever used in applied linguistics research. As you might expect, this scale has it all. The units of measurement are equal in amount of trait being measured, and there is a true zero. A good example is using a ruler to measure length. One centimeter means the same thing no matter where it is on the scale. In addition, a zero means that there is no length, which of course means that whatever we are measuring does not exist.

The one ratio scale measurement that I can think of that has been used in applied linguistics is reaction time. This is the time it takes for participants to react by pressing a button or speaking out after experiencing some form of stimulus. Reaction time is measured in units as small as milliseconds. The millisecond units are equal; if the measurement is zero, there was no reaction to whatever was presented to the participant. Jung (2016) studied the effect of glossing of second language tests on reading comprehension, L2 grammar, and vocabulary. Her research design was causal-comparative, pretest, posttest, and delayed posttest. She used a 14-multiple-choice item test to measure reading comprehension, a grammaticality judgment test for grammar, and a recognition test for vocabulary (i.e., interval scale). She supplemented these tests with reaction time data (i.e., ration scale) and binary confidence ratings. Jung presented 80 sentences to each participant on a computer screen. They were to press the z key if they thought the sentence was grammatical or the m key if it was not, as fast as possible. The reaction time from the onset of the sentence to the striking of the key was measured in milliseconds.

One final point regarding types of data, you will see two other terms to describe data: continuous and discrete. A *continuous* scale (or variable) means that the numbers in the scale go from low to high without a break (i.e., real numbers). In common English, there are decimals between numbers, which suggests that the trait being measured continues to increase without interruption; in other words, a person can have a meaningful 5.6 language proficiency. Test scores are treated as continuous data. A *discrete* scale (or variable) does not continue between numbers on the scale. Any nominal scale is discrete. Also, rating scales are discrete (though often treated as continuous). On a five-point attitude scale you cannot have a person with a 4.5 attitude. The person is either a 4 or a 5. Why is this important? Different statistical procedures work with these different types of scales, though often ignored.

At this point, you might want to digest what you have just read by doing the following exercise, not to mention taking a break.

Exercise B.1

1. Take any study and identify the variables under consideration.
2. Identify the type of scale that each variable is on: nominal, ordinal, interval, or ratio.

Shape of the Data Distribution

The shape of the distribution of the data is seldom discussed in results sections of published research, but it is very important. Based on the shape of the distribution of the data, researchers should choose which estimates of average and variation they will report in their studies. In addition, some inferential statistical procedures require the data to be distributed in certain patterns before they can be used appropriately.

The distribution of data is best displayed by a graphical display of how many participants/objects obtained certain measures beginning from the lowest measure to the highest (the frequency). To illustrate, Figure B.1 is a bar chart representing a subsection of data based on the total scores taken from a teacher evaluation scale. The graph shows the frequency of the scores, ranging from 70 to 80. The height of each bar corresponds to the frequency (i.e., the number on top of each bar). Note that five people scored 70, eight people scored 71, 16 scored 77, and so on. The shape of the distribution is noted by mentally drawing a line connecting the tops of the bars. These data show that there is a tendency for the frequency of people to increase as the total scores increase.

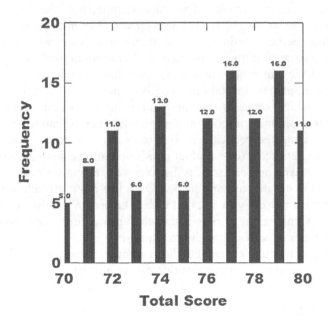

Figure B.1 Bar Graph of a Distribution of Data

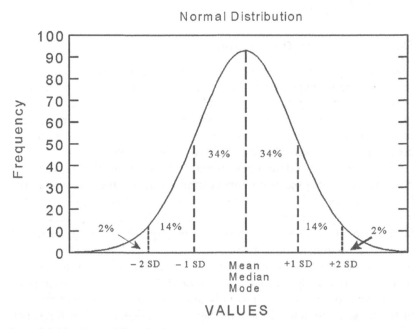

Figure B.2 The Normal Distribution

When referring to the shape of the data (see Table 7.3), three issues are of concern: symmetricality, skewness, and number of modes.[1] All of these terms are concerned with how well the shape of the data conforms to a normal distribution. An example is presented in Figure B.2. A *normal distribution* has specific properties and is used as a reference point for comparing the shapes of data distributions. The reason it is used as the reference for other curves is because many traits that we study are considered by many to be normally distributed in the population.

The distribution of the normal curve is perfectly *symmetrical* and has only one cluster of data in the middle. That is, by drawing a vertical line dividing the graph in half, as seen in Figure B.2, the shape of the curve on the right side is the exact mirror image of the left half. In addition, notice that the distribution has certain properties. Approximately 34 percent of the subjects are found from the middle (i.e., the mean, median, and mode) to either the first dotted line on the right (i.e., +1 *SD* above the mean) of the middle or the dotted line on the left side (i.e., −1 *SD* below the mean) of the middle. That is, 68 percent of the cases (e.g., people) are clustered in the middle between −1 *SD* and +1 *SD*. From +1 *SD* to +2 *SD* and −1 *SD* to −2 *SD*, each, are approximately 14 percent of the people being measured. The two ends of the distribution have roughly 2 percent on each side. To the extent that these distributions stray from being normal, these percentages between the *SD*s change accordingly.

When a distribution of data is not symmetrical, the issue becomes one of skewness. The *skewness* of the distribution has to do with how much the distribution strays from being symmetrical in terms of lopsidedness. When not symmetrical, a distribution is either *positively* or *negatively skewed*. If it is *positively skewed*, as shown by the distribution on the right of Figure B.3, the distribution will lean to the left, with the skewness index above zero. If the distribution is *negatively skewed*, illustrated by the left distribution in Figure B.3, it will be lopsided to the right side of the graph, and the skewness index will be less than zero, depicted by a minus sign. A good way to remember is to look for the *long* tail. If it is on the right side of the distribution, it is positively skewed. If it is on the left side, it is negatively skewed. The important thing to remember is that, if the data are fairly skewed, the researcher should treat the data differently when using either descriptive or inferential statistics. I discuss this further when I come to topics affected by skewness.

One other component important to the shape of the distribution of data is the numbers of *data clusters*. When the data have more than one cluster in the distribution, it means that there are subgroups of data in the data set. This is possible, for example, if a sample of participants consists of two ability groupings. This might be fine for some purposes, but descriptive and inferential statistics would be drastically affected by such distributions. How this works practically will be discussed next.

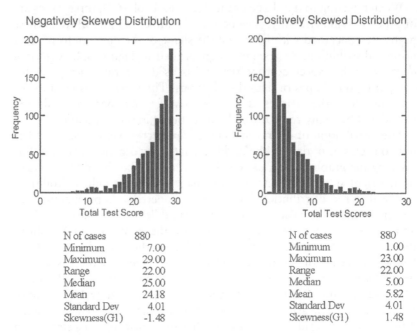

Figure B.3 Two Skewed Distributions with Descriptive Statistics

Besides the shape of the distribution, two other pieces of information are important: average and variation (see Table 7.3). They both play a crucial role in the analysis of data.

The Average

To understand the concept of *average*, think about how the word is used by almost everyone in everyday discussion. Teachers refer to their classes or students as average or above/below average. What do they mean? Aren't they saying that they are like the majority of individuals in a group? *Above average* refers to those who are above the majority, and those *below average* measure below the majority. In other words, *average* is used to mean the usual (or normal), and *above* or *below* average is used to mean the unusual or not normal. In this sense, average should be thought of as an area or zone that encompasses the usual. Figure B.4 illustrates this point. Note the large box in the middle, which represents the average, or what people are normally like. The smaller boxes on each side represent people who are above average and below average. The tiny boxes represent people who are exceptionally above (AA+) and below (BA−) average. Note that the boxes overlap to illustrate that the lines between average, above/below average, and exceptionally above/below average overlap. In other words, there is not a clear border between being classified as average or above/below average at these points on the distribution.

Among educators, *the average* is often thought of as a single score on some measures. Those who achieve that score are average and those who score above or below it are above or below average, respectively. However, this interpretation can be somewhat misleading. As stated in the previous paragraph, average represents an area of scores that are considered *usual*, which means that there is a spread of scores that would fit into the average zone. The single value that is referred to as the average is only an indicator of where this average zone might be. Because this zone can change with the shape of the distribution, there are three indicators used to mark this zone: *mean, median,* and *mode* (see Table 7.3). These three descriptive statistics are used to represent the average zone, but they should never be thought of as the zone. Statistics books refer to these as measures of *central tendency* for this reason.

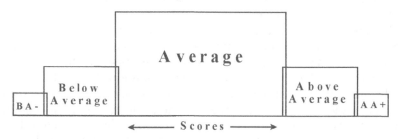

Figure B.4 The Concept of Average

Of the three, the *mean* is the most commonly used indicator of the average zone. As you may well know, all the scores are added up and divided by the total number of scores. Many studies that you read will report means in their descriptive data.

The *median* can also be found in some results sections of research articles, although less often. The median is simply the value that splits the distribution of values in half. It is a point in the distribution of data where 50 percent of the scores fall above it and 50 percent below. For example, if you have nine measurements, such as:

3   5   6   6   7   9   10   11   13

the value that would divide this distribution in half would be 7, which has four scores below and four scores above it. The values of the numbers are not added up. We only look for the point that splits the number of scores in half.

So what is the difference between the mean and the median? Often they are equal, in which case the mean is always reported. However, they are not always equal. For example, if you compute the mean by adding up all of the above values and divide by nine, you get 7.78, which is greater than the median of 7.00. The difference is due to the fact that the above list of values is not distributed symmetrically. It is slightly skewed to the right (i.e., positively skewed). If the shape of the distribution of data deviates from a symmetrical distribution to a large extent, the median would be the better indicator of averageness.

The third indicator of the average zone is the *mode*, which is the easiest one to understand but the rarest one used in research. It is simply the most frequent score in the distribution. In the above list of values, the mode is six because it is the most frequent score, occurring twice. Sometimes there can be more than one mode, as when two different scores are the most frequent. The shape of this distribution would be referred to as *bi-modal*, where there would be two clusters of data. When there is only one mode, the distribution of values is referred to as *unimodal* (i.e., one cluster of data), as illustrated in Figure B.2.

Why have three measures of averageness? The answer is based on the shape of the distribution of the data. When the data are perfectly symmetrical and unimodal, the mean, median, and mode are the same value (see Figure B.2). For example, if a distribution is normally distributed and had a mean of 25, then the median and mode would also be 25. In such instances, the mean is always the best indicator of average to report. However, if the distribution is skewed there will be three different values for the three indicators. You can see from the information under the graph for the negatively skewed distributions in Figure B.3 that the mean is 24.18, the median is 25, and the mode is 29. For the positively skewed distribution, the mean equals 5.82, the median equals 5.00, and the mode is 2.

You might still be asking why this is important. The significance of this becomes clearer when a researcher makes comparisons between groups of people using some form of inferential procedure. If the means of the groups are distorted due to skewness, then comparing the means may lead to false conclusions. More is said about this when I discuss inferential statistics. Suffice it to state here that journals should require researchers to include information regarding the shape of any data distributions used to help the consumer judge whether proper statistical procedures were used.

Data Variance

Not only are researchers in some studies interested in averages; they are also interested in how much people vary between one another in relation to the average. In fact, understanding variance is at the heart of every research question, whether qualitative or quantitative. Questions such as: On what traits do people vary? how much do they vary? and/or why do they vary? are the main foci of most research.

As with the average, there are also three measures of variation standard deviation, interquartile range, and range. As Table 7.3 shows, each one corresponds to one of the measures of average. The standard deviation corresponds to the mean, the interquartile range with the median, and the range with the mode. When reporting one type of average, the corresponding measure of variation should be reported as well.

The *standard deviation*, commonly denoted as *SD* (see Table 7.3), can be thought of as the average deviation from the mean. (Note: whenever you see the word *standard* in a statistical term, think *average*.) As with the mean, the *SD* is the most common measure of variation reported in published research for describing data. The *SD*s in Figure B.2 show plus or minus one and two standard deviations above and below the mean.

The less used measure of variance is the *interquartile range*. In essence, it is used to estimate the central 50 percent of the participants in the distribution, with the twenty-fifth and seventy-fifth percentiles marking the boundaries of that 50 percent of the participants. Although seldom used, there are studies that report this statistic. Fitzgerald, Stenner, Sanford-Moore, Koons, Bowen, and Kim (2015) studied the relationship between age and years of EFL exposure with English reading ability. They used a regression analysis to examine the relationships between the variables. To do this, they needed to test several assumptions about the data before they could use this procedure. The data passed all of the assumption tests. However, to back up the findings they used the interquartile ranges and medians to support their findings. This is the first time I have ever seen the interquartile ranges used this way and found it quite impressive. The last measure of variance is *the range*. This is simply the distance between the lowest value and the highest value in the distribution. In Figure B.3, you will find that the range for both of the distributions is 22. For the data on the left, the minimum score was 7.00 and the maximum score was 29.00. The difference between the two (i.e., the range) is 22. The principal use of the range is to compare it with the other measures of variation to estimate how homogeneous the scores are.

Why is it important for the consumer of research to know anything about the variation of scores? Returning to my first comments in this section on the importance of variance, both the range and the *SD* are distorted by data that are highly skewed or that contain unusual patterns of values. If those measures are used in such circumstances, the results of the study will be misleading. A well-written research article will alert the reader to any anomalies in the data and will explain how these are taken into consideration.

To digest the above discussion, this might be a good time to take a break by doing the following exercise before moving on to other topics.

Exercise B.2

Locate several research studies and do the following:

1. Determine what types of data are being used in each study.
2. Describe how the data are reported.
   a. What was reported about the shape of the data distributions?
   b. What measures of average were reported?
   c. What measures of variance were reported?
3. In your estimation, were the correct descriptive statistics used?

More About Inferential Statistics

Univariate Versus Multivariate Procedures

Different inferential statistical procedures are determined by the configuration of the independent variables (IVs) and the dependent variables (DVs). A study can have one or more IVs and one or more DVs. If there is only one DV then the statistical procedures are labeled *univariate*, regardless of how many independent variables there are. However, if a study has more than one DV, then the procedures are referred to as *multivariate*. In other words, the labels *univariate* and *multivariate* are only concerned with the number of DVs without reference to the number of IVs. Recall that independent variables can have two or more *levels*. For instance, gender has two levels: male and female. Levels of language ability may have three levels: low, intermediate, and advanced.

Based on the above, the following inferential statistical procedures are univariate: regression (simple and multiple), *t* test (dependent and independent), and all forms of ANOVA and ANCOVA. Multivariate procedures commonly used in applied linguistics (i.e., have more than one dependent variable) are factor analysis, multivariate analysis of variance (MANOVA), and multivariate analysis of covariance (MANCOVA). The following provides additional procedures to what was presented in Chapter 7.

More on Univariate ANOVAs

Multiway ANOVAs

In Chapter 7, we left off with 2 × 2 ANOVAs that each had two independent variables with two levels and one dependent variable. The following presents more complex configurations of ANOVA that you will also encounter in the applied linguistic research literature. For example, you might see a three-way or a four-way ANOVA. Again, remember that the number in front of the -*way* simply tells you the number of independent variables in the study.

When you have over two IVs, things can get messy. Let me summarize a study to illustrate my point. Tong, Lara-Alecio, Irby, and Koch (2014) studied the effects of embedding science instruction into English reading literacy for ELL fifth graders who had previously taken English reading literacy instruction embedded into science instruction. They had three research questions, but I will only focus on the third: "Did students' English literacy development in reading fluency, oral proficiency, and reading comprehension, measured by standardized English proficiency tests differ due to participation in these two interventions?" (p. 411). They also added gender as a moderating variable when answering this question. Tong et al. performed a four-way ANOVA ($2 \times 2 \times 2 \times 2$) on their data, with three between-subject factors: science intervention (treatment vs control), previous English intervention (treatment vs control), and gender (male vs female). Time of testing (pretest vs posttest) was the within-subject factor (i.e., repeated measure). This analysis tested four main effects: science intervention, previous English intervention, gender, and time of tests; six two-way interactions (e.g., gender × science intervention), three three-way interactions (e.g., time × gender × science intervention), and one four-way interaction (time × gender × science intervention × previous English intervention). (A group of my colleagues and I once did a study using a similar design. The first thing we did before running our statistical program was to pray that we did not have any complex interactions result in statistical significance. They are very messy to interpret.) However, Tong et al. did find statistically significant interactions, and they followed them all up with proper additional tests to unpack the various findings. Well done.

Repeated Measures ANOVA

Another type of ANOVA is one that uses repeated measures. This is similar to the dependent *t* test in that there are multiple measurements of the same instrument administered repeatedly to the participants. However, if there are more than two administrations and the data meet the assumption for parametric procedures, a repeated measure (aka within-group) ANOVA must be done. (Note, this is equivalent to the non-parametric Friedman test mentioned previously.) For example, Lee (2015) used a mixed-method design to examine strategies used by Chinese-speaking graduate students when reading familiar versus unfamiliar topics in an English multiple-choice-format reading comprehension test. All 36 participants of her study were given both the familiar and unfamiliar passages with attached tests. She extracted six general strategy categories from the verbal output using think-aloud protocols and semistructured interviews. Lee's data for the repeated measures ANOVA analysis were frequency data, which she wisely converted into more normal distributions using a square root procedure, since frequency data are notoriously positively skewed. She used a 2 × 6 repeated measures ANOVA, with two topics of familiarity, and six strategies. The factors were all within subjects (aka nested), meaning that each person had data for both factors. As with between-groups ANOVA, she tested for two main effects and one interaction. The main effect for topic familiarity was not statistically significantly different. However, the main effect for strategy was at the p < .0001 level. Lee followed this up with a Tukey pair-wise comparison to find out which strategy categories differed.

Between-Subjects and Within-Subjects ANOVA

Some studies use an ANOVA design that has one IV, where the levels contain independent groups of participants, and another IV that is *within* the participants. For example, if the first IV is gender, there are two separate groups of participants: males and females. However, the second IV could be time of testing, which could mean that each participant is given a pretest and a posttest. The result for this example is a 2 × 2 ANOVA, where the first IV is a between-subjects factor and the second IV is a within-subjects factor. In essence, the second variable is a *repeated measure*. In fact, some researchers refer to the within-subjects factor as such. Others refer to it as a *nested* variable.

   Jung (2016), mentioned previously in this chapter, used what she referred to as a mixed-model ANOVA, which is different to a mixed-methods research design. She did a 2 × 2 ANOVA using glossing as the between-subjects factor (glossed vs unglossed) and time (pretest, immediate posttest, and delayed posttest) as the within-subjects factor. She tested for the main effect for glossing (i.e., glossing vs nonglossing), and for time of test on the grammaticality test. She found a statistically significant main effect for time, and also found a significant interaction for glossing × time. Whenever one finds a significant interaction, the results are more informative than just looking at the main effects. Jung performed further analysis to find where the differences were in the interaction.

Analysis of Covariance (ANCOVA)

Do you recall back in Chapter 7 where researchers matched participants on some variable (e.g., intelligence) to eliminate its effect? There is a way to do this using a form of ANOVA as well—it is called *analysis of covariance* (ANCOVA). This procedure removes the variance from the dependent variable that is due to some extraneous variable, referred to as a *covariate*, and then looks at the relation of the independent variable to the remaining variance left in the dependent variable. This is commonly done when the researchers suspect that there might be a difference between the participants in the various groups prior to the treatment. No, this is not double talk; let me illustrate. Mistar, Zuhairi, and Yanti (2016) looked at the effect of reading strategy training on literal and inferential reading comprehension. They used two intact classes for their treatment and control groups. To control for possible preexisting differences between the two groups they used a local teacher-made test as a covariate. The dependent variable was a reading comprehension test that they developed for the study. The results of the ANCOVA analysis can be interpreted like any ANOVA, with main effects and interactions. The difference is that any preexisting differences prior to the experiment have been taken out of the results.

Multivariate ANOVAs

Univariate statistics has only one dependent variable, whereas multivariate statistical procedures have more than one DV. In cases where a study has one or more IVs and more than one DV, the researcher can perform a separate *univariate* ANOVA on each DV or analyze everything all at once using a *multivariate* approach. The purpose of doing the latter is to control for the Type I error, as with the rationale behind using ANOVA rather than a number of *t* tests. That is, for every ANOVA, there is an overall probability of making a Type I error.

The most common form found in the literature is the *multivariate analysis of variance* (MANOVA). This procedure basically uses any one of the independent variable configurations we have just discussed regarding ANOVA, only with more than one dependent variable, all at the same time. For example, if we wanted to look at whether people from different cultural backgrounds (IV one) varied on reading (DV one) and writing (DV two) ability, we could do two separate ANOVAs for each DV or we could do one MANOVA that does both at once. The rationale behind this is that the two DVs in this case are related, in that they are both reflective of verbal ability. In actual fact, when using the MANOVA approach, the common factor shared by the DVs is what is being compared in the independent variable. If an overall finding is statistically significant, it would suggest that somewhere in the analysis there is a significant difference. You will sometimes see values for *Wilks's lambda* or *Pillai's trace* reported for a statistically significant MANOVA, but they are converted into *F* ratios and interpreted as any *F* ratio would be.

If a MANOVA is found to be statistically significant, typically, separate ANOVAs would then be done on each of the DVs, followed by post hoc pair-wise comparisons to tease out the differences as I have already discussed.

Over the last decade, there have been more researchers using MANOVA to analyze complex research designs in applied linguistics. For example, Brantmeier, Sullivan, and Strube (2014) used MANOVA analysis in their study, which looked at the effects of embedded questions in scientific tests on three comprehension tasks. This resulted in three DVs: written recall, sentence completion, and a multiple-choice comprehension test. The independent variables were text enhancement adjuncts (three versions) and subject knowledge. They did separate MANOVAs on each text. Their first MANOVA revealed no main effect for adjunct version or interaction between adjunct version and subject knowledge for either text type. However, they found a significant main effect for subject knowledge for both text types. They pointed out that the lack of an interaction between adjunct version and subject knowledge was a key finding. Brantmeier et al. did another MANOVA with adjunct version and L1 reading ability as IVs, and the three forms of L2 comprehension as DVs. They found a significant main effect for adjunct version in one of the text passages. Since there were three DVs, they used the Roy–Bergman step-down test to find out which of the DVs contributed to the main effect. Sentence completion won the prize, so they had to do a Bonferroni-corrected pair-wise comparison for sentence completion to find out more information. They found that the no-adjunct condition differed from the written answer adjunct condition. As you can see, finding significant differences in a MANOVA is like opening Pandora's box. So why would anyone do this? The reason goes back to controlling for a Type I error, plus it is like opening Forrest Gump's box of chocolates. You don't know what surprise you will find. On the other hand, if you get no significant MANOVA you have saved a lot of time not having to analyze all of the possible comparisons that are contained within.

Finally, I close this section with *multivariate analysis of covariance* (MANCOVA), which is a MANOVA with one or more *covariates*. This is the same as ANCOVA, except it has more than one DV, thus MANCOVA. For example, the study done by Nielson (2014) tested three hypotheses to answer whether pretask planning offsets individual differences in working memory capacity (WMC) with L2 English learners. She had one IV, planning time (present vs absent), three DVs (recall, accuracy, and fluency), and one covariate (WMC). She used a number of different statistical tests, but the one of interest here is the MANCOVA, which she used to get the big picture of what was going on. Because there was no interaction with the covariate WMC and the IV, her results failed to reject the null hypotheses, meaning that WMC did not make a difference for planning time. Nielson confirmed this by doing a number of other types of statistics as well. Let me point out here that not finding statistical significances can be as important as finding them, although researchers might not think so. As with the other categories of statistics discussed above, there are a number of other multivariate procedures available. Because they are not commonly found in the research literature in applied linguistics, I have not included them here. However, when you do come across some type of statistical procedure that I have not touched on, remember that the same principles apply. If you want to know more about them, then use your favorite browser and you will find more than you than you will ever want to know.

Degrees of Freedom

When you see various inferential statistics reported in results sections, you might wonder what the numbers in brackets mean. For example what does (3, 76) mean in the ANOVA results of $F(3, 76) = 20.64, p < .0001$? (I have deliberately left this out of previous reporting of F values prior to this to keep things simple.) These are known as *degrees of freedom* (*df*), which you will see used along with various statistical results. One way that might help you to understand this is that it works like Sudoku. If you know eight of the numbers on a row or column, you automatically know the ninth. In other words, it has eight cells free to vary (i.e., 8 degrees of freedom). For a one-way ANOVA, the first number is the number of *levels* of the *one* independent variable being tested minus one and the second number is the number of participants being used minus the number of levels in the IV in the analysis. In the example above, there are four levels and 80 participants, therefore, $df = 3, 76$. It has nothing to do with how many dependent variables there are. The *df* is used by statisticians to determine whether the F ratio, or whatever statistic being used, is large enough to be statistically significant. If you want to know more about this, consult any elementary applied statistics text or enter the term *degrees of freedom* into your favorite Internet search engine, along with the word *statistics*.

Exercise B.3

Find a study that looked for differences between variables but that has more than one dependent variable.

1. Identify the independent variables and the dependent variables.
2. What type of data is being used?
3. What is the null hypothesis being tested (explicitly or implicitly)?
4. What statistical procedure(s) is used (MANOVA, MANCOVA, etc.)?

5. What follow-up statistics are used?
6. Are the results statistically significant? At what level? What does this mean regarding making inferences?
7. Are the interpretations given by the researcher(s) consistent with the findings?

Type II Error and Power

Recall from Chapter 7 that a Type II error is made when the null hypothesis is falsely accepted. That is, a study that fails to find a statistically significant relationship between variables or a difference between groups at the $p < .05$ may have made a mistake (i.e., a Type II error—there is an actual relationship or difference in the population, but the study missed it). The probability of making this mistake is indicated by beta (β) (see Figure 7.2). However, the probability of not making a Type II error is $1 - \beta$, referred to as the *power* of the test. That is, the probability of correctly rejecting the null hypothesis increases. Obviously, a researcher wants to have the most power in trying to support their hypothesis—usually the opposite of the null hypothesis.

There are three things that affect the power of a statistical procedure. One is the stringency of the probability of making a Type I error (i.e., the α level). The rule is that the lower the alpha (α) level, the greater the beta (β) and, thus, the lower the power ($1 - \beta$). Enough of the Greek; in plain English, this means that as the probability of falsely rejecting the null hypothesis decreases (e.g., $p < .05$ to $p < .001$), the probability of falsely accepting it increases. Logically, this means that, as the probability of falsely accepting the null hypothesis increases, the power of the test decreases (i.e., there is less chance of discovering a relationship or difference). In practice, this works out to mean that the researcher should choose the largest α level permissible to increase the chances of a statistically significant finding, although this increases the chance of making a Type I error. Remember, however, that $p = .05$ is as high as one can go for statistical significance.

The other two things that can influence ability of a statistical procedure to detect either a relationship or a difference are *sample size* and *direction of the prediction*. Sample size is positively related to power. That is, as sample size increases so does the power of the procedure and vice versa. Studies that do not find statistical significance, and have small sample sizes, have low power. Had there been a larger sample, the findings may have been different. Studies with large sample sizes may find statistical significance even with small correlations or small differences between groups of participants. For example, a correlation coefficient of .37 is not statistically significant for a study with a sample size of 15, but is for one that has 30 participants.

Direction of prediction is also a factor that can influence the statistical power of a procedure. Studies that test directional predictions have more power than those that do not. What is a directional prediction? If researchers predict that there will be a positive relationship between variables (or a negative one), they have proposed directional hypotheses. Based on theory or previous research, they may state that as one variable increases so will the other (i.e., it has a positive relationship), or as one increases the other decreases (i.e., it is negative). However, researchers may not be able to make predictions of a directional relationship but only a prediction of a nondirectional relationship (e.g., one variable relates in some way to the other, in either a positive or negative way). If a directional relationship is predicted, then the power of finding this prediction statistically significant increases over one that has no direction in the prediction. The reason is that the critical value[2] of the correlation coefficient is lower for a directional prediction than for the nondirectional prediction. For example, for a study (sample size = 30) that predicts a positive relationship between two variables, any correlation equal to or greater than .31 is statistically significant. However, if there is a nondirectional prediction, then the study must find a correlation equal to or greater than .36 to be statistically significant.

The same principle as the above holds for differences between groups as well. Researchers may predict that the treatment group will do better than the control group (i.e., a directional hypothesis), or they may only predict that there will be a difference without any direction (i.e., non-directional). The former will have more power predicting a significant difference than the latter—not because the former is a stronger prediction but because the critical *t* test value used to test the difference between the means of the two groups does not have to be as great as that of the latter.

Connected to the direction of prediction issue above, there are two expressions that you will encounter: *one-tailed* versus *two-tailed* tests of significance. Without going into probability theory, the following should be sufficient. If there is a directional hypothesis, you will see the term *one-tailed* test of significance. If there is no direction in the prediction or no prediction at all, then you will find a *two-tailed* test. If there is no statement about a one-tailed test, then assume that the procedures are using two-tailed tests. These two terms relate to the issue discussed above about how the critical value is chosen for determining statistical significance. It is enough to know that the one-tailed test uses the lower critical value and the two-tailed test uses the higher critical value, as illustrated above.

Effect Size Revisited

Almost all journals require researchers to include *effect size* with their inferential statistics (e.g., *Language Learning*). As the term suggests, it is an estimate of the extent to which one group differs from another, one variable correlates with another, and so on. This statistic directly relates to the *power* of a statistical procedure and the practical significance of the findings. It relates to power in that the greater the effect size, the greater the power of the statistical test. It relates to practical significance in that the greater the effect size, the greater the significance for practical use. Do not think that effect size only relates to quantitative research. Onwuegbuzie (2003) provided typologies of a number of effect sizes for qualitative data analyses. Though I have not seen these used yet in qualitative studies, I think that it is only a matter of time before they, or some form of them, are. The move to require effect sizes to be reported in quantitative research by journals took a long time.

There are a number of indices used today to show effect sizes. For correlations you will see eta-squared η^2, omega-squared ω^2, Cohen's f^2, and Cohen's q. For differences between groups you will encounter Cohen's d, Glass's Δ, Hedges's g, and more. The reason is that, for every type of statistical procedure used, there is a separate formula to compute effect size. In addition, there may be several ways to compute effect size, depending on one's preference. Google *effect size calculator* and see all the different methods. For example, as reported in Chapter 7, Moskovsky, Alrabai, Paolini, and Ratcheva (2013) examined the effects of teachers' motivational strategies on the motivation of students. They performed a chi-square analysis on their final placement matrix to ensure that there was no bias in the placement of participants. They found only one, region of origin, where there was a significant difference between treatment and control groups ($\chi^2 = 10.898$, $p < .005$). However, they reported that the effect size was small (Cramer's $V = .19$), so they did not expect any distortion of their results from this. Also, look at Chalhoub-Deville and Wigglesworth (2005), who used eta-squared (η^2) to show how their results, though statistical significant, failed to have practical significance.

Key Terms and Concepts

univariate ANOVAs
  analysis of covariance (ANCOVA)
  between-subjects and within-subjects ANOVA
  repeated measures ANOVA
multivariate ANOVAs
  multiple analysis of covariance (MANCOVA)
  multivariate analysis of variance (MANOVA)

Miscellaneous statistical terms
central tendency
covariate

degrees of freedom (*df*)
effect size
nested variable
normal distribution
one-tailed vs two-tailed tests of significance
positively or negatively skewed distributions
Pillai's trace
Power
scales: nominal, ordinal, interval, and ratio
Wilks's lambda

Notes

1. Usually there is only one mode (i.e., the most frequent score). However, if there are more, then this suggests that there may be several clusters of data.
2. The critical value is the value that determines whether it is statistically significant.

References

Brantmeier, C., Sullivan, J. H., & Strube, M. (2014). Toward independent L2 readers: Effects of text adjuncts, subject knowledge, L1 reading, and L2 proficiency. *Reading in a Foreign Language, 26*(2), 34–53.

Chalhoub-Deville, M., & Wigglesworth, G. (2005). Rater judgment and English language speaking proficiency. *World Englishes, 24*, 383–392.

Fitzgerald, J., Stenner, A. J., Sanford-Moore, E. E., Koons, H., Bowen, K., & Kim, K. H. (2015). The relationship of Korean students' age and years of English-as-a-foreign-language exposure with English-reading ability: A cross-age study. *Reading Psychology, 36*, 173–202.

Jung, J. (2016). Effects of glosses on learning of L2 grammar and vocabulary. *Language Teaching Research, 20*(1), 92–112.

Lee, J. (2015). Language learner strategy by Chinese-speaking EFL readers when comprehending familiar and unfamiliar texts. *Reading in a Foreign Language, 27*(1), 71–95.

Machida, N. & Dalsky, D. J. (2014). The effect of concept mapping on L2 writing performance: Examining possible effects of trait-level writing anxiety. *English Language Teaching, 7*(9), 28–35.

Mistar, J., Zuhairi, A., & Yanti, N. (2016). Strategies training in the teaching of reading comprehension for EFL learners in Indonesia. *English Language Teaching, 9*(2), 49–56.

Moskovsky, C., Alrabai, F., Paolini, S., & Ratcheva, S. (2013). The effects of teachers' motivational strategies on learners' motivation: A controlled investigation of second language acquisition. *Language Learning, 63*(1), 34–62.

Nielson, K. B. (2014). Can planning time compensate for individual differences in working memory capacity? *Language Teaching Research, 18*(3), 272–293.

Onwuegbuzie, A. J. (2003). Effect sizes in qualitative research: A prolegomenon. *Quality & Quantity, 37,* 393–409.

Tong, F., Lara-Alecio, R., Irby, B. J., & Koch, J. (2014). Integrating literacy and science for English language learners: From learning-to-read to reading-to-learn. *The Journal of Educational Research, 107,* 410–426.

Glossary

Accumulative treatment effect: The result of the accumulative effect owing to the particular order in which treatments are presented. Also known as the multiple-treatment interference or order effect.

Alternate-form reliability: The degree to which different forms of a test measure the same general attribute.

Analysis of covariance (ANCOVA): A parametric statistical procedure that removes differences between groups prior to treatment.

Analysis of variance (ANOVA): An inferential statistic used to compare the difference between three or more sets of data.

Applied linguistics: A discipline that focuses on practical issues involving the learning and teaching of foreign/second languages.

Applied research: Research that is directly applicable to practical problems in teaching and learning.

Automatic response: Occurs when a respondent selects only one choice throughout the questionnaire without thinking.

Average: A measure that best represents the central core in a distribution of data (i.e., mean, median, mode).

Basic research: Research dealing mainly with highly abstract constructs and theory which has little apparent practical use.

Case: One participant or record in a data set.

Case study: An in-depth study of an example(s) that represents a phenomenon in its natural setting.

Causal-comparative design: Characterized by variation in the independent variable found in nature rather than a result of experimenter manipulations, thus making the findings suggestive of cause/effect at most.

Central tendency: The term used by statisticians for average.

Chi-square: An inferential statistical procedure for comparing observed frequencies with expected frequencies.

Closed-form questionnaire: These items provide a set of alternative items answers, from which the respondent must select at least one.

Coefficient: A number that represents the amount of some attribute, such as a correlation coefficient.

Compensatory equalization of treatments: Occurs when attempts are made to give the control group extra material or special treatment in order to make up for not receiving the experimental treatment.

Competing group contamination: A result of anything that might cause the control group to behave differently than normal.

Confirmatory research: A study that is designed to test an explicitly stated hypothesis.

Construct: A concept that a given discipline (e.g., applied linguistics) has constructed to identify some quality that is thought to exist (i.e., language proficiency).

Construct validity: The global concept that encompasses all the facets of validity.

Constructed response items: Test items that require participants to recall and integrate information, such as a test of writing ability in which they must compose an essay.

Content coverage: The facet of validity that indicates how well the content of the measurement procedure aligns with the treatment objectives.

Convenience sampling: Using participants who are chosen because they are conveniently available for use in a study.

Conversational analysis: A research technique that analyzes verbal output from a totally inductive perspective without any prior knowledge about the context of the participants. The resulting verbal data are seldom coded or transformed into numerical data.

Correlational study: One that investigates relationships between variables.

Covariate: An unwanted variable that is controlled by statistical procedures.

Criterion-referenced tests: Interpretation of the results of such tests are based on one or more criteria for deciding the status of examinees.

Criterion-related: The facet of validity that indicates how well a measurement procedure corresponds to some external criterion, such as predicting the capacity to succeed or identifying current characteristics.

Cronbach alpha: An estimate of the reliability of a Likert-type questionnaire (i.e., degree of internal consistency of the items).

Degrees of freedom (*df*):   Numbers that are used for identifying the criterion for the determination of statistical significance—usually associated with number of groups and sample size.

Demoralization (boycott):   This potential contaminator occurs when participants in the control group resent the special treatment given to the treatment group and lower their performance.

Dependent t tests: An inferential statistic that assesses the difference between the means of two sets of scores for either the same group of participants or two groups whose participants have been matched (also called correlated *t* test or paired *t* test).

Dependent variable: The variable that is analyzed for change as a result of change in another variable (i.e., the independent variable).

Descriptive variable: A variable that consists of data in the form of observations and descriptions.

Descriptive statistics: Estimates of parameters that describe a population, such as means and standard deviations.

Differential selection: The selection procedure results in groups of participants who possess preexisting differences that may affect the variable being investigated.

Discrete-point item: This test item measures only one thing and is scored correct or incorrect.

Effect size: Used for determining practical significance in comparison to statistical significance.

Ethnography: A procedure whereby data are gathered from a number of sources in a natural setting, resulting in large quantities of verbal data.

Experimental design: A research design that involves manipulating the independent variable(s) and observing the change in the dependent variable(s) on a randomly chosen sample.

Experimental treatment diffusion (compromise):   Occurs when the control group gains knowledge of the factor(s) making up the treatment condition(s) and employs this factor(s) in its own situation, which distorts the results.

Experimentally accessible population: A population that is a subset of a larger population, but which is more accessible for obtaining a sample.

Exploratory research: A study that seeks to answer research questions without testing any hypothesis.

External validity: The degree to which the findings of a study can be generalized to a target population.

Extraneous variable: A variable that can adversely affect the dependent variable other than the independent variable(s).

F ratio: A value used to indicate statistical significance of differences between groups of data in inferential statistics such as ANOVA.

Face appearance: The facet of validity that indicates the degree to which a measurement procedure appears to measure what it is supposed to measure.

Friedman test: A nonparametric procedure for testing the difference between three or more sets of data gathered on the same people.

Full-participant observer: An observer who is or becomes a full member of the group being observed.

Grounded theory: A procedure which develops a theoretical hypothesis as the data accumulate in a study.

Halo effect: The biasing effect of judging the work of one participant on the work of a following participant.

Hawthorne effect: Occurs when participants behave unnaturally because they know that they are in a research study.

Highly structured interview: One that follows a predetermined set of questions with no allowance for variation.

History: Effects due to the influence of events that take place at different points in time on the dependent variable other than the independent variable.

Homogeneity of variance: The degree to which the variances of different groups of data are similar.

Hypothesis: A theoretical statement that proposes how several constructs relate to one another.

Independent *t* test: An inferential statistic that analyzes the difference between the averages (i.e., means) on one dependent variable for two independent groups of data.

Independent variable: The principal variable(s) being investigated regarding its influence on some dependent variable.

Inferential statistics: Statistics used to make inferences from samples to populations.

Informant: A person from the group being observed who gives verbal information to the researcher.

Information-rich strategy: Provides many examples of verbal data to add credibility to interpretations of verbal data.

Instrumental procedures: Procedures use some form of impersonal mechanism for obtaining research data.

Internal consistency: The degree to which all the items in an instrument measure the same general attribute.

Internal validity: The degree to which the results of the study are due to the independent variable(s) under consideration and not due to anything else.

Inter-rater reliability: The degree to which different observers/raters agree in their observations/ratings of the behavior of participants.

Interquartile range: An estimate of where the middle 50 percent of the scores are located in the data distribution—the distance between the first quartile and the third quartile of the frequency of scores.

Interval scale: The values represent equal amounts of the variable being measured, but have a relative zero such as temperature on a thermometer.

Intra-rater reliability: The degree to which observers/raters give the same results given the opportunity to observe/rate participants on more than one occasion.

Introspection: A procedure that requires participants to observe their own internal cognitive (or emotional) states and/or processing strategies during an ongoing task such as reading.

Item quality: The degree to which an item in a test or questionnaire is understood by the respondents due to the manner in which it is written.

John Henry effect: Occurs when the difference between the control group and the treatment group is due to competition rather than the treatment.

Kruskal–Wallis test: A nonparametric statistical procedure that analyzes the differences between three or more independent groups of participants.

Kuder–Richardson 20 and 21:   Two related formulas for calculating the reliability for tests consisting of items that are scored dichotomously (i.e., correct/incorrect, true/false, yes/no, etc.).

Longitudinal study: A study designed to collect data over a period of time.

Mann–Whitney U test: A nonparametric statistical procedure used to analyze the difference between two independent groups of participants.

Maturation: Effects due to natural changes in the participants that take place over time other than due to the variables being studied.

Mean: The most common index of average: the sum of all the scores divided by the number of scores.

Measurement–treatment interaction: Occurs when the results are only found when using a particular type of measuring procedure.

Median: A measure of average: the point that divides the number of scores in half.

Meta-analysis: A research method that analyzes the qualitative and quantitative results of a number of individual studies for the purpose of integrating the findings.

Mode: The least used index of average: the most frequent score.

Moderating variable: A variable that moderates the effect(s) of the independent variable on the dependent variable or the relationship between two variables.

Multiple analysis of covariance (MANCOVA):   ANCOVA with more than one dependent variable.

Multiple regression: A inferential statistical procedure used to determine which combination of independent variables best predicts or explains the variation in one dependent variable.

Multivariate analysis of variance (MANOVA):   ANOVA with more than one dependent variable—all at the same time.

Multivariate statistics: Procedures that analyze more than one dependent variable at the same time.

Multiway ANOVA: ANOVA procedures with more than two independent variables.

Negatively skewed distribution: Data that are lopsided to the right side.

Nested variable: One where the levels are within the participants rather than between them, such as a repeated measurement on the same subjects.

Nominal scale: One where the values of a variable represent categories, such as 1 = male, 2 = female. Other than identifiers, they have no quantitative value.

Nonparametric statistics: Inferential statistical procedures used for analyzing data in the form of frequencies, ranked data, and other data that do not meet the assumptions for parametric procedures.

Nonparticipant observer: One who does not personally interact with the participants in any manner while making observations.

Nonproportional stratified random sample: A sample of equal numbers of participants randomly sampled from each stratum in the target population.

Normal distribution: A symmetrical, bell-shaped distribution of data that has specific properties and is used as a reference point for comparing the shapes of data distributions.

Norm-referenced test: One where scores are interpreted by comparing them with scores from a body of people that represents the population.

Null hypothesis: One which states that there is no true relationship or differences between variables in a population.

Objectivity: The degree to which the data are not influenced by bias due to attitude, temporary emotional states, and so on, of the data collector.

Objects: Inanimate sources of data, such as a corpus of text.

Observational procedure: Any procedure that captures data through visual observation.

One-tailed test of statistical significance: A method for testing statistical significance that is based on one end of the probability distribution. It is used for testing directional hypotheses.

One-way ANOVA: The simplest form of ANOVA involving the use of one independent variable, usually with more than two levels and one dependent variable.

Open-form questionnaire items: Questions that allow respondents to give their own answers without restrictions.

Open-structured interview: One that follows a general plan but is not restricted to predetermined questions.

Operational definition: One that defines a construct in terms of observable behavior.

Ordinal scale: One where the values represent some type of rank order, such as first, second, third, and so on. It represents relative amounts of a variable (e.g., small, large, largest).

Pair-wise comparisons: Procedures that compare the differences between groups of data, two at a time.

Parameters: Measurements on an entire population.

Parametric statistical procedures: Inferential procedures used on data that meet the assumptions of normalcy of distribution and homogeneity of variance.

Partial-participant observer: One who has developed a personal relationship with the group being observed but is not a full member of the group.

Participant observer: One who has a personal relationship with those being observed by being a member of the group.

Participants: People from whom data are gathered—synonymous with *subjects*.

Pearson product-moment correlation: A parametric statistical procedure that measures the linear relationship between two sets of data, also known as the Pearson r, or simply r.

Position paper: A document in which a writer argues his/her particular viewpoint or position on some issues without doing a research study for support.

Positively skewed distribution: A data distribution lopsided to the left side.

Power: The probability of not making a Type II error.

Predictive utility: The aspect of the criterion-related facet of validity that indicates how well an instrument predicts performance.

Preliminary sources: Publications designed to reference and catalog documents in various disciplines. These are extremely useful for locating primary research.

Pretest effect: Occurs when a test given before the administration of the treatment interacts with the treatment by heightening participants' awareness of the importance of certain material.

Primary research: Research performed and reported firsthand by the researcher(s).

Proportional stratified random sampling: A technique that randomly selects cases that represent the proportion of each stratum of the population.

Purposeful sampling: A technique that selects samples based on how information-rich they are for addressing the research question.

Pygmalion effect: A type of researcher effect caused by the bias in the researcher's perception of the behavior of the participants due to preexisting expectations of the participants' performance.

Qualitative research: Research that is done in a natural setting, involving intensive holistic data collection through observation at a very close personal level without the influence of prior theory; it contains mostly verbal analysis.

Quantitative research: Any study using numerical data with emphasis on statistics to answer the research questions.

Quasi-experimental design: A research design that looks at the effects of independent variables on dependent variables; it is similar to experimental design, only the samples are not randomly chosen.

Range: A measure of how much data vary based on the distance from the lowest to the highest scores in the distribution.

Ratio scale: One where the values represent equal amounts of the variable being measured and that has a real zero, such as response time.

Regression analysis: A parametric procedure used to identify variables (i.e., independent variables) that either predict or explain another variable (i.e., the dependent variable).

Reliability: The degree to which a data-gathering procedure produces consistent results.

Reliability coefficient: A correlation coefficient that indicates the reliability of a data-gathering procedure.

Replication of research: The repetition of a study, typically using a different sample.

Representative sampling paradigm: A strategy for obtaining a sample that represents a target population.

Researcher effect: Occurs when data are distorted by some characteristic of the researcher either in administering the treatment or collecting the data.

Retrospection: A technique that requires participants to wait until after the task before reflecting on what they had done cognitively.

Rubric: A detailed definition of each level of a rating scale.

Sample: A portion of a larger population.

Secondary sources: These summarize other people's research rather than provide firsthand reports by the original researchers.

Semistructured interview: One that has a set of predetermined questions, but the interviewer is free to follow up a question with additional questions that probe further.

Simple random sampling: Occurs when everyone in the population has an equal chance of being chosen for the sample.

Skewed distribution: One that is lopsided—more scores on one side of the distribution than the other.

Spearman rank-order correlation (rho):   A nonparametric correlation that indicates the relationship between sets of data that are in the form of ranked data.

Spearman–Brown prophecy formula: A method for estimating the reliability of a test if the number of test items were to increase.

Split-half (odd/even) reliability: A measure of the internal consistency of a test by correlating one half of the test with the other, usually the odd items with the even ones.

Standard error of measurement (SEM):   An estimate of the average amount of error made by a measurement instrument.

Standardized test: A test which has been designed to be given under strict guidelines for administration and scoring across each occasion.

Statistical regression: An effect where the difference between scores on the pretest and posttest is due to the natural tendency for initial extreme scores to move toward the average on subsequent testing.

Statistical significance: When the chance of making a type I error is equal to or less than 5 percent.

Stratified random sample: One where a random sample is chosen from each stratum in a population.

Subject attrition (also experimental mortality):   Occurs when there is a loss of participants during a research study

Subjectivity: The degree to which the data are influenced by bias due to the attitude, temporary emotional states, and so on, of the data collector.

Subjects: People from whom data are gathered (synonymous with participants).

Target population: All the members of a group of people/objects to whom the researcher wants to generalize his/her research findings.

Test–retest reliability: An estimate of the stability of measurement results for the same instrument repeated over time.

Theory: An explanation attempting to interrelate large sets of observed phenomena or constructs into a meaningful holistic framework.

Think-aloud technique: A procedure wherein participants are required to talk about what they are thinking. Usually they are audio-recorded while talking.

Time of measurement: Occurs when the results of a study are not stable over different times of measurement.

Trait accuracy: The facet of validity that indicates how accurately a procedure measures the trait (i.e., construct) under investigation.

Transferability: The extent to which the findings of a study can be transferred to other similar situations.

Treatment fidelity: The degree to which a treatment is correctly administered.

Treatment intervention: Occurs when the results of a study are distorted due to the novelty or disruption of a treatment.

Treatment strength/time interaction: Occurs when the time needed for the treatment to have any noticeable effect is not sufficient.

Triangulation: A procedure using multiple sources of data to see if they converge to provide evidence for validating interpretations of results.

Two-tailed test of statistical significance: A method for testing statistical significance that is based on both ends of the probability distribution. It is used for testing nondirectional hypotheses.

Type I error: Occurs when the null hypothesis is rejected in a sample while it is true in the population.

Type II error: Occurs when the null hypothesis is not rejected in a sample while it is false in the population.

Utility: The facet of validity that is concerned with whether measurement/observational procedures are used for the correct purpose.

Validity: The degree to which a measurement/observational procedure accurately captures data and is used correctly.

Volunteers: Participants who have been solicited and have agreed to participate in a study.

Wilcoxon matched-pairs signed rank test (or the Wilcoxon T test):   A nonparametric procedure for analyzing the difference between two sets of data that are related in some fashion.

Wilks's lambda: A statistic used in multivariate statistical procedures for indicating overall statistical significance.

Index